ENGINES
OF WAR

ENGINES OF WAR

CHRISTIAN WOLMAR

ISIS
LARGE PRINT
Oxford

First published in Great Britain 2010
by
Atlantic Books, an imprint of
Atlantic Books Ltd.

Published in Large Print 2013 by ISIS Publishing Ltd.,
7 Centremead, Osney Mead, Oxford OX2 0ES
by arrangement with
Atlantic Books Ltd.

CIP data is available for this title from the British Library

ISBN 978–0–7531–5330–7 (hb)
ISBN 978–0–7531–5331–4 (pb)

Printed and bound in Great Britain by
T. J. International Ltd., Padstow, Cornwall

Dedicated to my daughter Misha MccGwire, to help her history studies, and in memory of Terry Brooks, the grandfather of my daughter Molly Brooks, who suffered on the Burma — Siam Railway.

Contents

Preface ix

Acknowledgements xix

1. War Before Railways 1

2. The Railways Called into Action 18

3. Slavery Loses Out to the Iron Road 49

4. Lessons Not Learnt 94

5. The New Weapon of War 132

6. The War the World Anticipated 184

7. The Great Railway War
    on the Western Front 224

8. Eastern Contrasts 281

9. Here We Go Again 339

10. Blood on the Tracks 397

Preface

While writing my previous book, *Blood, Iron & Gold: How Railways Transformed the World*, I stumbled upon the role of railways in war and saw that this had been greatly underplayed by historians, even those interested in railways. Researching this book, I realized that even my initial thoughts on the subject fell far short of the mark. The railways, I discovered, were as integral to the development of methods of warfare as they were to the numerous aspects of modern life that I had catalogued in *Blood, Iron & Gold*.

Most writers on the subject of railways and war — of which there have been remarkably few, as can be gleaned from my bibliography — have focussed mainly on how the railways coped with the extra demands placed on them, particularly during the two world wars. In this book, however, I have concentrated on what I felt was a far more interesting subject: how the creation of the railways led to a tremendous escalation of the scale of warfare and how increasingly they were used in a strategic way to conduct military operations. Over the course of the nineteenth century, it gradually dawned on military leaders that railways were a crucial weapon in their armoury, and as they exploited this great improvement in their logistics, their ability to amass ever larger and well-equipped armies increased exponentially. A recurring theme, which resulted from the growing military use of the railways during this century, was the constant tension between railway managers and military leaders who were often unable to understand that the iron road could not just be subjected to their whims. Railways, right from their beginnings, were used by governments to transport troops quickly in order to quell internal riots or uprisings and consequently the railway companies, unwittingly or not, became agents of the state at a very early stage in the history of the railways.

There was another, indirect, way in which the railways contributed to the escalation in the scale of warfare. As the tracks expanded across countries, they became a unifying force for nations, which in turn made conflict between them more likely since unification helped foment nationalistic feelings. The strong economic stimulus resulting from the creation of the railways also encouraged expansion and consequently aggressive intent towards neighbouring countries. Moreover, richer societies were able to devote more resources to waging war and building up their defensive and offensive capacities. Railways also enabled colonial powers to establish greater dominance over the countries in their possession, sometimes, as we shall see, with the result that the eventual rebellions were ultimately stronger. All these themes are explored in the book.

I have tried to make *Engines of War* as international as possible, examining a wide variety of conflicts, but inevitably I have had to ignore several wars in which railways played a role, such as, for example, the

Mexican revolution and civil war of the 1910s in which the railways were a frequent target. Inevitably, too, the easy accessibility of sources ensures there is a strong focus on Britain and something of a bias towards the British side of conflicts. I have, too, concentrated on the strategic aspects of railways, rather than their use — and overuse — by passengers at times of war, although this is sometimes referred to. I have also largely focussed on railways in the theatres of war, leaving out much detail about the exploitation of British railways by the government in the wars, partly because this has been better covered in previous books. Since the subject has been little covered by previous authors, there were a lot of potential avenues — or rather tracks — to explore, but I have tried to home in on facets of the story which best reveal how the role of railways in war has been consistently understated.

This book is set out broadly chronologically, with chapters that for the most part encompass a single war. I start by setting out a very brief assessment of war before the railway age in Chapter One, and the following two chapters cover, respectively, the Crimean War and the American Civil War. The latter is undoubtedly the first genuine railway war, fought by troops delivered to the front by railway and on battlegrounds frequently determined by the location of the train. Chapter Four mainly looks at the Franco-Prussian War, where interestingly the side with the best railways lost, but also examines the wars waged by Prussia in the run-up to that conflict. In Chapter Five, I look at a motley collection of conflicts which occurred between the Franco-Prussian War and the First World War, including various British colonial wars, such as its victory over Sudan rebels facilitated by the construction of a long railway across the desert, and the Boer War, fought over a single railway line. This chapter also covers the most important and bloodiest war of this period, the Russo-Japanese War, triggered by the construction of the Trans-Siberian Railway. In Chapter Six, I set out the build-up to the First World War, which involved massive investment in the railways across Europe, and assess A. J. P. Taylor's famous assertion that the rigidity of railway timetables triggered off the whole war. I devote two chapters to the First World War, in which railways played a significant part in virtually every theatre of that conflict. I analyse in depth the initial phases of the war, in which the railways played a crucial role and effectively determined the location of the front line. I consider the paradox that it was the increased mobility afforded by the railways which led to the stalemate lasting three and a half years on the Western Front, while the relative lack of railways in the east resulted in a less static war. I examine all aspects of the use of the railways, ranging from the often underestimated role of the light railways in delivering material to the front line as well as the far more famous attacks by Arab forces led by T. E. Lawrence on the Hejaz Railway on the Arabian peninsula.

While it might have been expected that railways would have played a lesser role in the Second World War given the technological changes in the intervening quarter of a century, this turned out not to be the case. I examine the reasons for this, and focus particularly on the German invasion of Russia, where the logistics were fundamental to the outcome. Finally, in Chapter Ten, I set out a few surprising and more recent aspects of railway warfare, notably the difficulties the Americans found in destroying the North Koreans' railway supply lines and the remarkable story of the Russian missile trains which carried weapons capable of blowing up American cities. And I finish by trying to draw out a few of the recurring themes of the book.

While I have made no attempt to give a comprehensive account of each war, I have attempted to set out the basic facts of each conflict to facilitate discussion of the role of the railways. Obviously, given the need to keep this book to a manageable length, it has been impossible to include great detail but I have tried, at least, to outline the cause of each war, the key battles and the outcome.

I suspect that even the least railway-minded reader of this book would agree that the way the military role of railways has been ignored in the past is quite remarkable and possibly can only be explained by the modern obsession with the motor car, at the expense of all other modes of transport. This example from a website featuring the Red Ball Express motor transport in the Second World War mentioned in Chapter Nine may be extreme but it is in no way unique in its ignorance: "Since the time of Alexander the Great large armies have crossed the world's military landscape with ponderous difficulty, their seemingly endless lines of animal-drawn carts and wagons trailing far behind. How different this is from the pace and dimension of modern warfare. The highly mechanized U.S. Army of WWII had the ability to cover vast distances at speeds unimagined by even the greatest of the Great Captains of old." No mention here of the previous century, during which rail transport had been the crucial line of communication, and how, for example, the railways delivered 23,000 Northern troops across half the breadth of America in just two weeks during the American Civil War, almost a hundred years before the Second World War. The same website goes on to quote an "observer" suggesting that the Second World War was "a 100 percent internal combustion engine war". That is just 100 per cent wrong, as is made patently clear in Chapter Nine, which shows that nearly 100 per cent of US troops travelled to their ships by rail.

Even in cases where I thought, on preliminary reading, that the role of the railways may have been minimal in a particular conflict, it emerged quite often that it was crucial. The Second World War, covered in Chapter Nine, is a case in point. Just like the generals who made such heavy use of the railways, historians have tended to relegate their role to that of backroom boy and only seemed to notice them when they went wrong. In fact, the railways were at times far more important in deciding outcomes than the HQs where those same generals spent their days. Hitler is simply the most glaring example of a military leader who dismissed the importance of logistics, but even a cursory examination of the Second World War demonstrates clearly that he made a grave error in ignoring this key aspect of warfare.

There are countless military histories where the role of the railways has been ignored or greatly underplayed. Indeed, at times railways have been written out of the histories, as, too often, have the wider problems of logistics, which, it is no exaggeration to say, were often a decisive factor in the outcome of a conflict. There is, therefore, quite an imbalance to redress, which is why readers may feel that I have gone too far the other way and overemphasized the role of railways in this account. I do not feel that this is the case, but I leave the reader to judge. Of course, I have tended to highlight features of those battles in which railways played a key part, and also stressed their role, but where necessary I have mentioned the relative roles played by other means of transportation, including road vehicles.

I am not a military historian and therefore am unfamiliar with many of the terms used in military histories. Indeed, I have always been bemused by them, not understanding the difference, say, between a division and a company, and with no idea of which is bigger. In a way my ignorance has been useful because so many books assume that readers know the difference when, in fact, I suspect a majority do not understand the precise meanings of these terms. Therefore every time I came across them, I interpreted them according to this list provided to me by the ever helpful librarians at the Imperial War Museum:

A *section* led by a lance corporal: 15
A *platoon* under a subaltern: 60
A *company* under a captain: 250
A *battalion* under a major: 1,000
A *regiment* under a colonel: 2,000
A *brigade* under a brigadier: 4,000
A *division* under a major general: 12,000
A *corps* under a lieutenant general: 50,000
An *army* under a general: 200,000

These figures are, of course, approximate and have varied over time and between nations, but I am assured that they are a good general guide.

I can make no claim to expertise on military matters, but one thing struck me consistently during the writing of this book. Virtually all the wars covered had very little clear purpose and, notably, resulted in a worse — or certainly no better — situation than before the conflict had taken place. There are of course exceptions, such as the American Civil War and the Second World War, but overall the readiness to go to war seems all too easily to overrule the caution that should be born of studying the history of warfare, a mistake which has been repeated several times during my lifetime. Writing this book has been a salutary experience and I hope that reading it will strengthen the view that war is an evil that is necessary only very rarely. With Iraq still suffering and the Afghan War still raging as I write these words, all I can say is: *Plus ça change*.

As with all my books, I have been greatly dependent on the availability of source material. Since the importance of railways in war has, as I mentioned, been largely shunned by military historians, and railway writers tend to focus on the technology and the mechanics rather than the effect of the railways, there are great gaps in our knowledge of this element of warfare. I have tried to fill a few through combing the library at the Imperial War Museum, but mostly I have relied on secondary sources, which at times are sparse and, inevitably, occasionally contradictory. There is, therefore, plenty of scope for lots of PhDs to be written on this hidden factor in conflict.

If there was any doubt that the use of railways in war is a neglected subject, I leave the last word of this introduction to Lloyd George. He noted that the histories of the First World War tended to ignore this aspect of warfare and in 1932 commented on the coverage in John Buchan's *History of the War*: "The Battle of the Somme has about 60 pages, and yet it did not make that much difference in the war; but the shells and the guns that enabled the army to fight it, all the organisation of transport behind the lines, do you know how much is given to this? 17 lines."

Acknowledgements

This book has stretched my resources to the full and I have been particularly dependent on advice and help from a variety of people. Thanks to the stalwarts who read and commented on the text: Jim Ballantyne, John Fowler and Tony Telford, who all contributed ideas and corrections that have greatly enhanced the book. I am especially grateful to Adrian Lyons, the former director of the Railway Forum, who contributed both his railway and his military expertise to ensure that the book remained on the right lines. Thanks are also due to the fantastic librarians at the Imperial War Museum, where I hope the roof is now fixed, and to various people who gave me advice or contributed stories, including Chris Austin, Michael Binyon, Liam Browne, David Drake, Nick Faith, Dr Guy Finch, Bernard Gambrill, John Harris, Phil Kelly, John Magala, Gordon Pettitt, Richard Phillips, Fritz Plous, Anthony Smith, Robert Summerling, Kim Winter and any others whom I may have forgotten. I am also grateful to my editor, Sarah Norman, and Toby Mundy at Atlantic Books, and all the other great people there who have been extremely helpful in bringing about the success of previous books, and to my agent, Andrew Lownie, who steers me through the nightmare complications of the modern publishing world. Thanks, too, to the University of Aberdeen, which has recently made me a research fellow. Finally, special thanks are due to my partner, Deborah Maby, who edited the draft and keeps me laughing. As ever, any errors are entirely my responsibility and please do contribute any thoughts and corrections to me via my website: www.christianwolmar.co.uk, which also has almost all my articles published since 2000.

CHAPTER
ONE

War Before Railways

We are used to thinking of railways as a benign invention which brought untold benefits to the world. For the first time ever, people were able to travel long distances cheaply and in relative comfort. The railways opened up vast new markets for the products of the factories springing up in the wake of the Industrial Revolution and were the catalyst for the far-reaching changes that created our modern way of life. They brought in their wake all kinds of positive developments which might not seem immediately obvious. The health of urban citizens improved greatly as fresh food became far more widely available and the railways, which during the second part of the nineteenth century were by far the world's largest businesses, were instrumental in improving education to ensure there was a supply of skilled labour to operate and maintain them. While today trains have been to a great extent superseded by the car and the aeroplane, they still play a vital role in many countries' transport systems, offering a particularly pleasant and relaxing way to travel, and, remarkably, the burgeoning network of high-speed lines is now attracting people back onto the railways.

Yet, there is another side to their history, one which has rarely been told and which shows that technology developed for one purpose can so easily be harnessed for another, one which might surprise or even appal its creators. Railways were first conceived as a way of transporting goods. Early "railways", such as the Stockton & Darlington completed in 1825, were primarily mineral lines with the principal task of taking coal from a mine to the nearest waterway. However, railway companies soon found it profitable to carry passengers, and it was the Liverpool & Manchester, a far more sophisticated enterprise, which truly inaugurated the railway age. Opened in 1830, the Liverpool & Manchester was the first railway in the modern sense of the word as it was a double-track line operated by locomotive haulage and linked two major towns with traffic, passenger and freight, flowing in both directions. The concept of hauling freight wagons and passenger carriages on permanent metal tracks using locomotives soon spread around the world, reaching the United States, France, Belgium and Bavaria by 1835, and a dozen other countries, including the far-flung Spanish colony of Cuba, by the end of the decade.

Most of these early lines were experimental but were developed with the knowledge that they would be the start of a network. Already, ambitious schemes to create country-wide and transcontinental systems were being put forward and, while no one quite realized just how fast this new invention would spread, the railways' early sponsors soon became aware of their potential. So did governments and, notably, their military leaders.

Almost as soon as the Liverpool & Manchester was opened, troops despatched to quell unrest in Ireland were being carried on its trains. While in Britain the development of the railway system was a haphazard process in which the government did not play an active role, elsewhere there was an immediate awareness of the railways' potential for military use. In Belgium, the development of the railways was seen as a key means of protecting the country against invaders, while in Prussia, as early as the 1830s, there was already discussion of their military value. According to a history of the role of railways in French-German relations, "the potential of railroads to alter the nature of warfare was quickly recognized . . . The first reflex in the 1830s was to assume that railways would bring a decisive edge for the defense; interior connections would enable a national army to concentrate its forces swiftly against any offensive thrust by an invading foe." Indeed, it is no exaggeration to say that the railways were an invention for which the military had been waiting for hundreds, if not thousands, of years. They would become a key development in the technology of warfare because of their ability to shift unprecedented amounts of matériel and huge numbers of people. It was, therefore, not so much that they could be used as a weapon, though armoured trains would play a significant role in several conflicts, but that they allowed a step change in the scale of warfare. Once railways became involved, the very nature of warfare changed, and wars increased in length, intensity, and destructiveness. However, as with other innovations, it took a long time for the military to understand their importance and exploit them fully.

Wars have been waged by human beings ever since they formed themselves into tribes or other groups and the history of warfare is one of growth in the scale of conflict nourished by technological progress, not just in weaponry but in the means of logistical support. To understand how railways affected the ways in which wars were pursued, it is essential briefly to examine how they were conducted before the dawning of the railway age. The earliest people developed weapons in order to kill animals both to protect themselves from predators and to obtain food, and, as they formed into tribes, to use in battles with neighbouring groups. Spears and arrows were initially made by sharpening wood and later became stone-tipped. When first soft and then harder metals were discovered, these were quickly used to improve the effectiveness of weapons. Otzi, the iceman shepherd who lived 5,300 years ago, was discovered in the Alps in 1991 with a copper axe, a flint knife and flint-tipped arrows and a bow, suggesting that weaponry was already well developed. It was around then that societies were becoming more economically advanced and thus increasingly militarized as they sought to protect themselves. Weapons were important but large-scale wars were only made possible by the establishment of settled societies that fed themselves through agriculture and were able to produce a surplus of food; as Jeremy Black, author of *War: A Short History*, explains, once certain groups became more affluent, they invariably had to protect

4

themselves against those who were less well-off: "Social change helped alter the nature of war. This change was linked to economic transformation with the move from hunter-gatherer societies to those focussing on specialized agriculture, both pastoral and arable."

Thanks to the surplus of food that could be used to supply warriors, settled societies were able to raise armies to fight in battles where mobility and speed became crucial assets. Horses were first domesticated as early as 4000 BC but it took another couple of thousand years before someone got the idea of using them in conflicts by hitching them to chariots carrying armed men into battle. Around 1700 BC, the Hittites, using chariots with spoked rather than solid wheels, which made them far lighter than previous versions, were able to dominate Anatolia and establish a kingdom in a large swathe of modern-day Turkey and Syria. Thanks to their efficient and manoeuvrable vehicles, these charioteers became the elite and the decisive force in battles. This is just one early example of the way that the progress of the techniques of war was to prove decisive in many conflicts. The three great empires of Classical times — Han China, Persia and Imperial Rome — all created standing armies but eventually found themselves vulnerable to tribal groups or invaders adept at waging mobile warfare using the horse with the minimum of support. Harnessing the speed and size of horses changed the nature of warfare. While initially they were unprotected and vulnerable, at some point between the fifth and tenth centuries — the precise date is difficult to determine because of the

absence of contemporary sources in the Dark Ages —
the horses began to wear light armour, which by the
thirteenth century had become heavier and thicker.
Massed charges of such heavy cavalry were the
blitzkrieg of the early years of the second millennium.
There were also developments in the technology of
archery, notably the longbow, which was decisive in
several battles of what became known as the Hundred
Years War (which actually lasted very intermittently
from 1337 to 1453), and later the use of gunpowder
and cannons became vital in enabling sieges to be
broken far more easily.

Technology, therefore, determined the success of
warfare with improvements first to bows, and later
guns, often proving crucial to the outcome. As ever, it
always took time for soldiers and their leaders to
understand how to use these new weapons and the
decisive factor would frequently prove to be organization rather than technology. Well-disciplined and drilled
infantry, for example, could see off cavalry even before
the development of the machine gun. Black suggests
the equation between weaponry and equine forces half
a millennium ago was in balance: "In Europe, it was
unclear that enhanced firepower would change the
nature of war. Instead, there was an emphasis on horse
armies, while Swiss pikemen acquired a formidable
reputation in the late fifteenth century, routing Charles
the Bold of Burgundy at Granson, Murten and Nancy
in 1476–7." In what has become known as the "military
revolution" between 1560 and 1660, the increasing
sophistication of weapons required, in turn, the training

of the soldiers using them and their incorporation into permanent armies. And once a country establishes such an army, transport requirements come to the fore. Whereas previously armies had consisted of perhaps a few thousand men, their numbers now increased exponentially. Louis XIV of France, for example, raised an army of 120,000 in 1673 to see off the Dutch and even in peacetime he had a standing force of 150,000 men, though only a proportion were actually permanently in garrisons.

This is where a hitherto neglected aspect of war, logistics — the science of managing the movement of men and matériel — begins to enter the equation to a much greater extent. Larger armies needed more skill and planning to move around. The very word "logistics", derived from the French *logistique*, initially referred only to military transport since, in pre-capitalist days, there was little movement of goods on anything like a military scale and the ability to develop expertise in logistics was as important as introducing new types of weapons. Compared to the fleet forces of previous generations, armies in the second half of the sixteenth century became massive lumbering enterprises that kept growing in size as they increased in complexity. According to Martin van Creveld, who has chronicled the logistics of battles between the Thirty Years War in the early seventeenth century and the Second World War, "a force numbering, say, 30,000 men, might be followed by a crowd of women, children, servants and sutlers [suppliers] of anywhere between 50 and 150 per cent of its own size and it had to drag this

7

huge 'tail' behind it wherever it went". Armies largely consisted of uprooted men who had no other home and consequently their baggage, especially that of officers, assumed monumental proportions. Van Creveld suggests that an army in the early seventeenth century might have one wagon, hauled by two or four horses, for every fifteen men and the proportion could, at times, be double that. However, even such a large fleet of wagons was not sufficient to keep an army, and especially the horses, provided with food. There was no question of supplying armies from a base, given the slowness of any method of transport and the huge volume of fodder required. This did not present a particularly great problem when moving through friendly territory since the army would establish a supply system using local markets to buy produce (although armies could be notoriously bad payers and undisciplined even in friendly territory). For the most part, soldiers were expected to buy their own food, and while there was plenty of scope for this system to break down or be subject to corruption, for the most part it worked reasonably well.

The difficulties really started when an army began moving through hostile territory. As van Creveld puts it, "from time immemorial the problem had been solved simply by having the troops take whatever they required. More or less well organized plunder was the rule rather than the exception. Consequently, armies "were forced to keep on the move in order to stay alive". The choice of which town to besiege, therefore, was made not necessarily as a result of a particular location's strategic importance, but rather the availability of local supplies of food. The best defence against being besieged was to have been the victim of a previous assault in which the attackers had eaten up everything in the immediate vicinity!

Once armies expanded in the early seventeenth century, relying on plunder or living off the land no longer became feasible for any length of time since the number of men was too great to allow them to obtain sufficient supplies. Either the armies had to be on the move the whole time or a reliable supply system to provide men with the basic requirements of food and shelter had to be created. Rivers initially proved to be the vital line of communication and the most successful armies of the seventeenth and eighteenth centuries tended to be those that made best use of navigable waterways or, like the British, Dutch and Swedes, of the seas.

These wars in pre-capitalist times were of a completely different nature to those of the nineteenth and twentieth centuries, examined in detail in this book, which would be prolonged and involve large numbers of players on both sides. Such lengthy conflicts would only be made possible, as we shall see, by the use of the railways. That the heyday of the railway age would also become the era of total war was no coincidence. The railways would give rise to a new style of war, with particularly long, bloody and damaging conflicts between countries lasting several years and involving much of the population of whole nations. In contrast, these wars of the pre-industrial age were really a series of short battles, invariably conducted in the spring and summer months to ensure the armies could live off the land and interspersed with lengthy peaceful periods. Even though they were, in hindsight, given names like the Hundred Years War or Thirty Years War, the actual fighting in each battle would normally be over in a matter of a day or even just a couple of hours, followed by a lengthy respite before the next one. Sometimes sieges lasted much longer but the limiting factor was not only, as one would assume, the supplies available to those being besieged, but also those available to the attackers. Even where there were prolonged sieges, there were no lengthy fronts of the type established in later wars to separate the combatants, as the attackers largely ignored the areas between the towns which they were besieging.

Improvisation was crucial to these mobile armies. For example, much ammunition could be produced in the field. There was ribaldry among soldiers who were required to urinate in designated areas so that the urea could be used for gunpowder production, while cannonballs were made from any old scrap melted down in field forges. However, the moving of artillery, especially siege "trains" — which, of course, were simply strings of heavily laden carts and carriages — was a massive enterprise requiring large numbers of oxen, which are even slower than horses, and consequently covering even five miles in a day was a great achievement. Bigger artillery needed very specialized facilities, such as massive carriages and special teams of horses, to move it around.

Armies, according to conventional wisdom, march on their stomachs, but actually, far more importantly, horses do and the availability of fodder was for a long time the limiting factor in the ability of armies to stay in one place. Feeding an army on the move was far easier than preventing a static one from starving. Armies were like those irritating flies buzzing tirelessly around in the summer, never able to rest or stay in one place for very long through fear of running out of food and forage.

Gradually, the more innovative military commanders began establishing networks of magazines, essentially supply depots of mostly ammunition but also some other provisions such as uniforms and blankets, to the rear of their battle lines. There was, though, no question that whole armies could be supplied for long periods from these magazines since the sheer scale of an army's requirements and the inadequacy of pre-industrial transport systems made this impossible. Van Creveld provides a precise calculation which shows the scale of the task. The biggest army brought together before the advent of the railways was the one raised by Louis XIV to fight the Dutch. Say it was divided into two for strategic reasons and each army (the expression "army" is actually used by the military to describe a force led by a general which could number anything from 50,000, in the seventeenth century, to 200,000 or more in the First World War) consisting of 60,000 men would have 40,000 horses and need a combined total of around one million pounds (nearly 450 tons) of food per day. Effectively, very little — van Creveld estimates just over 10 per cent — could be supplied from magazines some distance away. He finds no examples of seventeenth-century armies being supplied solely from distant bases and suggests that it would have been impossible to do so even for a modest-sized army. The transport of ammunition, interestingly, was never a crucial issue until the development of far bigger guns in the late nineteenth century. Van Creveld asserts: "So small were the quantities [of ammunition] required that armies normally took along a single supply for the entire campaign, resupply from base being effected only on comparatively rare occasions — most frequently, of course, during sieges." Food though was the limiting factor: "From beginning to end [of the wars of Louis XIV], the most difficult logistic problem facing Louvois [Louis's Secretary of State for War], his contemporaries and his successors was much less to feed an army on the move than to prevent one that was stationary from starving."

During the eighteenth century armies grew bigger and bigger and by its end Napoleon's *Grande Armée* peaked at a remarkable 2.5 million. But because these enormous groups of men lived largely off the local land, "taking the bulk of their needs away from the country", they were unable to stay in one place for any length of time. Van Creveld's back-of-the-envelope calculation demonstrates this unequivocally: "Had an army of, say, 100,000 men, wanted to bring up all its supplies for the duration of the campaign — usually calculated as 180 days [spring and summer] — from base, the resulting burden on the transportation system would have been so great as to make all warfare utterly impossible."

Consequently war before the nineteenth century was to be waged as cheaply and quickly as possible and armies were expected to live at the expense of their enemies by exploiting their territories.

Napoleon's surge through Europe in the late eighteenth and early nineteenth centuries marked a different kind of warfare, with an even greater emphasis on mobility and an end to the notion of sieges. Napoleon recognized the importance of logistics. His armies did suffer supply problems whenever they got bogged down, such as in Mantua in 1796 and before the battle of Austerlitz, his greatest triumph, in 1805, but his true military genius was in ensuring that he never stayed anywhere long enough to get into trouble. According to the historian David A. Bell, Napoleon personally took "charge of matters ranging from the number of carts needed to carry a regiment's paperwork to the amount of munitions carried by soldiers". He had an almost photographic memory and was able to work out the logistical needs of his army down to the minutest detail, yet that did not negate the simple fact that his huge armies could never be fed through supply lines but still relied on living off the land.

Napoleon's belief in the importance of mobility was the key to his success. As van Creveld puts it, "the French armies [were able to do] what their predecessors had normally failed to do, namely to march from one end of Europe to the other, destroying everything in their way". There were several factors that allowed him to do this. Under the *corps d'armée*

13

system, his armies were dispersed, making it easier to feed themselves from the countryside. He lightened the loads of his armies, dispensing with the large amounts of baggage and the vast numbers of hangers-on that had hampered the movement of troops in the past and he was helped by various external factors, such as the higher density of the population, which ensured there were more farms to plunder. He was, too, as van Creveld emphasizes, a unique military genius whose abilities were a key component of his success. It was only when he became bogged down in long-running campaigns such as in Spain or in the Tyrol, or reached out beyond the relative richness of the European heartland into Egypt and Russia, that his system collapsed and the troops began to starve.

While Napoleon may have revolutionized the manner of waging war, his troops were still dependent on living off the land. Although he did at times try to create massive magazines behind the front from which supplies were despatched, invariably the inadequate roads and lack of sufficient transport meant that they were never sufficient to supply his army. In a way, Napoleon straddles two types of war, pre- and post-railways. He made use of more sophisticated supply chains than had any previous military commander but he was still constrained by the inadequacy of transport facilities, which forced his troops to live off the land, limiting his ability to manoeuvre. Napoleon made mobility the key to success and, with simple tactics and brilliant strategies, he moved armies faster than anyone had before and punched harder than his enemies. At times, the Napoleonic Wars were railway wars without the railways. He even called his supply wagons "trains": they consisted of dedicated lines of wagons bringing up supplies behind the army. However, this supply system was still only sustainable for short periods of time and over relatively modest distances.

Napoleon's foolhardy incursion into Russia in 1812 demonstrates this perfectly. At first, Napoleon's brilliant organizational skills enabled the "trains" to supply his army of 650,000 men efficiently, but he was reliant on a quick victory because beyond a couple of hundred miles it was impossible to sustain the advance through supplies from the rear. His "trains" were not expected to keep up with the front-line soldiers on their rapid 600-mile march through central Europe. This suggests that, from a purely logistical point of view, the invasion was never sustainable because there was not enough food and forage for the soldiers to live off the land. Napoleon relied on the richer farming country nearer Moscow to sustain his troops, but inevitably the advance foundered as the men suffered from heat exhaustion on the march eastwards and hunger as the local peasantry fled taking their supplies with them (and burning what they left behind, a scorched-earth policy later revived by Stalin in 1941). He had hoped for a campaign of just three weeks and once it was extended there was no hope of victory. Moscow was always an overambitious target; once the retreat was sounded, starvation in the arctic conditions was inevitable and about half of Napoleon's army perished.

15

The rapid retreat from the burnt-out Moscow illustrated the point that such a huge army had to be permanently on the move. The French army had been far better organized than its opposition, but the Russians triumphed partly because they had a shorter supply line which kept more of them alive, but also because they were used to the conditions and more motivated as they were on home territory fighting off an invader. The Russian tactics were to resist briefly then retreat, hoping the French would follow and overstretch themselves in the process, a strategy the Russians would repeat when repelling the German invasion in 1941.

The ability of armies to move — and, ironically, to stay put — changed in the nineteenth century as the advent of the industrial age not only revolutionized weaponry but also the transport system. The railways would change the equation between mobility and ability to access supplies, but it would take time for the military to understand how. Wars are not won or lost solely by weaponry or even the numbers of combatants on each side. It is the mundane aspects of military operations that are crucial, such as food, supplies and lines of communication.

There were some counter-intuitive effects of the introduction of the railways, particularly in respect of the military's dependence on horses. The bulkiness of fodder meant that it had previously never been possible to transport it over any great distance because the animals would need to eat more than they could carry. Interestingly the arrival of the railways gave a new lease of life to the cavalry as large numbers of horses could be maintained by rail supply and the railways enabled production to be globalized, resulting in the production of massive quantities of cheap feedstuffs. Moreover, the cavalry could be transported to nearer the battlefield, keeping both men and animals fresh.

Napoleon's wars were the last significant conflict before the advent of the railways. How he would have loved to have had them at his disposal, transforming the logistics at which he was so adept. His less gifted successors, the military leaders of the middle of the nineteenth century, would find it harder to adapt to their arrival than he would have done. The railways would require a complete change of tactics and the ability — or indeed failure — to exploit their potential to the full was to be a decisive factor in several conflicts. As with all innovations, the military, ever conservative and often fighting a previous war, were rarely, as we shall see in the forthcoming chapters, able to appreciate immediately the advantage they offered.

CHAPTER
TWO

The Railways Called
Into Action

After Napoleon's defeat and exile, the absence of significant European wars in the first half of the nineteenth century coincided with the creation of the early railways and the beginning of their spread around the world. The construction of the first railways was stimulated by peaceful purposes for the carriage of both passengers and freight rather than for either defensive or offensive strategic objectives, but it was not long before some army commanders realized the railways' military potential for the simplest task, moving troops around the country. And in the early days of the railways, more often than not the troops were deployed against their own people, rather than a distant enemy.

Indeed, the railways had shown their usefulness in that respect right from the start. Soon after its opening in 1830, the Liverpool & Manchester Railway carried a regiment of troops from Manchester to the docks in Liverpool on their way to quell a rebellion in Ireland, then part of the United Kingdom. The thirty-one-mile journey took just over two hours, rather than the two days required to march that distance, and had the added advantage that the troops arrived in a far fresher condition. The railway's owners were canny enough to negotiate a cheap rate for the carriage of troops on active service, the world's first such agreement.

Britain's railway system built up relatively slowly in the 1830s, but nevertheless by 1839 there was a line between Manchester and London which General Sir Charles Napier used to reach the capital after being called from his northern headquarters by the leader of the ruling Whigs, Lord John Russell. Sir Charles impressed Russell by arriving within twenty-four hours of the summons and was exultant about this new service, writing in his diary: "Well done steam! Smoke, thou art wonderful, and a reformer." He had even more cause to be grateful to the railways a few weeks later when he needed the 10th Regiment of Foot stationed in Ireland to return rapidly to Manchester to quell yet another riot. Not only did the troops arrive speedily, but they were full of vigour and, according to Sir Charles, their numbers appeared to have grown on the journey: "One wing of the 10th came by morning train yesterday; the other by an evening train, which made everybody suppose two regiments had arrived.

Sir Charles, though, was something of an exception in his enthusiasm for the railways among British military men of the age. As an island nation with no enemies that could be reached without a journey by sea, the British did not really understand the railways' potential for military use and there was little interest in the subject during the early days of the railway era. The

19

usefulness of this new means of transport did not entirely escape the attention of the state, however, as legislation passed in 1842, one of the first laws affecting the railways, gave the military priority access to them. Two years later, a further Act imposed a duty on the railway companies to provide any trains required by the government for military purposes at a set fare that was well below the standard rate. Again, however, the thinking seems to have been around the railways' usefulness in helping to quell internal dissent rather than to transport soldiers to war in foreign lands.

In Europe, however, there was more understanding of the railways' military potential in conflicts between nations. In the early 1830s, even before any countries on the Continent had built significant lines, there were strategists who were aware that the railways could be used for military purposes. In the Austrian empire and the states that would eventually form Germany, countries with lengthy and easily crossed land borders, it was these arguments which were deployed to stimulate the early development of railways. Indeed, several early supporters of the railways in continental Europe emphasized their military value over all else. In 1833, Friedrich Harkort, a Westphalian entrepreneur and railway pioneer, wrote a pamphlet advocating a railway between Minden and Cologne which, while stressing its value for the economy, also underlined its military potential by calculating how much quicker Prussian soldiers could reach various key towns by rail rather than on foot. Such connections were vital for Prussia, since the settlement at the Congress of Vienna in 1815 after Napoleon's defeat had not given Prussia the Kingdom of Saxony that it wanted but rather a mountainous and woody tract of land in western Germany that became the Ruhr industrial heartland of the nation. It was separated from the main part of Prussia by a collection of small powerless states, which made good communications vital, especially as the local population were none too happy at being part of Prussia.

Harkort also promoted the idea of a much more overtly military railway, a line on the Prussian side of the Rhine which, he said, with some justification, would prevent the French ever reaching across the river since the railway would allow Prussian troops to be rushed to any spot under attack. Harkort, though, was before his time. As John Westwood asserts in his history of railways at war, "neither the Prussian military nor the Prussian press accepted Harkort's ideas, preferring to make fun of him whenever they could not ignore him". Writing nearly a decade after Harkort, Karl Pönitz found a more receptive audience with his 1842 treatise *Railways and Their Utility from the Viewpoint of Lines of Military Operations*, which elicited considerable interest in military quarters. The issue for Prussia, and later Germany, was always that it faced possible attack from two sides, Russia to the east and France to the west. Pönitz looked admiringly at Belgium: "The network of Belgian railways will be of as much advantage in advancing the industries of that country as it will be in facilitating the defence of the land against attack by France."

Pönitz had good reason to view Belgium as an example to follow. Right from its creation, Belgium had seen the railways and the military as having a symbiotic relationship. It was a new nation created by the split from the Netherlands in 1830 and the railways were seen not just as a way of establishing its national identity, but also as the means of maintaining its economic independence by providing an alternative transport system to the waterways dominated by its northern neighbour, which had, in the past, at times blocked off access to Antwerp. Belgium, where work began on the first railway in 1834, is not generally known for many world firsts but it was undoubtedly the unlikely pioneer in the understanding of the railways' military value.

Pönitz therefore put forward the notion of a series of six east-west railways across Germany built for military rather than commercial reasons. These would be linked by a series of radial lines that would ensure communication could be maintained even if some sections of the web were destroyed. Pönitz even went as far as to calculate how many troops each line would be able to carry and how long it would take them to get to the frontier, elementary arithmetic which subsequent military commanders frequently failed to work out. However, while his ideas were met with approval from some military leaders, Germany was not in a position to undertake such a massive enterprise. At the time it was a loose Confederation of thirty-nine independent states which, like rival neighbouring football teams refusing to share a ground, were wary of joining together despite the obvious advantages. In particular, they were suspicious of anything suggested by Prussia, the most powerful state of the Confederation. Moreover, most of their railway systems were in private hands and since a network designed primarily to suit military purposes could never be expected to pay for itself, a strong government involvement and considerable subsidy would be needed.

It would, therefore, take several decades and the Franco-Prussian War for Pönitz's ideas to bear fruit. In the meantime, the railways themselves were instrumental in bringing the states closer together economically — and therefore politically — by encouraging cross-border trade and making customs duties irrelevant, although the final union of the German empire did not take place until 1871.

The French, for their part, were even slower to recognize the military value of the railways. Indeed, according to the historian Armand Mattelart, the very notion of allowing them onto trains was "suspected of making soldiers effeminate". Certainly, there were debates in French government circles as early as in the 1840s about the strategic value of railways but there was little consensus. Moreover, while the planned lines radiating out of Paris would have enabled troops to be despatched to France's various frontiers — the Spanish, unlike the Germans and the Italians, had carefully chosen an alternative gauge for their railways so that they could resist any such invasion — the system was not designed with such aggressive intent in mind. After the initial rush following the opening of

France's first railway in 1832, the French had been rather sluggish in establishing anything like a railway network because of doubts among the intelligentsia about its value, prompting Helmuth von Moltke (the elder Moltke), later the long-serving Prussian Army leader but then only an ambitious staff officer, to remark sarcastically in 1844 that "while the French chamber debates railways, Germany builds them".

During most of the subsequent century, when railways were an essential component of warfare, the French military would have to make do for the most part with the tracks that happened to have been laid down for civilian needs. In the 1840s, it eventually started dawning on the French military hierarchy that the German railways might increase the potential for an invasion by their eastern neighbour, but they were never entirely convinced by the threat. The refusal to spot the obvious was well illustrated by the comments of the French consul in Mainz, in the Rhineland, who reported in 1849 that he felt "nothing indicates an offensive attitude, nothing that is hostile to France".He was to be proved wrong three times within the next century.

All in all, given that the various elements among government and military leaders on both sides had begun, albeit slowly, to acknowledge the value of railways in a potential conflict and each one saw the other as its most dangerous military rival, both France and Germany were guilty of complacency in their strategic railway preparations. It was only in the run-up to the Franco-Prussian War, as we shall see in Chapter

Four, that both sides belatedly began to examine how best to make use of the iron road in the event of war.

Any doubts about the value of the railways in a military context were to be dispelled by the terrifying events of the late 1840s. The ruling elites of Europe were, in the main, still absolute monarchs who had made scant concession to democracy; suddenly a wave of revolutionary and nationalist fervour swept the Continent and on numerous occasions troops were mobilized to crush these uprisings. Indeed, the most repressive regime of the age, the government of the Russian Tsar, was so fearful of people being able to travel more easily that it imposed regulations which required passengers to have a passport before being able to take the train linking Moscow with St Petersburg, ensuring that only the politically sound could move without hindrance around the country.

Of course, it worked both ways. The railways helped spread revolutionary ideas and were widely perceived as a democratizing force, opening up countries to people who had never been able to travel around them before. However, they also made it far easier for the strong arm of the state to impose itself on those who were perceived as a threat to the status quo. The ruling elites throughout Europe were soon routinely despatching troops by rail to maintain control and even began to build lines in the knowledge that a railway into a rebellious region was the key to nipping trouble in the bud. Therefore, while at first there had been an assumption that railways would be useful for governments in supporting an offensive or defending

25

themselves against outside aggression, now they were beginning to understand that their value was equally great in countering the threat within. As John Westwood, author of *Railways at War*, concludes, "the use which governments might make of railways for the movement of troops against internal dissidents had probably a greater appeal than the more purely strategic arguments".

The first significant transport of troops by rail was the despatch of 14,500 Prussian soldiers, together with their horses and wagons, to smash the Krakow rebellion of Polish nationalists in 1846, taking just two days to cover the 200-mile journey from their garrison at Hradish in Bohemia. Then, in 1848, Tsar Nicholas I, the most reactionary of the nineteenth-century monarchs — quite an accolade given the competition — got in on the act. He had no compunction in despatching 30,000 troops on the newly established Warsaw — Vienna railway to help his ally, the Austrian emperor, Ferdinand, quell a rebellion in Hungary in a particularly ruthless and bloody way. A few months later, the Austrians, in turn, made use of the railways to send reinforcements to reimpose their rule over Italy following a partial takeover by nationalists. That movement of troops stimulated the first recorded instance of railway sabotage when Venetian rebels, led by Daniele Manin, blew up some of the arches of the long viaduct linking their city with the mainland to try to prevent the Austrians reaching their island. They were unsuccessful as their sabotage only managed to lengthen the siege of the city, which ultimately fell to the Austrians in August 1849.

There were several significant troop movements on railways in the 1850s which made governments throughout Europe aware of the military potential of these networks, even if they were still unable to comprehend how completely the iron road would change the nature of war. The first of these involved the despatch of a 75,000-strong Austrian army, along with 8,000 horses and a thousand carts, from Vienna to Bohemia early in the winter of 1850. As Edwin Pratt, the first historian of the role of railways in war and whose seminal work on the subject, *The Rise of Rail Power in War and Conquest*, was published in 1915, puts it wryly, "owing to the combined disadvantages of single-line railways, inadequate staff and rolling stock, unfavourable weather, lack of previous preparations and of transport regulations and delays from various unforeseen causes, no fewer than 26 days were occupied in the transport" for a journey of a mere 150 miles, in other words barely six miles per day.

It would ever be thus. The limitations of a rail line, together with the failure of the military to exploit it properly, would lead to many similar stories. Nevertheless, van Creveld describes this movement as "perhaps the first time when the railways played an important part in international power politics by helping to bring about the Prussian humiliation at Olmütz [the agreement under which the Prussians were forced to give up their claim to leadership of the German Confederation]". The Austrian Emperor, Franz Joseph,

27

was sufficiently impressed to draw up a scheme for a strategic rail network and to devise plans for future movements of troops which could be carried out without disruption to existing traffic on the rail network. Unfortunately, despite this, the Austrians, as we see below, never quite got to grips with railway logistics while the Prussians, in contrast, would learn the lessons of their humiliation.

In spite of the hesitations and the nonsense about "feminising" soldiers, the French finally began to recognize the advantage of carrying soldiers by rail and, in fact, undertook two of the biggest early troop movements by rail, both times taking armies to the Mediterranean for embarkation to wage wars overseas. The first was used to take troops to the Crimean War in 1854 and the second, five years later, to fight the Austrians in Italy. The railway between Paris and Marseille was not even quite complete at the outbreak of the Crimean War but the troops were able to use large sections of it to hasten their journey southwards.

The French actually sent more troops to the Crimean War than the British, 400,000 as against 250,000, and large numbers of them travelled by train to the Mediterranean seaports for embarkation. However, it was the British who were to use a railway in a completely novel way during this war. Indeed, the Crimean War was the first in which a railway played a major part in maintaining lines of communication, partly as a result of the poor preparations made by the British, who had not learnt the lessons from Napoleon about logistics.

A transport corps, called the Royal Wagon Train, had been formed in 1799 and indeed operated during the Napoleonic Wars, but was disbanded in 1833 for reasons of economy, which meant that the regiments sent to the Crimea had to organize their own transport, at times without the benefit of any mules or horses. Notionally transport was the responsibility of the Treasury, which was separate from both the War Office, responsible for the Army, and the Master General of the Ordnance, in charge of supplying ammunition and equipment. The Treasury showed little interest in this task but this ridiculous and dysfunctional system was not scrapped until the 1870s, even though its shortcomings were exposed by the Crimean War.

The Crimean War was a misconceived and unnecessary venture, fought in difficult terrain and awful conditions by an army which lost far more men to sickness and disease than combat and earned the description by the historian Eric Hobsbawm as "a notoriously incompetent international butchery". The war was fought between Russia on one side and an alliance that encompassed Britain, France, the Ottoman Empire and the Kingdom of Sardinia on the other in a number of theatres, including the Balkans and Finland, and lasted from late 1853 until early 1856. However, the key battles were in the Crimea, notably the prolonged siege of Sevastopol by the British and French forces.

The ostensible *casus belli* was obscure in the extreme, a dispute about access to the holy sites of Jerusalem, which gradually turned into war because of

29

a failure of diplomacy and much ridiculous posturing. In fact, the Russians had long been on the outlook for an excuse to wrest control of the Black Sea — and consequently the land route through to India — from the crumbling Ottoman Empire, but they misread the diplomatic situation, not realizing that the Turks would receive so much support and expecting, wrongly, that Austria would be willing to fight on their side. Britain and France declared war after the Russians attacked the Turkish fleet in November 1853, wiping it out with the loss of more than 3,000 sailors. While this declaration was presented as a response to the horrors of the Russian attack, the two Great Powers had their own motives for becoming involved, as they sought to prevent the Slavonic parts of the Ottoman Empire, and even possibly Constantinople, from falling into Russian hands.

If the Russians were unprepared for a major and prolonged conflict, so too were the British, who had been at peace since the end of the Napoleonic Wars, more than a generation previously, and it was this lack of preparation which was to lead to the need for a railway as a key element of the supply route. The British army sent to the Crimea had lost its sense of purpose, having become obsessed with pomp and ceremony during the long years of inaction. As Anthony Burton, a railway historian, puts it eloquently: "The ordinary soldiers, poorly paid and badly fed, were no more than mannequins, displaying ever more gorgeous uniforms . . . The slightest falling away of standards — a dirty button, a foot placed out of sequence — was greeted with the vicious punishment of the lash. This was the army of popinjays and paupers that was sent to the distant Crimea to fight a real war in which blood would be spilled."

In response to the annihilation of the Turkish fleet, in the summer of 1854 a force of 60,000 troops, together with 3,000 horses and 130 heavy field guns, was landed on the Crimean peninsula (now in Ukraine) by the British and French, supported by their Turkish allies. The idea was to attack and capture Sevastopol, a fortress town and port of crucial importance in controlling the Black Sea. The hope, as with so many wars, was that it would be a quick campaign with the town falling after a period of bombardment and that the war would be over by Christmas. But it did not work out like that. There was an initial victory at Alma soon after the force landed but this was not followed up quickly enough and the wet summer turned into a freezing winter against which the troops had no protection.

The British had arrived utterly unprepared. They had sent an army 3,000 miles from home by ship scandalously ill-equipped and, as a wet summer turned into a freezing winter, the conditions for the troops became unbearable. The death rates from disease and malnutrition were staggering, the result, as Brian Cooke, the historian of the Crimean railway, suggests, of "the indifference and incompetence of a government and Army command which had sent out a large military expeditionary force almost totally lacking in any of the services necessary to support it".

The eight-mile road between the British base at the port of Balaklava and the front line, from where the bombardment and siege of Sevastopol were being conducted by 30,000 troops, was a terrible bottleneck. It was completely inadequate for the purpose of carrying thousands of tons of ammunition and other equipment and little thought had been given to the logistics. The army was dependent upon Russian ox wagons captured when the troops first landed and a few Turkish ponies, but according to Captain Henry Clifford, an officer stationed at Balaklava, "the cold, want of food and hard work have killed the oxen and ponies, and the roads are impassable".The troops were down to "a quarter of half rations of pork and biscuit". Later, he described how by December ammunition was running out because "our artillery horses [were] dying three and four a night".

As more and more supplies piled into Balaklava, unable to be taken up to Sevastopol, the state of chaos increased. There were numerous tales of food and forage rotting on board the ships while both men and animals starved. A letter in the *Illustrated London News* described what had, before the war, been a pleasant fisherman's harbour: "The harbour is a cesspool and the beach a bottomless pit full of liquid abominations — a putrid sea of black foetid mire, exhaling a poisonous stench even at this cold season and pregnant with the deaths of thousands the moment the hot sun of spring shall come forth to quicken the pestilence . . ." William Russell, the legendary *Times* reporter who has claim to being the world's first war correspondent, was blunt: "There is nothing to eat, nothing to drink, no roads, no commissariat, no medicine, no clothes, no arrangement: the only thing in abundance is cholera."

The British belatedly recognized that they would have to improve the line of communication up to the encampment outside Sevastopol to maintain the siege. The death of most of the horses and oxen from neglect and exhaustion, and the lack of timber to build what was called a corduroy road (a crude but firm path built with logs perpendicular to the direction of travel and covered with sand), suggested that a railway might be the obvious solution.

The idea was not, however, a product of military imagination; nor did it come from the government ministers who had become aware of the logistical failings. While previous military campaigns had been just as poorly organized and neglectful of human life, the difference this time was that there were journalists and photographers — "embedded" in the modern parlance — who were able to inform the public back home of the disastrous turn of events. Without this flow of information, the railway might never have been built. The suggestion to build it came, in fact, from railway interests back in Britain. The country had just been through its biggest ever railway boom, with the result that an astonishing network of over 6,000 miles of track had been completed by 1854, a mere quarter-century after the first major railway had opened. Many of these lines had been built by Samuel Peto, one of the great early railway contractors, who had also been responsible for lines laid in much more difficult conditions in places as far afield as Norway and Nova Scotia. Hearing of the transport difficulties through Russell's reports in *The Times*, Peto, a Whig MP and a widely respected figure, suggested to the Duke of Newcastle, the Secretary of State for War, that a railway be built from Balaklava to the encampment up the hill. It was not a notion that was universally welcomed among some of the senior military, who argued for simply improving the road. But the lack of animals and Peto's promise to build the line quickly proved decisive.

Peto teamed up with Edward Betts, with whom he had built several railways, and Thomas Brassey, the other prolific contractor of the day, and the trio promised that since they were working in the national interest they would carry out the work at cost without making any profit. After his suggestion to build the line was accepted by the Duke of Newcastle, the material for the railway was gathered together at remarkable speed. So was the workforce of around 250 experienced navvies — eventually nearly four times as many worked on the line at the peak of construction — who were not only motivated by the nationalistic fervour which they strongly espoused but also by the shortage of work since the collapse of the railway mania in Britain in the late 1840s. The flotilla of steamers carrying the men and material managed to leave in December 1854 for the two-month journey within a few weeks of the acceptance of the idea by the government.

The project certainly caught the imagination of the public, who liked the idea of these rowdy navvies being sent to the other end of Europe to save the British army. Peto was appointed chief engineer and was rewarded for his efforts with a baronetcy, although he did not actually travel to the Crimea. He left the work on the ground in the charge of James Beatty, an experienced rail engineer, who was paid the princely sum of £1,500 (the equivalent of around £1.2m today) to build the railway. Brassey and Betts stayed at home, too, but provided advice and financial support.

Arriving in a small advance party, the surveyor, Donald Campbell, had largely set out the route for the little railway by the time Beatty got there on 19 January. It was no easy task as the terrain and conditions were ill-suited for a railway. There was an initial problem over the location of the railway sidings at the wharf, but then Campbell decided to keep it simple by placing the railway in the centre of the main street in order to obviate the need for demolition of any existing buildings. Out of town, there was swampy land that required a few small bridges to ford the rivulets, but the most difficult section was about a mile after the village of Kadikoi, with a sharp incline up a valley reaching a col 600 feet above sea level to terminate on the plateau where the army was laying siege to Sevastopol. At its steepest, the gradient was one in fourteen, far too onerous for conventional locomotives of the day, and Campbell therefore realized that a stationary engine, using cables to haul the trains up the slope, would have to be installed.

The first group of 500 men arrived soon after Beatty. Most were ordinary navvies but there were also a hundred carpenters, a dozen engine drivers, three doctors and, remarkably, three scripture readers, whose injunctions fell on deaf ears on the trip as the navvies more than lived up to their infamous reputation. They had disembarked at Gibraltar (a timeless British military tradition), where they had got thoroughly drunk and a brave group had actually climbed up to join the monkeys on the Rock. At the next stop, in Malta, they had been banned from taking any money ashore to prevent similar drunken exploits, but they promptly staged prize fights to raise cash for their booze. News of these exploits had preceded them and their presence in Balaklava was met with hostility from some military top brass, who doubted their ability to build the railway. The officers were swiftly proved wrong. The navvies' effectiveness as railway builders could not be faulted and the military were impressed by their endeavours. Within a week of the navvies' arrival, rails were being laid on the road in Balaklava and much of the alignment of the whole route had been prepared. Captain Clifford was won over. While in his diary he describes the navvies on their arrival as "unutterable things", a few days later he wrote that "I was astonished to see the progress of the Railway in Balaklava . . . the navvies do more work in a day than a Regiment of English Soldiers do in a week."

Peto had rather rashly promised the Duke of Newcastle that the line would be ready within three weeks of the arrival of the workforce, but in the event it took slightly more than twice that time, still an amazing feat. Working conditions were appalling as the men, who toiled night and day, had to contend with several feet of mud using only spades, forks and wheelbarrows to help them. Although horses, mules and even camels were available, there was a shortage of animal labour as so many had succumbed to exhaustion and injuries caused by accidents.

Nevertheless, within ten days of the first landing, track had been laid to the village of Kadikoi, and as soon as the first section had been completed it was employed to carry material to the navvies building the remainder of the line and to help with the transport of supplies to the troops. The Grand Crimean Central Railway, to call it by its rather overstated and grandiose official title, was completed on 26 March 1855. While it was a crude and basic railway, its construction in just seven weeks during a fierce winter and early spring was a remarkable achievement. Although it was only seven miles long, Peto later pointed out that it comprised a total of thirty-nine miles of track, including branches, sidings and various sections of double track.

The operation of the railway was a cumbersome process, and sounds like something designed by the architects of the hugely complex railway privatization introduced by the Conservative government of the mid-1990s. The first two miles from Balaklava were worked by conventional steam locomotives imported from Britain and operated by Royal Engineers. Then the wagons were drawn up the steep incline from Kadikoi in batches of eight by the stationary engine, which again was under the charge of the Engineers. In the next stage, six horses, the responsibility of the newly

37

created Land Transport Corps, would drag the wagons in pairs up a further incline and finally a combination of gravity and further horse haulage would bring the wagons, each capable of carrying up to three tons, to the upland campsite. The return of the wagons to Balaklava was largely by gravity, which caused numerous accidents when brakes failed or were not applied sufficiently, including one which led to the death of poor Beatty. Although apparently not badly hurt at the time, he returned to Britain and succumbed soon after, aged just thirty-six, to an aneurysm which the autopsy revealed had been caused when he fell from the train. The navvies, who had six-month contracts, went home too. By then the army, so impressed by their work, had wanted them to stay to build fortifications, but the contractors insisted they were civilians and could not be obliged to remain. The navvies, too, were eager to return, though not before at least one had been killed by a Russian cannonball while partaking in the local spectator sport of watching the bombardment of the besieged town.

Despite the complex and at times dangerous operating procedures, the line represented a far better and safer alternative to the cart roads which still carried many supplies. As soon as it was completed, the railway was rapidly put into action at full capacity, although the army placed ridiculous constraints on its working, limiting its usefulness by stating that no supplies could be sent before 8a.m. or after 5.30p.m.

During much of the time the railway was being built, the fighting had stopped for the winter and it seemed for a while that it might never resume. The Tsar, Nicholas I, had died and was replaced by the more modernizing Alexander II, but in the early days of his rule he did not have sufficient confidence to call a halt to the crazy conflict. In Britain, too, there had been political changes. The government had fallen as a result of the scandalous conduct of the war brought to the public's attention by Russell's graphic reports. Lord Aberdeen, the Prime Minister, was replaced by Lord Palmerston but that only served to encourage the British to redouble their efforts, given the national embarrassment about the failings of the 1854 campaign and the far better performance of their allies, the French, who had only recently been the enemy. Now with the railway fully functioning, the assault by the Allies, bolstered by the arrival of the Sardinian army, resumed. Thanks to the railway, supplies of ammunition could be brought up the hill to enable the bombardment, which had been halted for six months, to recommence. The attack, which began on Easter Monday, 9 April 1855, was the fiercest bombardment in all military history until that time, and lasted ten days. The railway played an invaluable role in supplying this attack, which involved the firing of 47,000 artillery rounds, including a far higher proportion than previously of the heavier shells, which could now be carried up to the guns far more easily.

The results, however, were disappointing, and the siege was not broken. The Russians managed to repair much of the damage caused by the artillery fire and, more important, no proper plan for an assault on the town, which would have to be a joint effort with the French, had been drawn up. The hope had been that the Russians would simply melt away under the bombardment but, despite incurring massive casualties under the artillery barrage which had turned the town into a charnel house, they remained in place. Further similar bombardments in June and August again failed to break Russian resolve and it was not until yet another attack in early September that the siege was finally broken. On each occasion the railway was vital in supplying artillery fire on an unprecedented scale and the final bombardment was on an even greater scale, with 307 guns being used to fire 150,000 rounds in just four days. As Cooke concludes, the railway turned Sevastopol into "the first victim of the modern application of artillery to war. Never before had so many guns been concentrated into such a small area. Never before had ammunition been available in such prodigal quantities." While the railway might appear to have been a modest little line, its importance in military history should not be underestimated. As Cooke goes on to say, "the idea of a relatively sophisticated and complex system of transport being especially built to feed the guns was being adopted for the first time. It was to reach its zenith on the Western Front in the First World War." Whereas previously railways had been used to carry troops, here a specially built line became for the first time a vital part of the line of communication.

After the collapse of Sevastopol, the war meandered to a halt, its futility slowly dawning on the new Tsar, who signed a rather humiliating peace treaty in Paris in

March 1856. In the intervening months, however, the railway had been improved and was used to carry vast amounts of supplies to the British camp on the plateau as the generals had expected the war to continue and did not want the troops to spend a second winter out in the open. In the event, the utterly futile war cost nearly a quarter of a million lives, mostly to disease, and it may well have lasted longer had not the railway been built because the allies were intent on continuing their siege however much the Russians resisted.

Of course, not all the supplies arrived by rail. The road between Balaklava and the front line was eventually greatly improved but the railways continued to carry most of the heavy matériel, an average of 250-300 tons per day during the bombardments, the equivalent of perhaps a thousand carloads pulled by a couple of horses each, showing the huge capacity afforded by even such a Heath Robinson contraption. At its peak, the railway was worked by a huge group of 1,000 men, including many Turks, and carried 700 tons per day. The French, who fired more, but mostly lighter, shells than the British, did not have the benefit of a railway. However, their front line was more easily reached from their base, which was on the other side of the Crimean peninsula from Balaklava, partly because they had ensured the connecting road was well maintained.

As Brian Cooke sums up, "the railway did not save the British Army", since most of the poor soldiers who arrived in the initial wave of landings died of disease and starvation in the first winter, but it did have a huge

41

impact on the war through the simple expedient of allowing goods to be cleared out of Balaklava and used by front-line troops. More importantly, it taught the more far-seeing elements in the British military the importance of basic logistics since the army, until then, had seemed to assume that "if supplies of ammunition, food, fuel and clothing were delivered in sufficient quantities to the British base then they would distribute themselves automatically". Peto was extremely proud of what had been achieved. After listing the achievement of building the line so fast, he said: "I received a letter from Field Marshal Burgoyne on his return from the command of the Engineering Staff, stating it was impossible to overrate the services rendered by the railway, or its effect in shortening the time of the siege and alleviating the fatigues and suffering of the troops."

While the Crimean conflict is possibly best remembered for the work of Florence Nightingale, it marked another significant event: the first time that a railway was used to carry injured soldiers away from a theatre of war. While the railway was being built, the engineers and navvies had witnessed the appalling sight of the injured and dying being led down the hill to Balaklava, as Russell described in one of his dispatches: "A large number of sick and I fear dying men were sent into Balaklava today on French mule litters . . . many of the men were all but dead. With closed eyes, open mouths and ghastly attenuated faces, they were borne along, two and two, the thin stream of breath, visible in the air, alone showing that they were still alive. One figure was a horror — a corpse, stone dead, strapped

THE RAILWAYS CALLED INTO ACTION

upright in its seat, its legs hanging stiffly down, the eyes staring wide open, the teeth set on the protruding tongue, the head and body nodding with frightful mockery of life at each stride of the mule." Russell noted with satisfaction that now the railway was being used to bring down injured and sick troops: "Four wagons filled with sick and wounded soldiers, ran from headquarters to the town in less than half an hour. The men were propped up on their knapsacks and seemed very comfortable. What a change from the ghastly processions one met with some weeks ago, formed of dead and dying men, hanging from half-starved horses or dangling about on French mule-litters." As we shall see, it would nevertheless not be until the First World War that specially designed ambulance trains would carry out this task.

Just as the French Army had used the railway between Paris and the Mediterranean to move troops to the Crimea, their second major rail movement five years later took the same route, making use of the now completed Paris-Lyon-Méditerranée (PLM) to reach the country's southern seaports. This deployment was on a much larger scale than previous rail transportation of troops and would have a much more direct impact on the outcome of the conflict. However, it would also highlight the limitations of moving men rapidly towards a conflict without proper consideration of the rest of the army's logistical needs. The troops' destination was Lombardy to help the Italians chase the Austrians out of their country. Napoleon III had agreed to help the Kingdom of Savoy (Savoie) take Lombardy from the

Austrians in return for Savoy giving the strip of the Mediterranean coast that included Nice and the French-speaking part of Savoy south of Geneva back to the French.

Since neither the coastal nor the alpine railways between France and Italy had yet been built, the troops had to travel down to the Mediterranean to complete their journey by ship to Genoa. Pratt reports that in a three-month period from April 1859 the French railways carried more than 600,000 troops and 125,000 horses, with a maximum of 12,000 being transported in a single day, without, moreover, affecting the existing passenger traffic. While other historians have suggested that there may be an element of double counting in these statistics since the numbers do appear massive, Pratt's hypothesis that an army could be carried by rail six times faster than by road, as well as arriving in a far better state, is difficult to challenge.

The Austrians were surprised by the speed of the arrival of the French troops in Italy and their own preparations had been marred by their failure to learn from the mistakes of their 1850 experience when despatching troops between Vienna and Bohemia. Not only were they short of railway lines, but they had still not grasped how to make effective use of them. The station at Vienna, the staging point for reinforcements from the whole of the Habsburg empire, was choked with supplies, a situation that was exacerbated by the lack of rolling stock to take them to the front. This is a perennial issue at times of war because returning trains of empty wagons is considered by the military to be low priority when, in fact, as railway managers know, it is vital to ensure an efficient line of communication. On average, it took fourteen days for a unit to be taken from Vienna to the Lombardy battlefield, a journey that with efficient use of the railway should have been completed in just two. Admittedly, transport to the front was made more difficult by the steep gradients on the Semmering railway between Vienna and Trieste, the world's first mountain railway, since trains had to be split into three sections to get up the mountains, slowing down the whole process. Despite these difficulties, the Austrians made extensive use of their railways but the lack of a route that reached the front line directly meant the troops had to march a considerable distance from the railhead and consequently they arrived far more tired than their enemies.

The French on the other hand had quickly learnt how to make good tactical use of the railways. After disembarking at Genoa, the troops travelled on an Italian railway to head north to Alessandria, from where the Franco-Sardinian forces used local lines to defeat the Austrians on a couple of occasions. On 20 May 1859, the Austrians were beaten at Montebello because, as *The Times* reported, "train after train arrived by railway from Voghera [about sixty miles away], each train disgorging its hundreds of armed men and immediately hastening back for more". Then a couple of weeks later, the French used the railway to outflank the Austrians at Vercelli, forcing them out of the town and leaving them exposed to face defeat at Magenta.

It was, however, inadequate logistics on the French side that prevented a total victory. They were not able to force their opponents out of Italy completely because they ran out of supplies that would have allowed them to continue their attack. The soldiers went without food for twenty-four hours but, as ever, it was the lack of fodder for the horses that prevented them giving chase as the Austrians retreated after a third defeat, on 24 June at Solferino, tearing up railway lines and destroying bridges as they fled. The Austrians, therefore, would hold on to Venetia, the north-eastern corner of Italy, for a few more years.

Both the Austrians and the French made use of the railways during this war to take away their wounded and sick from the battle line but neither thought of providing any special facilities for their comfort or their medical needs. Injured and suffering soldiers were simply dumped on the floor of goods and cattle trucks or into third-class carriages with wooden benches, mostly with no medical attention available on board. Their suffering in these conditions did not go unnoticed. After seeing the inadequate transport arrangements, in Germany a Dr Gurlt suggested that hammocks should be suspended from hooks screwed into the roof of the goods wagons transporting the wounded so that they would not have to lie on the floor. The implementation of this well-intended idea proved to be flawed: not only were the roofs of the wagons too weak to support the weight, but the movement of the trains rocked the hammocks so violently that they dashed the wounded men against the sides of the vehicles. Instead, the Prussian war minister Albrecht Graf von Roon ordered that in any future wars the walking wounded should travel in normal passenger accommodation — the class determined by rank, of course — while the badly wounded should be given straw-filled sacks to lie on. Crucially, a doctor and attendant were to travel on each train with suitable medical equipment. Thus the notion of the ambulance train was born.

The different sides in future conflicts drew their own lessons from these early uses of the railways in war, not always the right ones. The French, for example, were misled by the ease of transporting the troops to fight the Austrians in Italy, as Allan Mitchell, a historian of the railways of France and Germany, suggests: "The tracks of the PLM were superbly suited for the purposes of that decade, capable of shipping men and supplies from Paris to Marseille." Yet, he asks, suppose France should be called upon to transfer military forces across the country, say, from Bordeaux in the west to Sedan in the east? That would, of course, happen in the Franco-Prussian War, when the limitations of the existing system would be exposed. Mitchell calls the 1859 experience an "optical illusion" which misled the French into thinking they could rely on their private railway companies in the event of war and that railways were an easy way of deploying armies that required little preparation.

The Crimean railway, too, was something of an exception in that it was specifically built for a military purpose, while in the subsequent history of the use of railways in war, there were very few such purely strategic railways and, rather, it was civilian railways that were used for military ends. As we shall see in Chapter Four, military considerations were at times allowed to influence the routeing and design of railways, with the result that the railway companies were helped financially to build lines in recognition of their military potential. Nevertheless, for the most part, railways were built for commercial or even political reasons but later happened to serve a military purpose as well, since they linked major towns or connected the system with ports. In the United States, as the next chapter shows, there was never any notion of the railways having a military purpose, but they were to play a crucial, and indeed decisive, role in the Civil War, the first conflict where the outcome was greatly influenced by which side was better able to exploit the iron road.

CHAPTER
THREE

Slavery Loses Out to the Iron Road

Barely half a decade separated the American Civil War, which started in 1861, from the Crimean, but these two conflicts could not have been more different. Whereas, with the Charge of the Light Brigade, primitive logistics and a prolonged siege, the Crimean belonged very much to the eighteenth-century tradition of conflicts, the American Civil War was, in the words of General Sir Rupert Smith, "the first industrial war"and, indeed, the first railway war. By making use of innovations in communications, weaponry and transport, principally the railroads, the belligerents, especially the North, developed a new type of war that was fought with much wider use of technology and in a way that relied on mobility and flexibility far more than its predecessors.

Conflict in America had been brewing for a long time. The "United" States were anything but. There was a fault line running through them dividing the slave states from the free ones, and a split had long seemed inevitable as both sides were unwilling to compromise. In the years before the war, the nation's politics were conducted almost entirely on the basis of the slave issue, with politicians becoming increasingly polarized on North-South grounds. The trigger was the secession of the Southern states following the election of Abraham Lincoln in 1861, but in truth war had seemed inevitable for some time as the South felt the continuance of slavery — and indeed its expansion to other states — was vital to its economic survival, while the North was equally adamant that slavery could not be allowed to continue.

This was not a war taking place in a far-distant land unobserved by European nations. Quite the contrary. Various European countries, notably the Prussians, sent observers to analyse these new techniques in practice and, while the right conclusions were not always drawn from their expeditions, the American Civil War exerted a powerful influence on subsequent European wars in the nineteenth century.

Nor was it a localized skirmish which pitted brother against brother in guerrilla-type battles, although inevitably there were occasions when this happened, but rather it was a war of secession where both parties were effectively independent states fighting for their very existence. In a way, the term "civil war" is a misnomer. The scale and breadth of the war were akin to far wider conflicts than the term might imply. Military operations took place over an area equal to the continent of Europe, and a great number of battles in territory which, especially in the west, was sparsely populated were only made possible by the extensive use of the railroads.

Since the opening of the country's first line, the Baltimore & Ohio in 1830, the growth of the American railroads had been spectacular. By 1840 there were 2,818 miles of line and at the end of the 1850s a total of 30,000 miles, more than the rest of the world put together. These railroads had very quickly changed the whole way of life in America in the most profound way. Within a generation of this transport revolution, the nation had changed from one in which most people lived in homesteads where everything from clothes to foodstuffs was produced by the household to one where traded goods were the norm. While as late as 1815 Americans produced almost everything they consumed, "a division of labor and specialization of production for ever larger and more distant markets" had emerged. With the advent of the railroads, a money economy developed in which farmers concentrated on a particular crop, which they then sold for cash, a class of merchants and dealers sprang up in the towns, and a machine industry began to produce tools and equipment that hugely increased efficiency.

All this was down to the railroads. They were, though, lousy. American railroads were built on the cheap because of the perennial difficulties in raising sufficient capital to build them and the huge distances involved. They were laid with lightweight — and therefore easily breakable — rails, resting on sleepers ("ties" as they are called in the US) frequently made of unseasoned wood that rotted easily, and placed on insufficient ballast. To keep costs down, the tracks followed the contour lines of hills and valleys to avoid the construction of expensive tunnels and embankments, and travel on the railroads was slow and meandering as a result. Nevertheless, for the most part they took passengers and goods safely to their destinations and were more reliable and quicker than any other means of transport. Rivers, the main alternative, were obviously limited in scope, while canals, which had briefly flourished, were equally unwieldy and closed in winter. As for the roads, they were mostly little better than muddy tracks.

In truth, the North was never going to lose. The Federal states had two thirds of the guns and benefited from a far more developed economy including most of the financial resources and four fifths of the nation's manufacturing capacity, since the South's major product, cotton, was exported to be made into cloth elsewhere. The North's population was nearly double that of the South and its territory included all the cities with a population of more than 100,000, with the exception of New Orleans. Most importantly, thanks to its more advanced state of economic development, the North was blessed with a far better transport system, including most of the country's canals and two thirds of its railroads, which, moreover, were much better attuned to the needs of its industry. Whereas in the South the railroads did not feed into ports and other waterways, in the North they were integrated with the wider transport system, though in 1861 it still took twelve hours and several changes of train to travel just over 200 miles between New York and Washington. Inevitably, too, there was a gauge issue and the North was helped by the fact that most of its lines used standard gauge, 4ft 8½ins, although there was some variation. By contrast, in the South, there was a clear division between 5ft gauge, which was used extensively by the states of the Deep South, and standard gauge that predominated elsewhere, hindering transport between the two areas. Moreover, the South was blighted by the sheer number of railroad companies, with its 10,000 miles being divided between 113 different concerns — fewer than ninety miles per company — which were reluctant to allow the trains of their rivals to use their lines.

In October 1859, before full-scale hostilities began, there was a little pre-war skirmish played out on the railway. This was the strange story of John Brown, immortalized in the song "John Brown's Body". With backing from a group of rich "free soilers", as abolitionists were called, Brown, together with a small band of barely twenty supporters, rowed over the Potomac river from Maryland to take over an armoury at Harper's Ferry in Virginia. While the arsenal quickly fell into their hands, it was a completely ill-thought-out mission with the laudable but fanciful aim of triggering off a widespread rebellion of slaves throughout the South. Ironically, the first casualty of the incident was a free black baggage master at the railroad station who was killed in error by one of Brown's sentries. Brown held up the midnight train for several hours to prevent the alert being given but then inexplicably allowed it to proceed, ensuring that by morning the armoury was surrounded by local militia. The armoury was quickly recaptured and Brown hanged a few weeks later, creating a martyr of this eccentric abolitionist and a song remembered today.

The real war began within days of the inauguration of Lincoln as the first Republican president in March 1861. John Brown's suicidal incursion and increasingly acrimonious divisions among politicians over the issue of slavery had served to inflame passions, but it was the election of Lincoln which made conflict inevitable. Lincoln had, during campaigning, stressed that he would accept the rights of the Southern states to maintain their slaves, and it was not until more than a year after war broke out that Lincoln would make the abolition of slavery a clear war goal. However, the Southerners did not believe him, fearing that the Republicans would incite their slaves to revolt and that their position would be untenable under a Lincoln presidency.

Within five weeks of Lincoln taking office, hostilities broke out. The trigger was an attack by rebel forces on Fort Sumter, a fortified island four miles off the coast, guarding the entrance to Charleston harbour in South Carolina. On 14 April 1861, after a lengthy stand-off, a Confederate militia attacked the fort to prevent it being resupplied, and easily overwhelmed the Federal forces defending it. That victory for the Southern forces marked the beginning of the Civil War, which was to last four years and claim the lives of 620,000 American soldiers, more than in any other conflict, and, in fact, remarkably, more than the total lost in all the other wars the country has fought before and since, including the two world wars of the twentieth century and Vietnam. While the high casualty rate was partly due to the fact that the more deadly rifle had largely replaced the musket and medical facilities were primitive in comparison with those in subsequent wars, the ability of the railroads to deliver large numbers of men to battle sites was an important factor.

The crucial nature of the railroads was understood from the outset by military leaders on both sides of the conflict and, indeed, by the population at large. Already a fortnight before the fall of Fort Sumter, Lincoln's government had taken possession of the Philadelphia, Wilmington & Baltimore Railroad, recognizing that it would become the lifeline of the Federal army protecting Washington, and soon afterwards an incident in Baltimore, Maryland, a state in a key position on the North-South border, demonstrated that the railroads would be a key aspect of the war. The failure of the railroad companies to have built a connecting route through Baltimore forced all passengers traversing the town to change trains or to undergo the tedious process of having their coaches horse-hauled through the streets on tramway tracks before continuing their journey. The fall of Fort Sumter had prompted Lincoln to ask for 75,000 volunteers to join the Federal Army, many of whom needed to pass through Baltimore on their way to Washington, which was on a branch off the main line of the Baltimore & Ohio. The first of these troops seeking to pass through the town were 2,000 men principally from Massachusetts and Pennsylvania, who had responded quickly to Lincoln's call and arrived at Baltimore's President Street station in a train of thirty-five coaches on the morning of 19 April. Although Maryland remained a Union state, many of its people were opposed to the unionist cause and the crowd began to shower the first coaches carrying the troops through the town with bricks and stones. When a second group of men was told to march the mile across town from the President Street station of the Philadelphia, Wilmington & Baltimore Railroad to the Camden station of the Baltimore & Ohio, they were provided with live ammunition but that did not prevent them being attacked by a local mob. They fired back, killing several innocent citizens but the death toll of sixteen included four soldiers.

The response of the authorities was a rather clumsy overreaction. In order to protect the area from mob violence or even from a full-scale battle between secessionist residents and unionist troops, they decided to destroy three railroad bridges on both the Northern Central Railway and on the Philadelphia, Wilmington & Baltimore, thereby cutting off Baltimore from rail communication with the North and preventing any troops from transferring through the city. This isolation could not be allowed to last long. Washington was in a crucial geographic position, a kind of advanced outpost into southern territory from the north but also the seat of government and the centre of Federal war preparations. The railroads were quickly repaired but Lincoln was wise enough to ensure that his troops no longer travelled through volatile Baltimore.

Instead, a route by-passing Baltimore was organized by Thomas Scott, the vice-president of the Pennsylvania Railroad, who was charged by Lincoln to sort out the situation and was aided by a young Andrew Carnegie, the Scot who was to become one of the richest men in the United States through his domination of the steel industry. The troops heading towards Washington from the North took the Philadelphia, Wilmington & Baltimore to the Susquehanna river, where they boarded a steamer to Annapolis to connect with the Annapolis & Elk Ridge Railroad and then the Washington branch of the Baltimore & Ohio. Various sections of line were taken over directly by the government and thus these enforced emergency arrangements led to the genesis of the United States Military Railroads, the government railroad organization which, while starting on a very small scale, became a major force in the Federal war effort, building several lines, taking over captured railroads and, crucially, as we shall see, repairing damaged ones. By the end of the war, the organization would control more than 2,000 miles of railroad and have laid nearly 650 miles of track.

The destruction of the railroad bridges also led to legislation passed in January 1862 allowing the Federal government to take possession of a range of important railroad and telegraph lines, including rolling stock, locomotive depots and all essential equipment, and placed all railroad employees under military control. For the most part, the legislation did not have to be used as its mere existence ensured that the Northern railroads fell into line, meeting military needs when asked to do so by the Federal government. It was, however, an important weapon in the legislative armoury, as acknowledged by the chairman of the Committee on Military Affairs in Congress, who argued: "The object is to move large masses of men without the knowledge or consent of anybody, without negotiating with railroad directors as to how many men are to be moved, or where they are to be moved, or what rolling stock is wanted." That was, in fact, rather simplistic. While he was right in emphasizing the importance of the railroads, his statement makes light of the inevitable tensions between railway managers and the military which would blow up in virtually every conflict over the next century. The relationship between the military and railway managers has to be one of co-operation and mutual respect, rather than a crass attempt to enlist railways into the Army's fold.

According to the official history of the war, there were 10,000 military encounters, of which nearly 400 were deemed serious enough to be called "battles", which precludes a detailed account of the role railroads played in the every campaign. However, since the very principle of supplying an army by railroad was established in the Civil War, the railroads were used in most of these battles by one side or the other, and usually both. Indeed, the railroads proved crucial in the war's first major battle, which, according to Westwood, "was the first battlefield victory achieved through the use of rail power", although this rather diminishes the role played by the railways in the war in Italy mentioned in the previous chapter.

As with many conflicts, the war was expected to be short and the North confidently expected to emerge easy winners. However, while the North was far stronger in almost every way, the Southerners proved more resilient than expected, with the result that the war lasted much longer than had been anticipated. They were helped by their stronger military traditions, which meant that much of the officer class was Southern and, when secession began, took up the rebel cause. In contrast, the early military performance of the North was poor, characterized by dithering and incompetence. More important, though, was the fact that people in the South felt they were fighting for the very survival of their way of life and therefore went to war with a greater readiness to die for the cause. Moreover, since most of the battles took place in the Southern border states, they also had the advantage of fighting on their own territory with the support of a population that was largely hostile to the "invaders".

The first major land battle, at Bull Run in July 1861 in Virginia, twenty miles south-west of Washington DC, was a victory for the Confederates which set the pattern for the early months of the war. The battle started as an attempt by the Federal government to put a quick end to the conflict by capturing the Confederate capital, Richmond — barely a hundred miles separated the two capitals — and an army under the command of Brigadier General Irvin McDowell advanced across Bull Run (a small tributary of the Potomac) to engage the rebel forces. The Confederate forces led by Brigadier General Joseph Johnston initially found themselves under pressure and retreated, but the turning point was when reinforcements arrived by rail from the Shenandoah Valley in the west. Although the line they used belonged to the Manassas Gap, which was a small railroad that could barely cope with the sudden load, and the locomotive engineers at one point refused to work the trains, claiming fatigue, enough troops arrived by rail to turn the tide. With the arrival of the fresh troops, the Confederates launched a counter-attack, inspired partly by General Thomas Jackson, who refused to retreat, earning him his famous nickname of "Stonewall", and the Federal troops fled back towards Washington. The Confederate victory gave the South confidence in its ability to win the war and any more talk of a swift end could now be dismissed.

Incidentally, the outcome of the battle also led to the first example of railway construction of the war. The Confederates remained in the area, digging in for the winter in entrenchments at Centreville, six miles from the crucial Manassas junction which linked the Orange & Alexandra Railroad with the Manassas Gap. The road from Manassas Gap to Centreville was fine in the summer but the wet weather of the autumn turned the red clay road into a quagmire of muck and mud, and the six horse and mule teams bringing supplies from the railroad to the encampment with 40,000 men was proving inadequate to the task. Work on the six-mile line, which was mainly carried out by slave labour, started in December 1861 and was completed by early February 1862. For a brief few weeks, despite difficulties obtaining rolling stock, the short railroad proved invaluable to supply the men at Centreville but on 11 March the line's brief existence came to an end as the troops were ordered to retreat from Centreville and they destroyed the line as they withdrew.

The major battles of the American Civil War are generally grouped into two sections, the Eastern and Western Theaters. While the Eastern received more coverage and is known for the most famous and bloody battles of the war, such as Gettysburg and Antietam, the Western was in many ways more important. There, the South was on the defensive throughout and with the odd exception, such as the battle of Chickamauga, the war in the west was a series of Confederate losses which ensured their overall defeat.

In the east, the brilliant generalship of Robert E. Lee kept the initiative with the South for the first couple of years, thanks to his clever tactics against generally superior forces. Cheekily, to keep the enemy on the defence, he even launched a couple of invasions of the North by marching into Maryland, but with hindsight that was hubris and he overreached himself, a mistake he repeated when he lost at Gettysburg in July 1863, the turning point of the war. However, time and again, it was the use of the railroads that enabled the North to keep Lee at bay and that was thanks to the superior organization of the rail network in the North.

The North did not have a general of Lee's genius, but it did have a railwayman whose contribution to the outcome of the war was arguably decisive. Once the legislation giving government oversight of the railroads was passed in January 1862, Daniel McCallum, a Scottish immigrant with much railroad experience, was appointed as military director and superintendent of the railroads, with virtually total power over them. Under McCallum, though very much a law unto himself, was a difficult but brilliant engineer, Herman Haupt, whose work for the United States Military Railroads in preparation for several battles, culminating at Gettysburg, would confirm the strategic role of the railways in warfare.

Haupt, who became known as "the war's wizard of railroading", came to the fore in the Peninsular Campaign, which was an attempt, launched in March 1862, to capture Richmond by circumventing the Confederate army in Northern Virginia, the first major offensive by the Union Army in the Eastern Theater. Haupt's background made him ideal for the task of harnessing railways for the purposes of war. He had passed through West Point, the main US military college, but resigned his commission soon after graduating to become a professor of mathematics and engineering, writing the definitive textbook on bridge building, and later he was appointed superintendent of the very important Pennsylvania Railroad. He was an extremely capable and hardworking engineer, but also a cussed, stubborn fellow — "pigheaded" was a frequent contemporary description — who would not allow anyone to stand in his way, which proved to be an excellent qualification for ensuring that the military realized the importance of railways in the pursuit of war at a time when this was still not widely understood. Haupt, according to a historian of the Northern railroads in the Civil War, "was responsible for developing not only the general principles of railroad supply operation, but also detailed methods of construction and destruction of railroad equipment", which would crucially later inform General Sherman's victorious march through the South in 1864–5 that finally would bring the war to an end. Haupt's two main principles were that the military should not interfere in the operation of the train service, and that freight cars should be emptied and returned promptly, so that they were not used as warehouses (or even, as happened, as offices). This second issue might sound prosaic, trivial even, but proved time and again in the Civil War and subsequent conflicts to be an absolutely vital requirement in ensuring the efficient use of the railroads in meeting military needs.

Haupt's initial task was to repair the Richmond, Fredericksburg & Potomac Railroad, a strategically located line which connected the two capitals, Richmond, Virginia, and Washington DC, as well as providing a link between the main Union Army of the Potomac and the smaller Army of the Rappahannock. Appreciating the importance of this railroad, the Confederate command had launched a fierce attack on the line in April 1862, wrecking it for several miles. Intent on destroying even more of the line than previous attacks had achieved, and seeing that the process of heating up rails and twisting them to make them malleable was too cumbersome and slow, the rebels devised an iron claw tool which could quickly tear up both the rails and their supporting sleepers. Half a dozen men could rip up and bend rails at such a speed that it only took a force of 500 to destroy comprehensively a mile of track in a few hours. As for putting locomotives out of commission, the simple expedient of firing a cannonball through the boiler was found to be far more quick and effective than dragging engines off the rails and hurling them down the nearest embankment. Bridges, too, could now be destroyed far more effectively than in previous raids, in which brushwood had simply been piled underneath the timbers and ignited. Now, on the Fredericksburg railroad, the Confederates blew them up by drilling holes in the main supports and inserting gunpowder "torpedoes" with a fuse. In this way, it took three men just ten minutes to bring down even the largest span bridges.

In response, Haupt worked what seemed a miracle. Even though he could call only on a few experienced men, as most of the troops from an agricultural background were useless for such complex work, he reconstructed the line and rebuilt bridges at an astonishing rate. Within two weeks, between ten and twenty trains were running daily on the fifteen miles between the two ends of the railroad. Lincoln himself was appreciative of Haupt's efforts, particularly his achievement in rebuilding a 400-foot bridge over the Potomac in just nine days despite, according to contemporary reports, having only green wood and saplings at hand and a largely unskilled labour force, and suffering from a lack of tools and bad weather. Lincoln praised Haupt, saying: "I have seen the most remarkable structure that human eyes ever rested upon. That man Haupt has built a bridge . . . over which loaded trains are running every hour, and . . . there is nothing in it but beanpoles and cornstalks." The greatest testimony to Haupt's work, however, was the oft-used but anonymous quote, attributed to local onlookers watching his men rebuild a bridge: "The Yankees can build bridges quicker than the Rebs can burn them down." While the destruction of the Fredericksburg line had been on an unprecedented scale, its rapid reconstruction demonstrated a truth that would be repeated in conflicts many times during the next century: railways were often far easier to bring back into use than those destroying them realized.

The assault on the Fredericksburg was not, however, the first major railroad destruction of the war. The Baltimore & Ohio, America's oldest railroad, which ran west from Washington and Baltimore to the Midwest, was the carrier most affected by the war as it virtually formed the boundary between the warring parties. There were several raids by Confederate forces on the Baltimore & Ohio, including a particularly destructive incident in June 1861, the razing of Martinsburg, the principal yards of the railroad, in an attack led by General "Stonewall" Jackson. The ruse which Jackson used to wreak maximum destruction of the yards demonstrated that the combatants in the early stages of the Civil War were still confused about whether it was to be a gentlemanly war, played out like those genteel eighteenth-century battles before Napoleon along well-defined rules tacitly agreed by both sides, or an all-out savage conflict with no attempt to limit the damage inflicted on the other side. Although the territory around part of the Baltimore & Ohio was occupied by Confederate forces, Jackson had allowed freight trains run by Union forces to continue using the railroad. This might have appeared to be a magnanimous gesture but was nothing of the sort. Recognizing that locomotive power would be crucial to the war, he devised a cunning scheme to capture as many engines as he could manage as well as wreck the railroad. He informed the railroad management that he did not want the trains keeping his troops awake at night and therefore it was arranged that they should only be allowed to enter the Confederate zone between 11 a.m. and 1 p.m. Amazingly, the Unionists accepted this flimsy argument and enabled Jackson to lay a perfect trap. On 14 June 1861, he allowed in all the trains to the fifty-four-mile section of line but then prevented them from leaving by ripping up the track. Before the Union forces grasped what was happening, he destroyed forty-two locomotives and 386 freight cars, taking with him by road another fourteen engines as well as much of the track for use in the South. His men wrecked the machine shops and warehouses at Martinsburg and as a result of the attack the Baltimore & Ohio's western section was closed for nine months. The rest of the line was kept going, however, thanks to the loyalty of its president, John Garrett, to the

Unionist cause. His dedication to keeping the line working, despite frequent attacks from the Confederates, ensured that it was used throughout the conflict in the interests of the North.

Most of the early destruction of the railroads was by the South, principally in pre-emptive moves to prevent the Federal armies from building up forces to launch attacks, but the North had been actively wrecking railroads too. There were a few early attacks by Northern forces such as the one on Harper's Ferry in February 1862, but the most famous of these early raids was the attempt by a young civilian scout, James Andrews, to destroy the crucial Confederate-controlled Western & Atlantic Railroad, which ran between Chattanooga and Atlanta. The raid 200 miles into enemy territory was prompted by General Ormsby Mitchel, the commander in middle Tennessee, whose target was Chattanooga, which was a key hub for both rail and river transport. Wrecking the Western & Atlantic would weaken the ability of the Confederates to defend the town, and Andrews was sent in with a group of twenty-one soldiers to capture a train and sabotage the line as he headed back north. On the morning of 12 April 1862, the group — two short as a pair had overslept — boarded a northbound train in the tiny town of Marietta, Georgia, twenty miles north of Atlanta. At Big Shanty, seven miles up the line, the train conductor, William Fuller, announced a stop of twenty minutes for breakfast, giving the raiders the opportunity to take over the train. Detaching the passenger cars, Andrews commandeered the engine,

The General, and headed north, cutting the telegraph wires in order to prevent the pursuers from alerting the stations ahead. Fuller, furious at the hijacking of his train, proved to be just as determined and heroic as Andrews. He pursued the train, first for the initial two miles to the next station on foot, then with a gandy dancers' handcart. It proved to be a versatile method of transport, as he was able to overcome a gap in the track which Andrews's gang had torn up, dragging the trolley through the ballast and rerailing it on the other side. Then, after being derailed again, he found a locomotive, the *Yonah*, which was fortuitously in steam, and when, again, there was a gap in the track, he ran another two miles to stop a train passing in the other direction to commandeer its locomotive.

And so the chase went on for a hundred miles, with the locomotives at times reaching speeds of 60 mph until *The General* ran out of fuel and the raiders dispersed into the local countryside. Because of Fuller's effort in keeping so closely behind, Andrews's men never managed to create any serious damage to the railroad. Their attempts to burn down bridges were thwarted by damp tinder and their efforts to tear up the track were confined to small sections, which were later easily repaired. They were all picked up quickly by the Confederate authorities and poor Andrews, just twenty-two years old, was soon hanged, along with seven of his gang. However, a group of others managed to escape back to the North, some helped by slaves, and most survived the war, one living until 1923. All the

nineteen military participants received the Congres-
sional Medal of Honor, the first soldiers ever to receive
this newly instituted award. On his side, Fuller, too,
was feted as a hero and spent his later years ensuring
that the story was told from his point of view, which
suggests that there may have been some rewriting of
history. Indeed, the raid has been mythologized,
inspiring several films, most notably Buster Keaton's
The General, which took the side of the Confederate
pursuers, with the Unionists depicted as ruthless train
wreckers.

Raids deep into enemy territory by cavalry
detachments with the aim of destroying railroads were a
tactic on both sides. On the Unionist side, the most
remarkable such raid was by 1,700 men led by Colonel
Benjamin Grierson, a former music teacher, in the
spring of 1863. They rode 600 miles through hostile
territory from southern Tennessee, through Mississippi
to Baton Rouge, Louisiana, which was held by the
Union, tearing up railroads, burning sleepers and
destroying storehouses. Not only did Grierson's raid tie
up large numbers of Confederate forces, but amazingly
only three of his men were killed and nine went missing
during the whole venture. Again, this tale attracted
Hollywood producers, with John Wayne starring in the
1959 version of the raid, *The Horse Soldiers*.

For the Confederates, the most effective was the
Morgan raid at Christmas 1862. With 4,000 horsemen,
General John Morgan attacked the Louisville &
Nashville Railroad, a strategic route which he knew
would be used by Union forces to push southward into

Georgia. Sweeping through Kentucky, he captured a railroad station in the small town of Upton and used the telegraph system to fool the Unionists further up the line into giving him information on the position of their forces. His men proceeded to demolish a series of bridges and warehouses on the railroad and after a week of havoc during which he wrecked much of the Louisville & Nashville, he withdrew, taking 2,000 prisoners with him. Even Haupt could not weave his magic quickly, as it took him the best part of six months to restore the line.

Despite Haupt's efforts on the Fredericksburg Railroad, the Peninsular Campaign failed, but in recognition of his railroad work he was appointed chief of construction and transportation for United States Military Railroads in May 1862. Learning from his experience of using untrained and reluctant troops, Haupt insisted on forming a specialized construction force to work on the railroads and was immediately given the task of reconstructing the short Manassas Gap Railroad in Virginia, near Washington, to allow the army to pursue the troops retreating under Jackson. In repairing and then operating the railroad, he was able to apply the two strict principles he had developed on control of the railroads and the rapid unloading of freight cars. Nothing was allowed to stand in his way to prevent smooth operation and the route was reopened in three days. Five bridges were reconstructed in one day and when he found an official using an empty boxcar in a siding as an office, he forcibly ejected the hapless fellow along with his money chests, furniture and papers so that the track could be used for railroad operations. Haupt then ensured that traffic flowed uninterrupted, quickly clearing a backlog of empty freight cars. Then, investigating the non-arrival of four trains at Piedmont, at the end of the line, Haupt found that the wife of a senior officer had stopped her train in order to find accommodation for the night and three others behind hers had not been able to get through. Going to the scene, he ordered the conductor to restart the train and then found the woman who had caused the trouble. His anger was expressed with great restraint. Writing in his autobiography, he recalls that the elegantly dressed lady came tripping across the field and "I did not display extra gallantry on the occasion, nor even offer the lady assistance. She had detained four trains in three hours in a period of urgency, and I was not in an amiable mood."

Haupt spent the next year reinstating and running railroads that were vital to particular battles, but he was not averse to destroying them, too, using the gunpowder torpedoes on bridges and the hook method to rip up track. He was put in charge of all the railroads of Virginia and in a series of operations demonstrated the importance of maintaining efficient running. He formulated precise working arrangements. As well as ensuring that cars were unloaded quickly, supplies were never to be forwarded until required and trains had to run to a schedule from which they were not allowed to deviate even if that meant departing half empty. Haupt understood what railroad operators around the world have subsequently learnt — that a delay in one part of a system almost invariably leads to hold-ups elsewhere. Railways must be run with military precision or they risk degenerating into chaos.

Haupt established a system of priorities: subsistence stores were given first priority, forage second, then, in order, ammunition and hospital stores. Interestingly, only fifth in line were veteran infantry regiments, followed by raw recruits, while artillery and cavalry troops were not to use the railroads at all. Haupt reckoned that provided his principles were adhered to, a single-track line could maintain a supply chain for an army of 200,000 men, a remarkable number and, according to Haupt, ten times greater than would be possible if his rules were not maintained.

Haupt was nothing if not an innovator. When the Army of the Potomac was moved to a position near Fredericksburg, the railroad connection initially involved a lengthy detour around the Rappahannock river. Instead, Haupt devised the notion of using huge barges, fitted with rail track, to cross the river, creating a connection between the Orange & Alexandria and Aquia Creek railroads. Using this method, the normal sixteen-car trains were able to be transported directly without having to unload their contents onto the barges, saving both time and manpower.

A little insight can be given into the chaotic state of the war, much of which was taking place on Washington's doorstep, and was brought even nearer by the existence of the railroad. During the second battle of Manassas (Bull Run), the Secretary of State for War, Edwin Stanton, ordered Haupt to provide a train to take civilian volunteers from Washington to the battle site in order to help the wounded. Haupt had only wanted medical staff to be transported but instead an unruly group of 800 men, half of them drunk, arrived near the site late at night and proceeded to demand priority over the wounded on the return train.

The importance of sticking to his rules was likewise demonstrated by Haupt's supply operations for the battle of Gettysburg, where General Lee's second advance into Northern territory was halted. In May 1863, Lee had beaten the Unionists at Chancellorsville and the South was at the height of its conceit, with genuine hopes of being able to triumph in the war. Overconfident, Lee had continued to march into the North with visions of possibly even reaching Philadelphia until the Unionists confronted him at Gettysburg, which was to become the bloodiest battle of the war. As soon as it was realized that there would be a major confrontation, Haupt went to Baltimore to organize the running of the Western Maryland Railroad, a line running northwest from Baltimore to Westminster, thirty miles away, where it eventually connected through to the Gettysburg front in Pennsylvania. The Western Maryland was a lousy little single-track line, laid with scrap-iron rails on poor-quality sleepers and with no adequate sidings or even a telegraph system. Haupt quickly drafted in 400 men to bring the line up to standard and used it to send a series of huge convoys to the front and to bring back wounded soldiers. Because of the shortage of rolling stock and the lack of sidings, Haupt established a service of three trains per day, each consisting of five ten-car sets carrying 1,500 tons of supplies, which returned to Baltimore with between 2,000 and 4,000 wounded soldiers each. His system was so effective that it not only helped the Unionist forces to victory but, seeing the potential, encouraged General George Meade, the commander of the Army of the Potomac, to use supplies from the railroad to pursue Lee and beat him decisively. That would have required repairing a series of railroads pulled up by the retreating Confederates, which Haupt prepared to do, but, in the event, Meade, worried about the state of his troops after the bloody battle and their susceptibility to disease further south, did not pursue Lee's retreating army, possibly prolonging the war.

Haupt left the Army soon afterwards owing to his involvement in a long-running dispute over the construction of a tunnel in Massachusetts, but his influence remained through the principles of operation he had established, which most senior officers in the North — but by no means all — had come to accept. Many of those running sections of railroad for the Northern forces had been trained directly by Haupt. With the Southern attacks into the North stymied, the only remaining question for the Unionists was to work out how to conquer the South.

Railroad construction was to play a major part in both the east and the west as the North counter-attacked and began to enter enemy territory. The last two years of the war, 1864 and 1865, saw feverish activity by the United States Military Railroads, which built and rebuilt railroads, as well as operating and maintaining them. Almost every attack was preceded by the establishment of a railway supply route, often requiring sections of new line, as well as significant troop movements by rail. Already in the Mexican War in 1846, American railroads carried troops down to New Orleans to do battle, but now the scale of such movements would be unprecedented. For example, when General Ulysses Grant planned to capture Richmond from the South, he needed to build two new military railroads, totalling twenty-two miles, before the attack could commence. Not only were countless railroad lines laid, but others were pulled up in order to supply rails and sleepers for the new ones. Troop movements involving tens of thousands of men were carried out in waves of trains on single-track railroads which before the war might have accommodated just a couple of trains per day. To give just one example, in the course of a fortnight in May 1865, 18,000 men were carried in forty-five trains, each with around ten coaches (which works out at around forty soldiers in each one), on the 120-mile trip between Danville and Manchester in Virginia. Such mass movements became routine and, since Haupt's rules were largely maintained, normally passed off without causing chaos.

In the Western Theater, broadly defined as the area west of the Mississippi river, the situation was very different from in the east. The amount of territory covered was far larger, and the role of the rivers, which were navigable for vast stretches, was far more significant. Nevertheless, although railroads were sparser, they still played an important role in several key battles, often in conjunction with river transportation. Battles in the Western Theater required several lengthy troop transfers by rail, including the greatest movement of the war, a 1,200-mile journey from east to west along the boundary between the rival armies in the early autumn of 1863. It was prompted by the defeat of General William Rosecrans's Army of Tennessee at the battle of Chickamauga, Georgia, in September 1863. The defeated Unionists retreated to Chattanooga, Tennessee, a vital rail hub, and Grant, who took over the command from Rosecrans, urgently needed 20,000 reinforcements for the defence of Tennessee and for future attacks in Georgia.

The initial estimate was that it would take up to two months to transfer such a large body of men to relieve Chattanooga. However, McCallum, the superintendent of the military railroads, devised a route which would enable a far speedier transfer, involving the use of no fewer than seven railroad journeys broken only by two short ferry trips across rivers: the Orange & Alexandria, the Baltimore & Ohio to Wheeling, where a ferry took the troops across the Ohio, the Central Ohio to Columbus, the Indiana Central to Indianapolis, the Jeffersonville, Madison & Indianapolis to Jeffersonville where another ferry took them across to Louisville, the Louisville & Nashville, and finally the Nashville & Chattanooga. It was, in the words of the historian of the Northern railroads during the war, "the most dramatic rail operation of the entire war" and certainly the most impressive anywhere in the world up to that point. Remarkably, the whole operation, involving 23,000 troops, was completed in just two weeks and they made a crucial difference. Thanks to the arrival of these reinforcements, the siege of Chattanooga, where the Union troops were suffering from hunger and lack of medical supplies, was relieved by a battle in November and the town became a crucial staging post for the Unionists' invasion of the South.

This ability to transfer troops so rapidly gave the North a distinct advantage over the rebels. During this huge operation, the Unionist railroads were under military control, with the remit to prioritize the movement of troops, whereas for the most part the Southern military was never allowed to co-ordinate the railroads in that way: "Only at times of obvious crisis were the Southern military authorities able to run through trains." One such exception was the operation to reinforce Chattanooga before the battle of Chickamauga, which involved six railroads and a distance of 750 miles with 25,000 men being transported from the north-eastern corner of Mississippi to Atlanta in a period of ten days. Similarly, the rebels employed the railroads for several troop transfers, and although they did not cover the vast distances of the major Unionist movements, several involved huge numbers of men such as the 40,000 mobilized in Mississippi in the early stages of the war travelling on a variety of railroads. However, for the most part the rebels found it harder to make efficient use of the local railroads because of the military's inability to impose itself on the railroads' management in the way that McCallum could in the North. Without that strong government control, there was continued animosity between railroad administrators and local army officers, and no arbiter to sort out disputes. Nor were the lessons pushed so hard by Haupt ever learnt in the South: "Army officers . . . were all too frequently ignorant of how delicately interlocked railroad operations were and consequently brought trains to a standstill amid chaos which might take days to sort out."

Money, private enterprise and weak government were at the root of the problem: "Southern railroad managements regarded themselves as true patriots, but claimed that their first duty was to their shareholders." Therefore, they were eager to squeeze as much money out of the Confederate government as possible, which meant charging high tariffs rather than the low ones promised at the outbreak of war, exploiting their monopoly position and keeping hold of precious locomotives that could be better used by other railroads. For example, one of the railroads involved in the build-up to the Chickamauga battle, the Richmond & St Petersburg, immediately raised its charges when it saw that the line was an essential part of the military build-up. Overall, the Southern railroads promised much but delivered far less.

Moreover, there was a perennial labour shortage. As men left to join the Army, they were replaced by unskilled workers and sometimes hired slaves, but at times companies were so desperate that they poached each other's employees, bidding up the prices they were paying to the slave owners. The Confederate government failed to understand the importance of keeping experienced railwaymen in their jobs to ensure the smooth operation of the railroads.

There was also a fundamental ideological reason why the determination of the North to ensure the railroads served the needs of the war was not matched in the South, and that was because the very essence of the secession ethos militated against strong central government. As Westwood succinctly sums it up: "In the South, nothing could be strictly imposed, and every compromise failed accordingly. Because the Confederates' quarrel with the North centred around their demand for freedom from interference from Washington, they were psychologically incapable of accepting that their railroads should be subject to interference from their own government." Even though, in the early years of the war, the Confederate President, Jefferson Davis, appointed an assistant quartermaster to take charge of all rail transport in Virginia, he was not given the power to force the railroads to co-ordinate their workings or acquiesce to military demands. Over the course of the war, various efforts were made to try to bring the railroads to heel, but each time the politicians were too concerned about their local interests and angering the railroads to force through legislation. It was only in February 1865, just three months before the end of the fighting, that a Railroad Bureau with substantial powers was eventually created.

The Confederates' military effort was also hampered by their failure to maintain their key rail supply routes as, towards the end of the war, a lack of experienced repair gangs and the difficulties of obtaining equipment (not only did the South have little industrial capacity but the Union naval blockade effectively cut off the Confederacy from the rest of the world) meant that by then the railroads were barely able to support any significant troop movement. The condition of the Southern railroads declined markedly in the later stages of the war: "By the final year of the war, a passenger train which averaged more than 10 miles per hour was exceptional." Troops were taking three days to travel a hundred miles, infuriating the military leadership.

Not surprisingly, when these generals began to write their memoirs after the war, it was the Southern railroads which were often blamed for the South's military failures. While this is somewhat unfair because the Southern railroads still contributed massively to the war effort, even though they were undoubtedly inferior to their northern counterparts, there is no doubt that the lack of control of the railroads by the military was a major handicap.

Moreover, the South ultimately proved less adept at destroying railroads, which became a key aspect of warfare in the conflict. It was impossible to make a railroad irreparable since, with sufficient labour and ingenuity, the most devastated line could, in time, be restored. However, the Unionists proved far better at causing widespread destruction that required far more work to bring the lines back into use: "Confederate raiders never acquired the pure destructive skill of the more mechanically-minded northern soldiers," John F. Stover, a railway historian, wrote dismissively.

Inevitably, the railroads were to play a key role in the final assault that ended the war. The successful supply of Sherman's army during his campaign from Chattanooga to Atlanta which finally led to outright victory in this bloody and prolonged war was the most outstanding achievement of the military railroads in the Civil War. Sherman recognized this. In his memoirs, he confirms, with military precision, the point made in Chapter One, that without the railroads it would have been impossible to have conducted a campaign on the scale of his final assault on the South. The Western & Atlantic, which together with the Nashville & Chattanooga and the Louisville & Nashville created a near 500-mile-long supply line from Louisville to Atlanta, proved absolutely essential to his campaign and in particular for feeding the horses: "That single stem of railroad supplied an army of 100,000 men and 32,000 horses for the period of 196 days, from May 1 to November 19 1864. To have delivered that amount of forage and food by ordinary wagons would have required 36,800 wagons, of six mules each . . . a simple impossibility in such roads as existed in that region." A cat-and-mouse struggle over the line was fought throughout this period with Confederate forces, led by General John Hood, one of the South's best commanders, mounting frequent attacks on the railroad. The Construction Corps of the United States Military Railroads was kept permanently busy, at times starting to reconstruct sections of line while the destruction was still being carried out a few miles away. The speed with which they conducted their work was remarkable, especially as the destruction techniques had become increasingly thorough. When, in October 1864, Hood destroyed thirty-five miles of track and 450 feet of bridges, the line was restored within a week by a workforce of 2,000 led by E. C. Smeed, who had been one of Haupt's most able deputies in Virginia, and was fully operational within two. McCallum, in his memoirs, pays particular credit to the railroad workers in these gangs on whom the entire success of the military operation was dependent: "All [the railway workers] were thoroughly imbued with the fact, that upon the success of railroad operations, in forwarding supplies to the front, depended . . . the success of our armies . . . that should failure have taken place either in keeping lines in repair, or in operating them, General Sherman's campaign . . . would have resulted in disaster and defeat." McCallum stressed that the dangers and hardships endured by the railway workers was greater than for any other class of civilian employees and that they showed courage equal to that of the soldiers, at times working on the restoration of lines continually for up to ten days with barely any sleep and little food.

Sherman's reliance on the railroad in fact led him to become "the greatest railroad wrecker of all". Precisely because he had made such intensive use of the railroads, he realized their importance and consequently made sure that he targeted those in the enemy's control or which risked being used by them. Indeed, his most thorough act of destruction was on the very railroad which he had used to supply his army. In the final part of his attack after the fall of Atlanta, which was abandoned by the Confederates once the last rail line had been taken over by the Unionists, Sherman then decided to march on through the South without relying on the railroads, fearing that, deep inside hostile territory, his rail supply line would be ever vulnerable to attack or, worse, takeover by the enemy, who would then be able to chase his men by rail. Instead, during the final weeks, he built up supplies using the Western & Atlantic and then uprooted it behind him, preventing the Confederates from pursuing him. His troops ripped up eighty miles of track, heating and twisting the rails, dismantled a bridge and destroyed the surviving railroad installations at Atlanta. The destruction continued as he marched 300 miles east to Savannah in Georgia, his troops ripping up a similar length of railroad, much of it vital to the Confederate war effort. Sherman may have eschewed the iron road for the last part of his march, but his success was only made possible thanks to the supplies he amassed by rail in preparation for the final assault.

It was not only railroads which suffered under his scorched-earth policy. This was an all-out assault on his enemies' resources, and farms, factories and warehouses all went up in smoke. Shops, crops and whole plantations were devastated as he cut a sixty-mile swathe through the country, and when Sherman headed back north after reaching the coast, he undertook the most decisive piece of railroad destruction. Instead of making a direct attack on Charleston, Sherman ordered the destruction of sixty miles of track around Branchville, a small junction town on the South Carolina Railroad. Thus, with ease, Sherman severed Charleston from all its sources of supply and according to Edwin Pratt, "left the garrison with no alternative but to surrender". It was the last straw for General Lee, who, bereft of supplies and desperate to ensure that the divisions created by the war could ultimately be healed, surrendered in April 1865, thus ending the first railway war.

Railways may be alternately destroyed and overstretched at times of war, but they also tend to make handsome profits as a result of conflict. The Civil War was no exception. The railroad companies prospered thanks to increasing their business both directly by transporting troops and supplies and indirectly from private manufacturers with government contracts. Of course, there was damage to be repaired, not only from the direct attacks in the war but also because of the failure of the soldiers to understand that the railroads needed to be treated with care and respect. As a minor but not uncommon example, on the way to the battle of Chickamauga the Confederate troops ripped off the side walls of the boxcars in which they were travelling to improve their view and ventilation. More amusingly but still with serious consequences, Haupt found that unless told not to do so, soldiers were wont to bath and wash their clothes in water needed for the supply of engines, with the spectacular result that "many engines were stopped on the road by foaming boilers caused by soapy water".

Overall the war secured the railroads' position as a vital part of the nation's infrastructure, with a proven record of being able to cope in extraordinary circumstances and with exceptional loads. The nation's system expanded by 5,000 miles during the conflict, reaching 35,000 miles of track by 1865, and each year gross income increased, with profits rising almost as fast. The first edition of the *American Railroad Journal* in 1864 called 1863 "the most prosperous ever known to the American Railways".

In addition to Haupt's strictures on how best to operate railways in wartime, there was no shortage of lessons to be learnt from the conflict. The most obvious was that the railroads were a major weapon of war, and maintaining them in a workable condition was, at times, more important than battlefield military strategies. Constructing and rebuilding railways, too, became crucial aspects of military planning. The second lesson, deriving logically from the recognition of the vital nature of rail transport, was that the destruction of the enemy's railroads became a key military aim. In the absence of aeroplanes, this necessitated raids into enemy territory. Consequently, the Civil War was the first one in which the destruction of the other side's industrial capability, as illustrated by Sherman's final march, was a clear strategic aim that marked a new type of "total war" made possible only through the ability of the railroads to move troops and supplies rapidly. As Sherman's last cruel advance showed, railroad destruction became, as one historian puts it, a new weapon of war. Indeed, Pratt is in no doubt as to the importance of targeting the enemy's railways: "It was the American Civil War that was to elevate railway destruction and restoration into a science." While in the early stages of the war it was the Southern rebels who attacked the railroads which could be used to invade their territory, later on it was the Unionists who wreaked havoc by targeting the Confederates' railroads on a much larger scale.

Another enduring lesson was that the relationship between the railroads and the military had to be settled from the outset, as had happened in the North. The Southern railroads remained a law unto themselves for most of the war, sometimes accepting non-essential civilian traffic when troops or ammunition were desperately needed at the front. Rail transport became much sought after and forwarding agents were not averse to bribing railroadmen to expedite their shipments. While the military needed overall control, it also had to be alive to the complexities involved in railroad operation. The process had to be through negotiation rather than military commands, as it was "no use for generals to threaten to shoot stationmasters who would not provide the trains they demanded".

The fact that railroads were bi-directional was another obvious but not always understood fact. The military men tended at first to think only of getting to the battlefield, but the railroads had a vital role in both evacuating it quickly, especially after a defeat, and removing the wounded from the site. Initially, the example of special ambulance trains which had begun to be used in Europe was ignored, greatly contributing to the death toll, but soon the importance of providing good transport for the wounded was accepted. After the first major battle, Bull Run, the railroads were unprepared for the task of removing the injured from battlefields and provided nothing more than freight cars with straw on the floors. The agonies endured by the suffering men prompted several railroads to consider fitting out ambulance coaches but the process proved slow. The first railroad to adopt the idea was the Wilmington & Weldon, in the South, which produced an ambulance train capable of carrying twenty patients within a week of the first battle of Bull Run, and in the North hospital cars were running in the spring of 1862 between Boston, Massachusetts, and Albany in New York State with a hair mattress, pillows and blanket for each berth. However, most railroads — and indeed the two armies — failed to understand the huge demand for trains with medical facilities likely to be placed on them in a major theatre of war. Weber, the historian of the Northern railroads, says that during the Peninsular Campaign of 1862 the wounded had to lie on the bare floors of the wagons and, according to a contemporary source: "The worst cases are put inside the covered cars — close, windowless boxes — sometimes with a little straw or a blanket to lie on, oftener without. They arrive a festering mass of dead and living together."

The situation improved, thanks to the efforts of a government agency, the Sanitary Commission, which commissioned special "ward" cars, each holding twenty-four removable stretchers suspended from uprights with heavy rubber bands, that enabled patients to be brought directly from the battlefield. They were used on various lines but were never available in sufficient numbers to ensure that all the wounded could use them. Soon whole hospital trains were in use, led by the Orange & Alexandria Railroad, and when General Sherman attacked Atlanta, he had three such trains, each capable of carrying up to 200 men, operating between Louisville and Atlanta. These trains had special markings and, with one exception in April 1863 when rebel raiders burned a hospital train after allowing the wounded to leave the cars, were not attacked even when passing through enemy territory.

Armoured trains were another innovation that made their first significant appearance in the American Civil War. The idea of armoured trains was almost as old as the railways and the earliest were probably the improvised trains used by the Austrians to help quell the revolts mentioned in the previous chapter. The first American armoured trains were built to patrol the railroads north of Baltimore against Confederate saboteurs, which was, according to the standard work on the subject, "the earliest example of armored trains performing their classic role of antipartisan warfare".

In the South, General Lee, ever innovative, conceived of using them in an offensive way with a rail-mounted gun. At the battle of Savage Station in June 1862, a 32-pounder mounted on a flat car and protected by strong oak planking on the sides and roof, was pushed along by a train. It was, however, of limited use since it was confined to the railroad line, ensuring it had a restricted field of attack. The Federals also showed interest in the idea and an "ironclad railway battery car" was manufactured at the Baldwin Locomotive Works in Pittsburgh in August 1862. It was a bizarre beast, a 30-foot-long flat car with a 6in cannon mounted on a revolving platform, and protected on the sides. Haupt was not impressed, and shunted it into an old siding, but the idea gradually took hold and several of these cars were eventually produced and saw active service in the later stages of the war, being hitched to the front of a locomotive to give maximum vision and reach, and pushed along. Armoured trains were, though, a sideshow, as they would, with several notable exceptions, remain.

The most fundamental lesson of the use of railways in the Civil War was, of course, the sheer logistical advantage which they offered. General Sherman's calculations, mentioned above, demonstrate that the railroads enabled armies to be bigger and to be supplied from bases much further away than previously. Trains could not only carry far more than mules, but they travelled faster and ensured the supplies remained in a better condition. While Civil War-era steam locomotives were unreliable, they were more dependable than irascible mules that not infrequently lived up to their reputation for stubbornness. Moreover, new locomotives could be built faster than mules could reproduce! The military historian Christopher Gabel suggests that "the advent of the steam-powered railroad boosted logistical output by at least a factor of ten".

89

On the wider question of the precise effect of the railways on warfare, the Civil War raised issues that were rather more complex than they might initially appear and over which military historians still argue. While there is no doubt that the railroads created a highly efficient new form of supply which enabled armies to be equipped for the first time from bases far away, the precise effect of this innovation is difficult to unravel. For example, once the troops disembarked from the trains at the railhead, the logistics were no different from those faced by Napoleon or even the Romans. It was back to mules, horses, carts and marching. As Gabel points out, "up to the railhead, supplies and reinforcements travelled on the industrial-age railroad. Beyond the railhead, transportation depended upon muscle power. In other words, it was often easier to move troops and supplies hundreds of miles from the home front to the railhead than it was to move even a few miles beyond it. Like water behind a dam, armies gathered in large, nearly unassailable masses around their railheads." Thus the military leaders in the Civil War learnt that it was often easier to move troops hundreds of miles on rail than it was to get them to the battlefield perhaps just ten or fifteen miles from the railhead. Haupt quickly understood that bunching and crowding at railheads had to be avoided at all costs, but ensuring that obstructive generals used to getting their own way understood this vital point proved, at times, impossible.

The railways not only brought supplies and troops to the front, but as their importance became increasingly recognized by the military authorities, several battles were fought over attempts to establish control of a particular line. Both sides, as we have seen, embarked on orgies of destruction, targeting crucial lines in enemy territory, leading to ever more sophisticated methods of wrecking railways in an effort to make it as difficult as possible to bring them back into use. The railways determined, therefore, not only the location of several of the main battles, but also their outcome. As with the French troop movements to Italy, the American Civil War not only showed that it was possible to conduct a military operation at some distance from the supply base, provided there was a railway, but also that there had to be a well-organized system of detraining troops and transporting goods away from the railheads, or otherwise the advantage of having a rail line would be lost. The Civil War, which was bloody and prolonged, also showed how the railways allowed a major increase in the scale of warfare, the numbers of men involved and the level of logistical support. Together with the advent of the telegraph, introduced as an adjunct to the railways, the whole speed and pace of war were transformed.

Certainly the efficiency of the supply lines made possible by the railroads increased the intensity and length of the war. Not only did they allow both sides to build up and maintain far larger troop concentrations than ever before, but they obviated the need for foraging by armies. In much of the Western Theater, there was no agricultural development which would have allowed armies to live off the land in that way and therefore it was only thanks to railroad supply lines that battles could take place there. Thus the railways made it possible for more frequent and intense offensives to be launched during a war, but an unexpected consequence was that the railways made it more difficult for an outright winner to emerge from these battles because losing armies either could be resupplied more easily or they could cut and run. As Gabel points out, "an army sitting on a railhead, when threatened with attack by an enemy relying on wagons, often could be reinforced by rail before the muscle-powered attacker could destroy it". Alternatively, when the North got the upper hand, the fact that its armies could amass vast quantities of supplies and troops meant, quite possibly, a swifter end to the war than might otherwise have been the case.

Finally, there is the even wider question of whether the Civil War would have occurred at all, or with the same result, had it not been for the railroads. The railway historian Slason Thompson argued that "it is not impossible that [secession] might have succeeded in 1850 when over 40 per cent of the nation's inhabitants formed a truly 'solid' South and the opposition 60 per cent was scattered from Skowhegan, Maine to the Mississippi with no completed means of transportation at either end". While such suggestions may be speculative, there is real substance to the fact that the Civil War was a product of railway technology. Given that, there is a juicy irony. While in the Civil War the railroads exacerbated the scale, length and intensity of the war, within less than a decade they would be feted for bringing the nation together. The start of the construction of the transcontinental line to join the two coasts had been delayed by the outbreak of the war, but got under way in 1863 in the west while the conflict was still raging and two years later in the east when it ended. The skills developed by the United States Military Railroads in building new railroads and quickly rebuilding destroyed ones helped ensure the rapid completion of the transcontinental. After the war many of the civil engineers and lower-level engineering employees who had worked for the Union railroads joined the Union and Central Pacific railroad companies and were responsible for the erection of those huge timber trestles that were thrown across every gap from ravines in Nebraska to deep chasms in the Rockies. What Lincoln had termed "beanpoles and cornstalks" had a large role in ensuring the two coasts linked up. When the line was completed in 1869, the iron road which had exacerbated conflict soon became etched in the public consciousness as the iron sinews that bind the nation together. And it is that peaceful aspect of the railways which lives on in popular memory today. However, all too soon, railways in Europe would be harnessed for bellicose purposes. Despite the fact that several military officials from Europe had crossed the Atlantic to observe the war, many of these lessons were not taken on board by the military, who had to relearn them in numerous conflicts leading up to the First World War.

CHAPTER
FOUR

Lessons Not Learnt

The early years of the second half of the nineteenth century saw a series of three major wars in central Europe, culminating in the Franco-Prussian War, in which the railways played an increasingly significant role. Prussia, which was in the vanguard of a new German nationalism and would be the prime mover of unification in 1871, was involved in all of them and would use the railways to particularly good effect.

The first of these conflicts, the German — Danish War, which broke out in 1864 while the American Civil War was still raging, was fought in such a limited area and on such a small scale that the railways played little part, though that was partly the result of a failure by the Danish to understand their potential. The war was triggered by a foolhardy Danish attempt to integrate the duchies of Schleswig and Holstein in northern Germany more fully into Denmark, in breach of previous treaties and against the wishes of its big southern neighbour. The Prussians made immediate use of the railway when, in the space of just six days in January 1864, they quickly despatched by rail an infantry division comprising 15,000 men and 4,600 horses — around a third of the Prussian forces deployed in the war — from Minden in North Rhine-Westphalia to the outskirts of Hamburg 175 miles away. Later, considerable amounts of supplies were rushed up north using the railway from Hamburg but otherwise the railway played little part in the conflict. Even these modest movements, however, showed that congestion and chaos could easily develop at railheads if proper arrangements were not made for unloading and onward transportation of supplies. During this short war, the Prussians made several attempts to speed up the process of taking off supplies from trains by using mobile unloading ramps but these experiments met with little success, and the perennial problem of failing to clear railheads quickly of both troops and supplies was never adequately addressed in the two subsequent Prussian wars. A French military attaché, *partipris* of course but nevertheless worth quoting, noted that the mobilization by the Prussian and Austrian allies "was less impressive" than the Italian campaign seven years earlier when Napoleon sent his troops to Lombardy.

The result of the German — Danish War was never in doubt, as Prussia and Austria — allies this time but soon to be enemies — united with far greater forces to teach the small Scandinavian monarchy a lesson. As soon as the Prussian President, Otto von Bismarck, announced his intention to occupy Holstein, the Danes gave it up and retreated to Schleswig, hoping to hold off the Prussian — Austrian army long enough for the Great Powers — Russia, France, Great Britain — to intervene. It was a miscalculation as none of them wanted to become involved despite fears of the growing strength of the German Confederation, leaving the Danes to fight on their own. The Danes made a further retreat in early February 1864, abandoning the Danevirke, an ancient earth fortification dotted with fortresses that proved impossible to defend with the forces available. Although Schleswig-Holstein was not well served with railways, this retreat from the Danevirke would have been far easier and resulted in fewer casualties had they used the line running up to Flensburg, twenty-one miles away, a major town with a population sympathetic to the Danes. Instead, the retreat, which began at night in order not to alert the enemy, has been likened to Bonaparte's march from Moscow half a century previously as it was carried out in terrible conditions, with many men succumbing to the cold. Instead of a journey of a couple of hours on the train, the men marched for up to eighteen hours fighting rearguard actions against the enemy with the loss of more than 600 men killed or captured.

There is much conjecture among historians as to why the railway was not used. One possibility is that the departure of the train, which was in steam and waiting at the railhead near the Danevirke, would have caused too much noise, alerting the enemy to the retreat. Another is that the train crew, like many local people, were of German ethnic origin and therefore unlikely to help evacuate the Danes. The most likely, though, seems to be that the Danish did not understand the value of the railway for logistics, even though retreating by road was much slower and entailed the abandonment of sixty pieces of artillery which could then be used against them.

After the debacle of the Danevirke retreat, it was only a matter of time before the Danes, despite enjoying some success at sea, were defeated and, following various truces and negotiations, the outcome of the war was never in question. Under the Treaty of Vienna signed at the end of October 1864, the Danes ceded Schleswig-Holstein to the Prussians and Austrians, costing Denmark 40 per cent of its land mass and population. It is unlikely that the Danes' failure to take advantage of the railway in their retreat made any difference to the result of the war, but using it might have saved some lives.

The second of these Prussian wars set the two allies in the Danish war against each other over its spoils, Schleswig-Holstein, and was on a much larger scale. Like the American Civil War which had just ended, this was a civil war setting the North against the South, but there the similarity ended. There was none of the passion raised by the American Civil War as the conflict was in effect a manoeuvre by Bismarck to force the Habsburgs, who ruled Austria, to concede the leadership of the German Confederation to the Hohenzollerns, who ruled Prussia. And rather than lasting four years like the American Civil War, it was all over in a mere seven weeks with just a single major, and decisive, battle, at Königgrätz.

The railways were crucial to the planning of the war and the deployment of the troops to the front line.

Prussia had sent observers to the American Civil War, and detailed information about Haupt's successful organization of the railways had percolated across the Atlantic thanks to a German translation of General McCallum's war memoirs, which contained a detailed account of the role of the railways in that conflict. The Prussian Army chief of staff, Helmuth von Moltke (the elder Moltke), widely recognized as "the greatest military organizer of the nineteenth century after Napoleon", had long been aware of the railways' importance in war. He had shown a "precocious interest in railways", even though his use of them eventually proved not always as effective as this preoccupation with the iron road might have suggested. As early as 1843 he had written an article extolling the virtues of the railways as a weapon of armed conflict: "Every new railway development is a military benefit, and for national defence it is far more profitable to spend a few million on completing our railways than on new fortresses."

Consequently, the Prussians began to organize their railways systematically to prepare for the advent of war. They planned to create a dedicated section based closely on Haupt's idea of having a separate corps of men to build — and, importantly, destroy — railways. This was only to be established in the event of war breaking out, but as soon as the conflict began early in the summer of 1866, a railway section (*Feldeisenbahnabteilung*) was set up for each of the three Prussian armies, composed of a mix of military and civilian personnel, a radical innovation for the age.

The military members were drafted in from regiments of engineers, while the Prussian State Railway supplied qualified men able to operate and maintain the railway. The three Prussian railway section units were mobilized as soon as war broke out and each had its own repair train, with a locomotive at each end. In a complex and bizarre procedure, as the train ran slowly down the track it was preceded by a hand trolley propelled by four men and carrying an officer and a bugler. When an obstruction was discovered, the bugler would sound the alarm and the train brought up to undertake repairs. If the enemy started attacking, the train could be hauled clear by the locomotive at the rear.

The very nature of the Prussians' military strategy relied on successful exploitation of the railways. Moltke's appointment had coincided with the reform of the conscription system to ensure it covered a far greater proportion of the male population than previously and included reservists who could be called up with little notice. The Prussian Army was proclaimed to be "the nation armed" and was therefore dependent on rapid mobilization from all around the country, which was only made possible by the effective use of the telegraph and the railways. According to van Creveld, the historian of war logistics, during the campaign against Austria, "the railway network dictated not merely the pace of Prussia's strategic deployment but also its form".

Much has been made of Moltke's genius in organizing the mobilization of his forces, but the efficient bringing together of an army of nearly 200,000 men and 55,000 horses to confront the Austrians on the Bohemian battleground was more down to luck and the existence of sufficient railway lines rather than careful planning. His use of the five railways was even given a name, "the strategy of external lines", to describe a tactic that was subsequently employed in both 1870 and 1914. While it appeared very clever and carefully planned, the scheme was in reality born of necessity and hastily cobbled together as war loomed. The Prussians had originally intended to concentrate their forces around the border town of Görlitz in Saxony but they mobilized late, even though the war had been long planned by Bismarck, and consequently the Prussians had to make use of all five lines leading to their frontier, with the result that their forces were deployed on a 200-mile-wide arc. There is no doubt that the deployment was efficient and successful. The troops and their horses were brought to the front in just twenty-one days on these five railways, and the speed of mobilization undoubtedly contributed to the Prussian victory. Moltke boasted that Prussia had the advantage of being able to transport the army on these five lines, mobilizing them twice as quickly as it would take Austria, which had only one line.

Moltke, like most successful military leaders, was lucky. If he had been forced to continue using the railways for a prolonged conflict his army would have found itself desperately short of supplies as the lessons of the supply difficulties during the Danish conflict had not been learnt and the facilities were inadequate. To compound the difficulties, Moltke had failed to ensure that his rail expert, Count Herman von Wartensleben, stayed in Berlin to sort out the inevitable mess and instead took him to the front. This deprived the system of a directing mind, allowing the local quartermasters, who had no strategic view of the situation, to rush in excessive amounts of supplies to the front line irrespective of whether the railheads could handle them or not. The resulting blockages were exacerbated by the shortage of rolling stock, which was caused by empty wagons not being returned but used for storage. Despite being aware of the importance of the railways, Moltke appears to have been far too relaxed about the whole process. According to van Creveld, during the deployment of the troops, "it is said that an officer visiting Moltke during this period found him lying on a sofa and reading a book", which was reportedly a popular novel of the day, *Lady Audley's Secret*, an early, rather racy, detective novel.

The operation of the railways after the initial mobilization of Prussian troops hardly paints Moltke in a good light. Van Creveld points out that within a few days of the start of the war, on 15 June 1866, the railways were virtually paralysed: "it was estimated that no less than 17,920 [the precision is admirable] tons of supplies were trapped on the lines, unable to move either forward or backward, while hundreds upon hundreds of railway wagons were serving as temporary magazines and could not therefore have been used for the traffic, even if the lines had been free to carry them". All Haupt's rules were being broken and the consequence was a reversion to the type of pre-railway war that would have been familiar to Napoleon. As bread went stale, fodder rotted and cattle died of malnutrition, field commanders sent off their troops to forage in the countryside and supply themselves by requisitioning. While these efforts met with success since it was summer and the area was fertile, had the war been prolonged Moltke would have struggled to feed the soldiers and the horses.

Despite all the experience gleaned from the Americans, the Prussians "made relatively poor use of military transportation by trains and only very marginally owed victory to them", while the Austrians had no equivalent organization, believing that it was up to the railways to ensure that the lines were functioning and in good condition. While some Austrian officers had pressed for the creation of a special railway unit, the war ministry showed no interest, arguing that repairing the track, even in wartime, was a matter for the railway company. This is not to suggest that the Prussians, or the other combatants, did not realize that railways were now a crucial instrument of war, but rather that they failed to understand their limitations and the need to ensure their optimal operation through disciplined management.

Fortunately for Moltke, the war was effectively won at Königgrätz, the first battle, where the Prussian strategy of a dispersed army worked well. The Austrians had mobilized first but too slowly to mount a frontal attack on the Prussians, who then, arriving on their five lines, were able to overwhelm the enemy. The consensus among historians, however, is that "in retrospect, Moltke's decisive victory at Königgrätz appeared to be more the product of calculated strategy and superior tactics than was actually the case". Both commands were blundering around, unaware of the precise location of the others' troops, and the decisive engagement resulted from one of the Prussian armies fortuitously stumbling upon the bulk of the Austrian force and then being saved by the unplanned but timely arrival of reinforcements. The Prussians had superior weaponry, too, in the form of a new type of gun, and therefore, far from Moltke's genius being the decisive factor, "the conflict was decided by horses, infantry-men, and the needle gun".

After the victory at Königgrätz, which earned Moltke his reputation as a brilliant strategist, the Austrians had no stomach for a long fight and the war was quickly brought to an end, with the railways playing little further part. The Prussians tried to pursue the retreating Austrians by rail, using the line from Dresden to Prague, but found it was blocked and guarded by fortresses. Moltke's exhortations to clear the line because it was "essential to our very difficult supply situation" fell on deaf ears. The fortresses proved impossible to overcome and building emergency lines around them would have taken too long. The Prussians therefore simply continued their pursuit southwards by circumventing the fortresses, leaving van Creveld to conclude that during the second part of the campaign "the railways were unable to exercise the slightest influence on the course of operations".

In fact, this is a slight exaggeration since the railways were still for the most part usable owing to the failure of the retreating Austrians to destroy them effectively, partly because they were unwilling to damage structures which were a source of national pride. What damage they did cause was pretty haphazard. Bridges were at times only partly blown, leaving several spans intact, or packed with explosives which were then unaccountably not detonated. The delay in blowing up a particular bridge — over the Elbe at Lobkowitz — proved very useful to the invading Prussians, as it left them the use of the line for a crucial ten-day period at the end of July. The bridge was eventually brought down on 27 July but earlier destruction would have delayed the Prussians by six weeks according to their own strategists, greatly prolonging the war. The Austrians also failed to understand the importance of removing rolling stock, leaving many carriages and wagons in Prague for the Prussians to use. According to Westwood, the explanation for these failings lies in a combination of "lack of engineering experience, underestimation of the ease of restoring partially damaged structures and emotional reluctance to destroy what were regarded as the technical achievements of the age".

As the conflict, with its outcome clear, was coming to an end in August 1866, Moltke, in a letter to Bismarck, stressed the point about how remarkably easy it was to repair minor damage to the railways and that "the only obstruction of any duration" had been caused by the fortresses. He recommended, therefore, that wherever possible Prussia's railways should be made to pass through the perimeters of existing fortresses, a remarkably feudal view, but he did not suggest that more fortresses should be built. Instead, Moltke appreciated that "it was with rails, rather than brickwork, that the future lay". Moltke skated over the difficulties resulting from his own mismanagement of the railway system but stressed that these errors would not be repeated in the coming war with France. This time, neither side had any doubt as to the railways' importance in the supply chain and their ability to deliver massive numbers of troops and matériel. The large scale of the Franco-Prussian War, in comparison with the two previous conflicts, made it, according to Allan Mitchell, the author of a comparative study of the French and German railway systems, "the first and only major railway war of nineteenth century Europe",which put to the test the planning for military use of the railways carried out in anticipation of the conflict by both countries. In comparison, he argued, the previous European battles involving the railways had been mere skirmishes. However, the role of the railways, while undoubtedly important, was not as crucial as some historians have suggested, since for a major part of the conflict many lines were effectively unusable.

Indeed, despite considerable preparations, mistakes were made on both sides, and, except in the first crucial phase of the war, Moltke's actions again do not seem to have been sufficiently informed by the logic of his own emphasis on the strategic importance of the railways. As we saw in Chapter Two, the structure of the railways in the two countries was very different. Those in France emanated, fan-like, from Paris, while the Prussian/ German lines ran mostly on a north-south or east — west axis. In terms of density, the railways were about equal, with Prussia having the fourth most dense in the world and France the fifth. Both types of railway, too, could be harnessed to military objectives, but the east — west lines in Germany proved to be the most important. After the war, both sides accused the other of having constructed their railways with the aim of facilitating war. They were both right to some extent. In neither country did military objectives determine the shape of the network but in both they played a significant part in their development, through negotiation, lobbying and, ultimately, money.

In France, where half a dozen large railway companies had emerged in the 1850s, the railways were privately operated but their construction was supported at times with substantial state investment. The routing of new lines was governed by *commissions mixtes* consisting of both public and private interests but there were several instances where the Army determined the route of a railway. However, military interests were by no means always paramount as three-way rows developed between the companies, eager solely for profit, the Ministry of War, pushing for the most militarily strategic route, and the Ministry of Finance, worried about the cost of deviating from the commercial solution sought by the private sector.

The same considerations were being assessed over the border in Prussia, by the same players. Military advisers wanted rail lines built under the protection of fortresses, at a safe distance from frontiers and on the "opposite" side of waterways — in other words, the bank furthest from the likely enemy, whose identity was known to both sides long before the start of the war. Money, too, was often a deciding factor, though the military clearly won the argument over the construction of several lines, notably the *Ostbahn*, which could take troops to and from the north-east.

The Prussians, in fact, were at a disadvantage because they had a far greater number of railway companies, under different state administrations, and there was therefore far less uniformity in the system. The Minister of Railways in Saxony complained rather wittily that it would be "to the general good in peacetime, and of benefit to the military man in wartime, if the superintendent met at Cologne was dressed like the superintendent at Köninsberg, and if there was no danger of a Hamburg station inspector being taken for a superintendent of the line by somebody from Frankfurt". Rather more alarmingly, he added that there were parts of the network on which a white light meant "stop" and others where it signified "all clear", a real risk to the safety of people travelling on the system.

In the run-up to the war, there was widespread feeling in Prussia that the French had the better railways. That was backed up by compelling evidence in a pamphlet, published as late as 1868, by an anonymous Prussian officer who concluded that "the overall French [railway] performance exceeds the

Prussian by far". He cited the fact that only a quarter of Prussian lines were double-tracked, compared with over two thirds in France, creating far greater capacity. Moreover, he found that French stations were roomier, allowing faster loading and unloading and that the French had more rolling stock. He also suggested that the domination of the system by half a dozen large companies made it more unified with greater standardization of equipment.

Meanwhile, in France, senior officers who were eager to stir up hostile opinion against Prussia were warning that the French railways were inadequate to the task of defending *la Patrie* and that the Prussians had the better system. In fact, neutral observers such as van Creveld, the logistics expert, suggest that the French system was better: "On practically every account, the French railway system in 1870 was actually better than the German one." Nevertheless, even though the anonymous Prussian officer was right, the difference in the two systems would not prove decisive because the French were ultimately let down by their administrative arrangements.

In the late 1860s, as war drew closer, both sides attempted to tailor their railways to the needs of the coming conflict. Moltke was, again, lucky. He had a counterpart in France, Maréchal Adolphe Niel, the Minister of War, whose "intentions were quite similar and his vision no less lucid". Niel, like Moltke, attempted to reorganize the railways to ensure that in the event of war, they would be under central military planning. In this he was supported by his sovereign,

Napoleon III, but his reforms stalled in the face of resistance from conservative elements within the government. However, before that opposition could be overcome, Niel died. It was to prove a most untimely death which left a series of half-introduced reforms that would only add to the chaotic situation on the French side after war was declared. Without a man of Niel's drive to push through change, the central commission he created, which was essential to the military's ability to take control of the railways in wartime, was more or less forgotten and consequently was not in a position to be activated when war commenced.

In Prussia, the whole approach to war was more scientific and thorough. Moltke had reorganized the Prussian general staff, taking on highly trained military personnel drawn from the cream of army officers. Nothing was left to chance. There was endless analysis and planning, with railway and logistical issues being accorded high priority, and the whole approach was completely unlike the military organization of any other European nation. Nowhere else was there this emphasis on a scientific approach to warfare. This resulted in a bizarre political structure with an army that held a place of almost feudal status in society being supported by a highly technocratic and effective machinery.

As part of this process, Moltke quietly introduced a key reform affecting the railways. The translation of the report written by McCallum on his experience of running the railways for the North in the American Civil War was influential in convincing the Prussians that they must adopt the same structure. On this basis,

Moltke was able to push through a reform enabling the military to strengthen its control over the railways, in particular those running on an east-west axis. He created a central committee of civil and military officials attached to the main railway office in Berlin to co-ordinate mobilization in the event of war. Even more crucially, for every major east-west railway across the territory of the North German Confederation — the area effectively controlled by Prussia after the 1866 war — he created individual line commissions controlled by the military which reported to the general staff of the central committee in Berlin. According to Allan Mitchell, the concept was crucial to the war effort because "this arrangement removed the principal obstacle to rapid troop movement: the necessity of crossing several state borders or of using the tracks of private companies". Once war was declared and these commissions took control, it became possible to move soldiers long distances without changing engines or personnel, effectively giving the military control of the railways.

The line commissions remained inactive until the outbreak of war, when their first task was to issue emergency schedules to the key stations along the line. These schedules, which had been prepared in advance, were far more detailed and sophisticated than a simple timetable, setting out precisely the composition of each train, the number of men to be moved and even refreshment stops: "The execution of these schedules was to be so precise that many trains would be able to make connections *en route*, dropping and attaching cars to ensure that units would be complete, in their order of battle, when their trains arrived at the concentration areas."

The war was actually declared by the French, the culmination of years of tension between the two sides over a variety of issues. The actual *casus belli* was obscure in the extreme, the candidacy of Leopold, a prince belonging to the Hohenzollern family, the rulers of Prussia, for the throne of Spain, which had been rendered vacant by the Spanish revolution of 1868. Under pressure from Napoleon III, who did not want France to be encircled by a Spanish — Prussian alliance, the candidacy was withdrawn but then the French emperor overplayed his hand, by trying to extract a promise from the Prussians that a Hohenzollern would never sit on the throne of Spain. Bismarck, who had put forward Leopold's candidacy in the first place, then manipulated the situation by publishing the French demands in an edited form to inflame passions on both sides of the border. Bismarck's intentions were clear. He felt he needed a war to guarantee the unification of Germany under Prussian control and had long worked towards this outcome. Napoleon, a foolhardy emperor with none of the nous of his illustrious namesake and uncle, was rash enough to declare war on 19 July 1870 despite the thinness of his cause and the fact that Prussian forces were likely to be at least as strong, if not stronger, than the French. He had sprung the trap set by Bismarck, who later, in his memoirs, wrote: "I knew a

Franco-Prussian war must take place before a united Germany was formed."

Napoleon's cause was imperilled right from the outset by the chaotic mobilization of the troops on the French side. It was not the fault of the railway companies. Already, four days before the official outbreak of war, the five big main-line companies — Est, Nord, Ouest, Orléans and Paris-Lyon — had been effectively taken over by the military as they were ordered to place all their equipment and personnel at the disposal of the war ministry. All freight and most passenger services were cancelled, the number of telegraph operators doubled and military timetables distributed. Having already made contingency plans, by the next day the Est company had prepared the first troop train, which was ready for despatch by 5.45p.m., but the chaos that was to dog the whole French mobilization was already evident. The troops, who were accompanied by the same sort of enthusiastic crowds who were to greet their successors heading for war in 1914, with cries of "Á Berlin", had arrived at 2p.m. only to find that the train was not due to depart for several hours. As a result, they did what such groups of men invariably do: drank their way around the local bars and caused mayhem. By the time the besotted soldiers arrived back at the station, many were collapsing from the effects of alcohol and, more seriously, had lost or given away their ammunition often as "souvenirs", though much of it was later claimed to have supplied the revolutionaries in the following year's Paris Commune (although that sounds like fanciful military propaganda).

This was a portent of things to come. Sure, nearly a thousand trains were despatched from Paris over the next three weeks, carrying 300,000 men and 65,000 horses, as well as countless guns, ammunition and supplies. Moreover, the French got to the frontier first. After a mere ten days, 86,000 men had reached the border, while hardly any Prussian soldiers were there to face them on the other side of the Rhine. However, the bare statistics mask an incompetent and ill-organized process that would seriously handicap the entire French war effort. Instead of the tightly planned schedule prepared by the Germans, French regiments were split up because they arrived piecemeal at the stations and men separated from their own commanders were often reluctant to take orders from officers on the train from another regiment. Some trains were despatched half-full, because of the non-arrival of a company, while others were overloaded as men who had missed their regimental train piled onto the next one. The unwillingness of officers to take control of the boarding and detraining of their men, as required by the regulations, and leaving it to the poor overworked railway officials, added to the confusion and delays. Systems to unload trains might not have been worked out properly, but measures to ensure the provision of coffee to the men at stations with the help of the steam from the locomotive as a kind of improvised espresso machine had been set out in great detail: "A receptacle of at least 150 litres is to be taken, in which sugar, coffee and water are placed, with each ration of 24 grams of coffee and 31.05 grams of sugar [it is not explained how such precise measurement can be made!] being allowed 42 centilitres of water. By means of a copper tube of diameter 0.012 metres fitted to a locomotive pressure gauge, a jet of steam is directed into the receptacle, with the tube deep in the water so as to agitate all the liquid. The operation is finished when the steam no longer dissolves . . ."

The momentum gained by having been the first to the border was, therefore, quickly lost, and any possible advantage for the French foregone. An early analysis of the use of railways by a Captain Luard written four years after the war sums up the French failings neatly: "In a fortnight, from the date of the order for mobilisation being given, the Germans placed 15 *corps d'armée* complete on the frontier, and did it methodically, so that everybody arrived at the right place at the right time, whereas the French sent everybody labelled *Á Berlin* and much confusion resulted when they arrived at the terminus of the line. The German organization appears to have been more perfect throughout than that of the French, and the results were consequently more successful." Pratt, the original historian of the railways in war, is scathing about the French effort on the railways, pointing to "the absence of any adequate organisation for regulating and otherwise dealing with the traffic, so far as concerned the military authorities themselves". A French general complained after the war: "you could

see your railway trains encumbered by men crisscross-
ing their way in all directions and in all parts of France,
often arriving at their destination just when the corps to
which they belonged had left, then running after this
corps, only to catch it up when it was beaten, in retreat,
or besieged in an inaccessible fortress."

The confusion on the ground was matched higher up
the command chain. Because Niel's idea of an
overriding military commission in charge of the
railways had failed to take root, orders for running
trains came from everyone and everywhere ranging
from the Ministry of War and its various *bureaux* to
local authorities and *préfets*, right down to officers and
non-commissioned officers seeking to prioritize their
needs over others. All of these were not averse to
threatening railway officials with dire consequences
should they disobey, however impractical their orders
or trivial their requests: "the assumption that trains
could be made to operate simply by issuing orders was
never abandoned by some high officers, even after
painful experience".

Orders would be countermanded and then reinstated
with great frequency. The accumulation of wagons and
matériel was legion and their use as storage was
widespread, blocking up sidings and preventing their
re-use by other parts of the Army. Officers took
advantage of the lack of central command to retain
wagons both to provide storage for their supplies and to
transport their equipment should their regiment be
moved. This, of course, was the obvious consequence of
the failure to have an overall control system. The needs

of one part of the Army were not necessarily concomitant with the efficient pursuit of the conflict: an obvious conclusion, but one which the military command in 1870 seemed unable to comprehend.

The French strategy of invading Prussia before the enemy could mobilize was risky but, as Westwood suggests, "it might have won the war if only the French railways had been properly used". However, they were not. Perhaps the French situation is best summed up by a despairing brigadier — who was in charge of 4,000 men — complaining that when he reached Belfort he had "not found my Brigade. Not found General of Division. What should I do? Don't know where my regiments are." Many of the men, it turns out, were having much more fun. Behind the lines, a floating mass of supposedly lost soldiers had built up enjoying the hospitality of the jingoistic locals and making scant effort to find their regiments. The numbers involved were such that a group of up to 5,000 men had accumulated at Reims in eastern France, the capital of Champagne country, and had to be physically restrained from plundering the supplies in the wagons which had accumulated there.

Metz, a few miles from the border, was the destination of much of this early traffic as it was initially the headquarters of the Army. Napoleon went there on 28 July to take control of the newly named Army of the Rhine which was already 200,000 strong and expected to expand as reinforcements arrived. After a series of defeats during August, Metz became besieged and supplies were limited, but the lack of organization on the railways made the situation far worse. Metz, in fact, had a large station with four miles of sidings and should easily have been equal to the task, but right from the start, with the arrival of the first infantry trains, there were delays in detraining owing to the absence of orders, and the supply wagons were mostly simply shunted into the sidings and effectively "lost". According to Pratt, "everything was in inextricable confusion. Nobody knew where any particular commodity was to be found or, if they did, how to get the truck containing it from the consolidated mass of some thousands of vehicles." Consequently, when Metz eventually fell, the town was still awash with wagons, both full and empty, which the Germans were able to put to use. Pratt estimates that no fewer than 16,000 wagons were captured by the Germans at Metz and other parts of the French rail network, which, as he wrote, meant that "not only had the French failed to get from these 16,000 railway wagons the benefit they should have derived from their use but, in blocking their lines with them under such conditions that it was impossible to save them from capture, they conferred a material advantage on the enemy, providing him with supplies, and increasing his own means both of transport and of attack on themselves".

The strategic importance of Metz led the Germans to draw up contingency plans, knowing that the town was a fortress and expecting, wrongly as it turned out, that the French would retain it well into the war. As a contingency, the Germans allocated 4,000 men to build a twenty-two-mile line around the city using material

117

captured from the French. The railway was not a great success as it had steep inclines, limiting its capacity to just three or four vehicles per train, and sharp curves that resulted in derailments. The only notable structure, a bridge over the Moselle, was so poorly constructed that it was washed away in the autumn rains, but fortuitously for the Germans that was on the day Metz capitulated, obviating the need to rebuild the line.

This "Iron Cross Railway", as it was dubbed by the locals, was an illustration of the thoroughness of the German planning. In contrast to the French, German mobilization had proceeded remarkably smoothly. Even though the Prussians did not, unlike the French, have a standing army, and therefore had to call up all its men, Moltke's work over the previous four years bore fruit. As van Creveld suggests, "it was only necessary to push a button in order to set the whole gigantic machine in motion". Crucially, Moltke insisted that the soldiers should be got to the front first, and their supplies would follow. The process was helped by the fact that thanks to the layout of the railways, and the work of the line commissions, six railway lines were available to the Prussian forces, and a further three to its allies in southern Germany. Moltke had reckoned they would reduce the time taken to move troops to the French border from twenty-four to twenty days, but in the event, after war was declared, nearly 400,000 men reached the border in just eighteen days after mobilization was put into effect on 14 July (which significantly was before war had even been officially declared). Once mobilization started, the line commissions took over and many normal passenger trains were removed from the schedule in order to prioritize military moves. So effective was the Prussian mobilization that it is possible to argue that the war was actually won before the firing of a single shot, thanks to Moltke's ability to harness the railways to his military ends. The early battles all ended in a series of defeats for the disorganized French and the war was effectively over with the surrender of half the French army and capture of Napoleon III at the battle of Sedan on 31 August 1870.

After that victory, the Prussians headed west to besiege Paris, though they hardly made use of the railways during this advance. The Germans had expected to fight the war on or around the border and had even prepared contingency plans to surrender much of the Rhineland, whereas in fact they found that, thanks to French incompetence, they were soon heading for the capital. The war, consequently, took place on French rather than German territory, much to the surprise of Moltke, upsetting his transportation plans, which had relied on using Prussia's own railways. The distance between the front and the Prussian railheads soon became too great to allow for effective distribution, and supplies of food for both men and horses came from foraging and purchases of local produce. This was the result of a failure of planning and a lack of flexibility. The Prussians had expected to use railheads in their own country and did not have sufficiently well worked-out contingency plans to move them forward on to the French railways when that became the obvious solution. However, they were rescued by another piece of luck for Moltke; as his tactics had by good fortune resulted in the troops being spread over a wide arc, it was easier for them to live off the land, which they did with ease as eastern France was fertile. Warfare had returned to the bad old days of a pre-Napoleonic-type of war.

Efforts were made to advance the railheads but the Prussians found that many of the French railways had been rendered unusable thanks to the sabotage at which the French became remarkably adept. The most comprehensive damage was caused to the Nanteuil tunnel on the line between Reims and Paris, which was blown up with great precision by French military engineers who managed to bring down twenty-five metres of tunnel, the explosion filling the remaining structure with fine sand. The Prussians worked for two months to unblock it, but just as they finished, a storm brought down a fresh influx of sand. They then tried to create a detour around the hill by drafting in labourers from Germany as the local population refused to work on the scheme, but even after its completion the trains remained blocked further down the line, at Lagny, near Paris, by French artillery.

This was the pattern throughout much of France. The French demolished large numbers of bridges and tunnels not only on the Est railway, whose area covered most of the battle sites, but also on the main lines of the Nord and, as the conflict spread to the west, the Ouest, the Paris-Orléans and the Paris-Lyon-Méditerranée.

The destruction was not always successful as there was a reluctance, born of national pride as in Austria, to blow up complete structures and at times commanders delayed pushing the button until too late. Luard, the early historian of the use of railways in war, also suggests that the French missed opportunities to wreak more havoc through guerrilla-type attacks: "At one period indeed, there is little doubt that a well organized raid on the railway between Toul and Blesure [on the main line between Alsace and Paris] would have had every chance of successfully interrupting for some time the main artery by which the supplies of all kind were sent from Germany to the armies before Paris, and might possibly have led to the raising of the siege of that city."

At other times it was sheer incompetence that left the railways intact: "In one case, while engineers were inspecting a bridge prior to laying charges, the train which had brought them steamed off, taking their explosives with it." As in the US, the French discovered that simply removing track was ineffective, since the Prussians were not averse to shifting rails from the nearest branch line to replace those which had been removed. It could turn out to be a game of cat and mouse. After the French defeat near Wissembourg on 6 August, the last French train left the nearby railway centre at Hagenau at 3a.m., tearing the tracks up behind it to prevent pursuit, but by the morning of the next day, barely thirty hours afterwards, the first Prussian train arrived on newly relaid track to remove the wounded.

Indeed, instances of retreat always pose the most insuperable problems for the railway managers. Suddenly, hoped-for loading points become unavailable as the enemy invades and lines are cut. The military is always seeking to use the railways until the last available moment while the railway managers want to leave as quickly as possible to ensure the rolling stock is brought to safety rather than left for the enemy to use. And all this is taking place as morale is plummeting and tempers become frayed.

Another reason for the reduced role of the railway after the initial phase of the war was that the fortresses protecting the railways remained a formidable obstacle, despite Moltke's recognition of this issue in his note to Bismarck after the Austrian war. In the early months of the conflict, several fortresses blocked the main lines towards Paris, preventing the Prussians from operating through-trains. The fortress at Toul in Lorraine was particularly troublesome and it was only when the occupants finally surrendered in September that the siege of Paris could be supplied by rail. Even then, however, because of lack of capacity, the trains were mostly used for ammunition, while the besieging troops had been sent out to forage for food. Other fortresses at Strasbourg and Schlestadt delayed the German advance, but when they were captured at the end of October, the Prussians could finally enter Mulhouse permanently. They had made several earlier forays there which, according to Westwood, "were registered by the local railway authorities, who would run the train service when the French held the city, and suspend it when the Prussians were in occupation". One fortress near the border, Bitche, held out until the end of the war, preventing the Prussians from using a local peripheral line.

The Prussians were hampered, too, by the activities of the *francs-tireurs*, the guerrilla army of irregulars which sprang up in the wake of the defeat of the conventional forces. The *francs-tireurs'* most notable success was the blowing up of a troop train between Reims and Metz in October 1870. This was real Wild West stuff as they laid an improvised mine between the tracks which was detonated by the weight of the locomotive. When the surviving troops tried to flee the wreckage, they were massacred by the French forces waiting in ambush.

In order to draw attention away from their own errors, the Prussians were wont to blame everything on the *francs-tireurs* and their efforts to counter them led to reprisals that were widely regarded as atrocities by foreign observers. The Prussians hit upon the idea of using local prominent people as hostages on the front of the locomotives of their trains. There was much resistance to this ghastly scheme, even among Prussian officers who, according to the historian John Westwood, would invite the dignitaries into their well-appointed carriages because "evidently many felt ashamed of the order and tried to make things easier for the hostages", not least because it was a particularly harsh winter. In the event, there are no reports of any hostages coming to harm but French prisoners of war were subjected to journeys on open wagons which resulted in their

123

freezing to death. While this may suggest that the strategy was successful, it is more likely that in fact attacks by the guerrilla forces were less frequent than the Prussians had suggested. The Prussians claimed that 100,000 of their troops were needed to guard the railways in France, a figure that was widely quoted at the time but appears to be an overestimate because that would represent nearly 10 per cent of their forces, and, as we have seen, it suited the Prussians to exaggerate the difficulties posed by the *francs-tireurs*. In another case, Fontenoy, a village which had the misfortune to be near a bridge on the main line between Prussia and Paris destroyed in a successful attack of sabotage, was burned down even though there was no evidence that the villagers had sheltered the guerrillas.

In fact, many of the derailments, minor accidents and track failures were due to the incompetence of the Prussian running of the railway rather than the result of attacks by partisans. Through the invasion, the Prussians gained control of 2,500 miles of French railway but operating it effectively was beyond them. They were, after all, working in a foreign country with strange equipment and with little help from French railway workers, who mostly abandoned their jobs once the Prussians arrived rather than collaborate with the enemy. In such conditions, accidents were inevitable but the *francs-tireurs* were a useful scapegoat though they could hardly be held responsible for the fact that chimneys kept being knocked off Prussian locomotives because French bridges were too low for them.

The post-war recriminations on the French side were lengthy and deep-rooted with an almost painful attention to detail. Numerous tomes were published by French retired generals and former railway managers blaming each other for the failure of the war. Even years after the conflict, there were debates in the newspapers as to why, for example, a freight train carrying roofing material for barracks had been allowed to disrupt military schedules during the retreat from Nancy. Interestingly, it was the railwaymen who won the post-war battle of words. While the old generals attacked the performance of the railways, the rail managers were able to cite so many precise examples of military incompetence that their view prevailed. The most influential memoirs were in a book by François Jacqmin, the general manager of the Est railway, who in *The Railways during the War of 1870–71*, contended that there were two essential conditions to run a rail system in wartime. First, there had to be a unified control of the railways for military purposes, whether it was the transport of troops or supplies, and secondly there had to be a "permanent association" of the military and technical elements: in other words, a joint command which would ensure, for example, that before any order for transport was given it should be guaranteed that it was possible to carry it out "without prejudice to other transport orders already given or likely to become necessary". As usual, it was basic stuff but seemingly so hard to take on board. The much chastened Ministry of War did, however, listen and Jacqmin's advice, as we shall see in Chapter Six, would form the basis of the French preparations for the 1914 war.

On the Prussian side, there were the usual plaudits for the strategies of the victors. Moltke was hailed as the military genius who delivered the victory, but the compliments served only to disguise the failings that, to neutral observers, were all too obvious. As in the two previous conflicts, Moltke had ignored Haupt's basic set of rules, which, had they been followed, would greatly have increased the effectiveness of the railways and created a much more effective supply line for the second part of the war. Pratt is again pretty damning, suggesting that "a common mistake has been the attributing to Germany of a far higher degree of credit in regard to the alleged perfection of her preparation for the Franco-Prussian war of 1870–71 than she is really entitled to claim." Moltke, though, emerged with an even greater understanding that railways were the key to modern warfare. According to Barbara Tuchman: "'Build no more fortresses, build railways', ordered the elder Moltke who had laid out his strategy on a railway map and bequeathed the dogma that railways are the key to war."

The Prussians had, out of necessity, learnt that the old methods of keeping an army's supplies replenished were still necessary if there was no railway line of communication. They had discovered that a large mobile army could still live off the country in the same way that Napoleon's troops had seventy years before, provided it was in summer and they were in a fertile agricultural area. Moltke's troops had survived because they had dispersed across a wide front rather than concentrated in a small area. Moltke, therefore, might have been of the age of the railway and understood its advantages, but the strategic movement of his troops in this war was still determined, at times, not so much by the existence of the railway but, rather, by the ability to forage for food.

Once armies came to a halt, however, life without railways was extremely difficult. When the Prussians besieged Metz, their supplies had run very short and the logistical bottleneck was only solved thanks to the considerable effort of the train companies, and the proximity of the railheads. The armies besieging Paris had faced even greater difficulties and the military function of the troops had effectively been abandoned for a two-month period while they were sent out into the countryside to harvest the crops and bring them to the front. It would be the last time in history that an army would be forced to carry out such a function.

If France did have, according to neutral observers, the better railways, how come it lost the war? In one word, incompetence. The French learnt that while the railways were adept at enabling far larger armies than previously to be delivered to a battle site, thereby increasing the scale on which wars could be fought, when things went wrong the enormous numbers involved meant that the scale of chaos increased commensurately. According to a renowned war historian, Brian Bond, despite French troops having a better rifle than their Prussian counterparts and the country boasting a better railway network, "these assets

127

could not offset the disastrous higher direction of the war by Napoleon III, compounded by the machinations of his empress [Eugénie, the conservative Spanish countess who was a friend of Queen Victoria and lived until 1920] and the irresolution of its principal army commanders, Bazaine and MacMahon". Bond points out that the Prussians actually lost more men in the opening frontier battles which proved decisive, and had the French resisted these early attacks more fervently, the result might well have been different. Instead, the Prussians were allowed to get between the two French armies and Paris, leading to the ultimate humiliation at Sedan.

Despite the overall disappointing performance of the railways — or rather, the failure of the military to make proper use of them — they were crucial, decisive even, during two key phases of the war. Firstly, as we have seen, the railways ensured the rapid mobilization of the Prussian troops, as had been planned, with the result, according to Allan Mitchell, that the outcome was never in doubt "once the initial encounters had been decided on the Franco-German border. German victory was sealed by superior rail transportation"; and secondly, the bombardment of Paris by a sitting army would never have been possible without supplies arriving by rail as the assault required "the concentration in a small space of very large masses of men and heavy expenditure of artillery ammunition".

The Franco-Prussian war dispelled the hopes of assorted idealists and strategic thinkers that the creation of the railways and their ability to deliver supplies to entrenched defenders would make the waging of war so difficult as to deter any attempt at aggression once and for all. Friedrich List, an early German railway pioneer and something of an idealist, had hoped that railways would put an end to war because the "greater speed in movement would always assist the defender". A British writer, W. Bridges Adams, had expressed similar thoughts in an 1859 magazine article arguing that the railway was "emphatically the offspring and tool of civilisation . . . a weapon of defence and not of attack, and is easily rendered useless to an invading enemy". While Moltke had been influenced by this thinking, "reasoning that whereas a defender would have full use of his own network, the attacker would not be able to rely on any lines in advance of his front", his own war experience would expose the flaws in this line of thinking. While the railways definitely gave the defenders the edge in a conflict because of the logistical difficulties faced by an invader, ultimately that advantage would be lost if the railways were not properly managed. This puts the French performance in context and it is impossible to resile from the fact their mismanagement of the railways was a story of stunning incompetence that cost the country the war — and changed the course of history.

Worse, the victory of the invading forces gave the military strategists the wrong impression about the railways. As we shall see in Chapter Six, military planning over the next forty years running up to the First World War was based on the mistaken notion that railways gave the offensive side the advantage. The French blundering on the railways therefore not only caused their defeat but helped stimulate the military build-up that resulted in the First World War. Had Moltke's successors, Schlieffen and the younger Moltke, realized that the victory was more the result of French errors than Prussian brilliance, the tragedy of 1914, stimulated by the twin notions that attacking first was essential and that swift victory was possible, might never have happened.

As in the Austrian conflict, a longer Franco-Prussian war or a more static one, like 1914–18, would certainly have dented Moltke's reputation for genius. Indeed, van Creveld is highly critical of Moltke's performance: "An interesting aspect of the railway problem is the failure of Moltke and the general staff to learn from experience. Every one of the obstacles that arose in 1870 had already been rehearsed in 1866, and yet they were allowed not only to recur but to become infinitely worse." As we have seen, the rules set down by Haupt would have solved many of these problems. The Prussian army was not enormous and each corps — of around 50,000 men — could have been supplied with food, ammunition and forage with, say, six or seven trains per day, easily within the capacity of one well-organized single-track line.

Thanks to the railways' ability to deliver vast numbers of troops — albeit inefficiently on the French side — the Franco-Prussian War was a remarkably bloody affair with more than 180,000 soldiers killed, around 10 per cent of the participants, a high number given the conflict lasted barely ten months and most of the fighting was over within six. The next major war in Europe would, of course, be even bloodier. In the intervening period, however, the railways would figure in a number of colonial and minor wars where gradually the lessons of how to use them to best effect would be learnt.

CHAPTER
FIVE

The New Weapon
of War

The world in which the 1914 war would break out was very different from the mid-Victorian age of 1870. Europe largely industrialized in the intervening period, partly thanks to the stunning growth of the railways, which would nearly triple in size from 65,000 miles to 180,000 in those four and a half decades with, in particular, northern and central European countries seeing rapid expansion of their networks. With the exception of a few minor wars, there was peace in Europe throughout this period, but it was an uneasy one, constantly at risk of being broken by the frequent bouts of sabre-rattling, stimulated by xenophobic governments and encouraged by the media. There was no shortage of potential sources of conflict, notably the continued weakening of both the Habsburg and Ottoman empires, as well as the militarization of Germany and the fluctuating state of alliances, but these tensions, for the time being, did not break out into all-out war.

On the fringes of Europe, however, and in the colonies, there were several wars, notably in Africa, during which the various aspects of the performance of railways in wartime were tested. The growing power of Japan, contrasting with the weakness of China and Russia, resulted in a series of conflicts culminating in the massive Russo-Japanese War, in which that most ambitious of military railways, the Trans-Siberian played a central role. In several other places, too, railways were being designed and built specifically for military purposes while elsewhere the perennial problems of destruction and sabotage, lack of logistical nous and rows between military and railway administrations were in evidence during conflicts. There was, too, a growing realization that civilian railways could easily be turned over to military use with little adaptation — a longer platform here, a set of sidings there — with the military therefore trying to dictate the location and extent of railways. In India, for example, work on the railway network was greatly speeded up after the quashing of the bloody mutiny in 1857. The British rulers saw the railways quite explicitly as an adjunct to military force. There was a clear equation: the more railways that were available to move troops quickly around the country, the fewer garrisons would be needed and consequently, while the cost of building railways was high, it might well be cheaper than not having them in the long run.

From the point of view of the railways, the two most important conflicts during this period both occurred outside Europe. The Boer War proved to be a testing ground for the British use of railways in war, and not only pitted a guerrilla force against an army making heavy use of the railways but also saw the most intensive use of armoured trains in any nineteenth-century war, while the Russo-Japanese War was in every respect a railway war.

The Russians were involved, too, in one of the few conflicts on European soil during this period, when they demonstrated the clear advantages of building railways to further a military campaign in their war against the Ottoman Turks in 1877–8. This short but bloody war was a legacy of their defeat in the Crimea a quarter of a century previously and triggered by the ongoing collapse of the Ottoman Empire controlled by Turkey. The war came at the end of one of those perennial Balkan crises, which have continued into the twenty-first century, and resulted in a brief conflict between Serbia, Russia's ally, which was seeking independence, and the Ottoman Empire.

After protracted negotiations over the future of Serbia had failed, Russia declared war on the Ottoman Empire in April 1877, hoping for a short and victorious battle which would culminate in a triumphal march into Constantinople. It was not to be. As in so many wars, the enemy had been taken too lightly and the difficulties of fighting battles a long way from home underestimated. The logistics proved problematic. In order to provide the route through to Constantinople, the Russians had enlisted the support of Romania, which had until then been an autonomous part of the Empire, and obtained running rights on Romanian railways for trains carrying their troops. Unfortunately for the Russians, the main railway line in Romania was a basic affair, a single track running from the border town of Galatz on the Danube to the capital, Bucharest, and then through to the Bulgarian border, eventually reaching Varna, the Turkish supply base on the Black Sea. The Russians needed to proceed quickly through the country because they feared that the transport facilities would be unable to sustain an adequate long-term supply line for the army since the roads were impassable in winter and the railway line in a poor condition. However, they were soon held up by stern resistance at Plevna in Bulgaria, where the extremely able Turkish general Osman Pasha managed to hold out against superior Russian forces in a siege that lasted until the end of the year.

Pasha's resistance had stymied the Russian advance, so to keep the troops supplied the Russians had to hastily build a line to connect their railway system with the Romanian line at Galatz. The 189-mile line from Russia's South-Western Railway at Bender, on the Dniester river, to Galatz had originally been planned as a commercial scheme, but now became an urgent military project and when completed was by far the longest military railway built up to that date. The work, organized by a private contractor called Polyakov who had a poor reputation, started in July soon after the army got stuck at Plevna. Polyakov, however, excelled himself and the line was completed in only three months, an achievement that was even more remarkable given that industrial-relations difficulties with a very devout labour force which downed tools on holy days and Sundays resulted in work proceeding on only fifty-eight days. Moreover, it was not a basic line designed for temporary use but, rather, a well-constructed railway with stations and stable embankments, one of which was three miles long, built with the intention that it would remain useful, for both military and civilian purposes, long after the war was over. Polyakov himself scoured Europe for locomotives and wagons to operate on the line. It could not connect directly with the Russian network, however because of the difference in gauge as Romanian trains ran on the standard 4ft 8½in gauge in use throughout most of Europe while the Russians had adopted 5ft.

Galatz, the transfer point, became a logistical nightmare. The trans-shipment of 200,000 men plus all the other war matériel, including 1,250 large guns, from one railway network to the other resulted in lengthy delays and slowed down the whole line of communication. Moreover, on the return trip, the need to change trains at Galatz meant that Russian wounded were seen to be "stacked like logs" while awaiting ambulance trains, and graphic newspaper reports about the soldiers' suffering inflamed public opinion in Russia, which had already been angered by the growing number of casualties in the face of the sterner than expected Turkish resistance.

The Russians built another railway for their war effort, a forty-mile stretch between Fratesti and Simnitza in Romania, which was an essential link between Bucharest and the Danube. This shorter line also took around three months to build, its progress hampered by a shortage of construction materials. Nevertheless, it proved vital in taking military traffic from the roads that became impassable with the winter rains and snow. The Russians had also envisaged building a third section of railway, a seventy-five-mile line in Bulgaria, but while much of the preparatory work had been completed, the lack of materials along with labour problems prevented its completion before the end of the war. Nevertheless, Pratt, the original historian of railways in war, was most impressed at the efforts of the Russians, suggesting that they had done a far better job in railway construction than the Germans in the Franco-Prussian War a few years previously: "Whereas the Germans had, in 1870, with the help of a Construction Corps more than 4,000 strong, taken forty-eight days to build twenty-two miles of railway between Pont-à-Mousson and Remilly, the Russians in 1877 built, by contrast, 189 miles of railway in just over double the same period." Pratt suggests that the achievement in building the two lines was noted by military strategists across the world: "So the development of the rail-power principle in warfare was carried still further by this construction, during the course of the Russo-Turkish conflict, of a greater length of railways, designed for military use, than had ever been built under like conditions before. The world gained a fresh lesson as to the importance of the role played by railways in war, and it was offered, also, a striking example of what could be done in the way of rapidly providing them in a time of emergency."

137

Despite incurring far greater losses than expected and enduring troublesome logistical problems, the Russians eventually won the war after the Ottoman Empire offered a truce at the end of January 1878. The main objective of the war had, however, not been achieved. The stern resistance at Plevna had ultimately stopped the Russians from reaching Constantinople, preventing a Christian army from taking over the Turkish capital, which would have had enormous historic and long-term importance. There followed the now customary post-war commission examining the role of the railways, which were inevitably blamed for many failings that had not actually been their responsibility. The Romanian railway was a primitive affair, with badly maintained track, lack of rolling stock and illiterate railway staff, while the Russian South-Western was fiercely criticized for its supposed inefficiency even though problems such as the gauge difference at the frontier and the usual failure to return empty wagons could not be laid at its door. Neither had the South-Western's poor reputation among the military recovered from an early incident when a troop train plunged into a ravine because track workers had failed to replace a rail they had removed. The commission found that many of the problems resulted from pre-existing issues on the railway, such as the shortage of locomotives, compounded by the reluctance of other railways to lend their own stock. Even when more locomotives were offered by other railways, the South-Western could make use only of types with which its maintenance staff were familiar. Thus, as

Westwood puts it: "an important consequence of this war was the adoption of a government standard locomotive". In the 1890s, a new government standard design for engines was adopted by the Russians and more than 9,000 of these locomotives were manufactured and deployed during the First World War.

The problems caused by the change in gauge between Russia and Romania did not go unnoticed in European military circles either. Indeed, when the first Russian line was built in the 1830s, the Tsar had deliberately chosen the 5ft gauge for defensive reasons, knowing that it was different from the standard gauge being adopted throughout most of Europe. Russia had been more fearful of invasions, having only recently been attacked by Napoleon, than concerned about attacking its neighbours. The difference in gauge was, indeed, a useful asset as a defensive measure against invaders, as the Germans would find out in their invasion of Russia in 1941 (outlined in Chapter Nine), but the conflict with Turkey showed it was a hindrance when the Russians sought to use the railways to supply an offensive into neighbouring countries. Moreover, the extreme smallness of the gap — a mere 3½ inches — between the two gauges used by the Russians and Romanians did not make conversion any easier since it proved impossible to add another rail just inside an existing one as there was not enough space. Therefore changing the gauge either way — from smaller to larger or vice versa — involved dismantling and refixing a rail, a requirement which greatly delayed the Germans in their advances towards Leningrad and Moscow in the

Second World War. For the Russians with their wider gauge, though, there was the added difficulty that while narrow-gauge rolling stock can, relatively easily, have its axles extended to allow running on the wider gauge (though this is difficult for steam locomotives), the reverse procedure is impossible. Moreover, the fact that structures such as platforms, telegraph poles, tunnels and bridges were designed only to accommodate the smaller Romanian trains meant rapid conversion of the line to 5ft was impossible and trans-shipment, which was slow and heavily dependent on manpower, was the only option.

Outside Europe, there was in this period a succession of colonial wars which were, in various ways, to illustrate the importance of the railways as a weapon of warfare. Just before the Franco-Prussian War, there had been one of those small obscure wars in far-off places that were a recurring feature of British colonial rule. The Emperor of Abyssinia (now Ethiopia), Tewodros II, was a weak and indecisive character who had locked up the British Consul and various missionaries on a pretext. After the failure of various diplomatic initiatives, in 1868 Britain sent a massive army at huge expense to rescue the consul and, more importantly, restore honour. The Bombay Army, under the command of Sir Robert Napier, was selected for the expedition on the grounds that the troops would be used to the fearsome climate and conditions. This was imperial warfare on a large scale. Intent on not repeating the errors of the Crimean War, where too few troops had been despatched, the force numbered

15,000, with nearly twice as many camp followers and three times as many animals, including a force of forty-four elephants trained to haul the heavy guns. It was far more than was needed to defeat a weakened emperor who had already lost control of much of his country to rebellious forces and it created enormous logistical problems.

The landing site was at Zoulla on the East African coast, a desolate and ramshackle place with little infrastructure, and this is where a railway played a small part in the outcome of the conflict with the construction of a line similar to the one in Balaklava to help unload the ships and bring supplies inland. Initially only a short tramway was envisaged, but soon plans were drawn up for an eleven-mile line from Zoulla to Koomayleh, where preparations for the arduous 300-mile expedition to attack Tewodros were under way. There was no question of building a railway all the way — as would happen later in Sudan — since the territory was mountainous and the expedition had the very limited goal of freeing the hostages and taking them back home, with no attempt at permanent occupation. Nevertheless, even this short stretch, the first line to be constructed by the Royal Engineers, required a great effort to build, and took six months to complete, far longer than envisaged. Neither the Royal Engineers, nor the Chinese workers who provided most of the labour, could be held responsible for the delay and the difficulties. Rather, it was the equipment sent from India which let them down as it was second-hand,

141

purloined from a variety of railways on the sub-continent and incomplete, with, for example, no spikes to hold down the rails, which were themselves of variable quality and design. Even after the completion of the line, the Engineers were only able to bring four of the six locomotives provided into steam because of defects and the sixty wagons sent from India were old-fashioned and prone to break down. In any case, by the time the railway was completed, the troops had already defeated the emperor in the decisive battle of Magdala, had secured the release of the hostages at Addis Ababa and were on their way back. Nevertheless, at least the railway saved the troops from having to march the last few miles back to the docks after their victory.

A couple of decades after this experience on the East African coast, the Royal Engineers enjoyed a much more productive time in neighbouring Sudan, where the highly ambitious military railway they built, in three stages, enabled the British to regain control over a rebellious land. Egypt had come early to railways, the first country in Africa to build them when a line between the capital, Cairo, and Alexandria on the Mediterranean coast was completed in 1856. There were immediate thoughts about extending the line through to Khartoum, the capital of Sudan, but it was impossible to make progress because of the shortage of capital. However, in 1884 a start was made on a line at Wadi Haifa, the Nile port on the Egyptian — Sudanese border, by British and Egyptian soldiers and labourers, overseen by a company (about 250 men) of Royal

Engineers, but work stopped when the 700 local labourers deserted. The idea was abandoned shortly after, with just fifty miles completed, when news reached Egypt of the fall of Khartoum and the death of General Gordon at the hands of the Mahdi rebels in January 1885. Work also stopped on a separate line which was being built simultaneously to link the Nile with the Red Sea at the port of Suakin. Again the Royal Engineers had been involved but attacks by Dervishes on the mostly Indian labour force led to the abandonment of the project after just twenty miles had been laid, despite the construction of fortified posts at regular intervals along it and the introduction of night patrols using a bulletproof train armed with a 20-pounder gun. Both these projects were overtly military in intent and it was hardly surprising that it was local hostility which halted their construction.

A decade later, however, work restarted on the Sudan Military Railway from Wadi Haifa to Khartoum. Since Wadi Haifa could be reached by ships on the Nile from Luxor, the line was the last link in the line of communication between the two capitals, Cairo and Khartoum. However, this time the scale of ambition was far greater as not only was the line planned to be a military railway enabling the British to retake Sudan from the Mahdis, but it was also part of the ambitious Cape to Cairo project promoted by Cecil Rhodes to build a railway line across the whole continent. After much prevarication following the disaster of Gordon's fall, Herbert (later Lord) Kitchener, then the commander-in-chief of the Egyptian Army, obtained permission from the British government to build the line in order to quell the Mahdi rebellion once and for all. The original fifty miles of railway had, by then, been completely wrecked but progress was impressive thanks to the leadership of a remarkable young Canadian military railway engineer, Lieutenant Edouard (Percy) Girouard, who would, too, play a major role on the railways in the Boer War and later use his railway expertise in the First World War.

The plan this time was to build a line to Khartoum from the Sudanese frontier at Wadi Haifa on the Nile, which could be reached by ships from Luxor, in order to carry and supply the troops. Kitchener chose a route that went straight across the desert, rather than following the winding Nile valley, which would have involved linking navigable parts of the river with sections of railway. The railway was the mechanism through which the war was conducted. There are few stories of railway construction more beautifully and painstakingly described than Churchill's account of the Sudan Military Railway in his book *The River War*, originally published in 1902, in which he stresses time and again that it was the railway which won the war. Churchill took part in the campaign against the Mahdis, in a rather bizarre role as both officer and war correspondent, and wrote eloquently about Kitchener's plan: "No more important decision was ever taken by Sir Herbert Kitchener, whether in office or in action" than this " 'selection of line of advance' ". Girouard made up a huge list of requirements for what would become a 576-mile railway and travelled to London to buy the plant and rolling stock, while a workshop was set up at Wadi Haifa.

This time the Royal Engineers, under Girouard, excelled themselves as they were put in charge of the disparate workforce, who ranged from Dervish prisoners to various tribesmen and a few former soldiers. Construction, which started on the first day of 1897, proceeded slowly at first because of the lack of equipment and the need to train the workforce in the skills of railway building, and by May only forty miles of track had been laid. Then, however, a military-style operation was put into effect with the aim of building at least a mile and a half (2,500 yards) per day, a target that at times was easily exceeded, with three miles being the record. It was perhaps typically British to fail to take advantage of the cooler weather in the winter and spring, but rather the main effort of railway building was concentrated in the summer months. The timing, however, was determined by political and military, rather than logistical, considerations as the goal of retaking Khartoum became a key imperial goal. Despite the torrid conditions and the fact that the supposedly "flat" desert actually rose up to 1,600 feet and back down, construction proceeded remarkably smoothly. The routine to drive through what Churchill called "a smooth ocean of bright-coloured sand" was simple but exhausting. The crucial innovation was a moveable "Railhead", "a canvas town of 2,500 inhabitants, complete with station, stores, post-office, telegraph-office, and canteen, and only connected with the living world of men and ideas by two parallel iron streaks, three feet six inches apart [the cheaper Cape gauge had been chosen rather than the standard 4ft 8½in] growing dim and narrower in long perspective until they were twisted and blurred by the mirage and vanished in the indefinite distance".

The "town" had only three days' reserve of water, and had the line been broken for a longer period, its population would have rapidly perished of thirst. They were kept alive by the two regular trains that arrived along those iron streaks every day and determined the routine of the construction. The first train would arrive at dawn and again Churchill describes it best: "Every morning in the remote nothingness there appeared a black speck growing larger and clearer until a whistle and a welcome clatter, amid the aching silence of ages, the 'material' train arrived." As well as water both for its own needs and for those of the workers, it carried 2,500 yards of rails, sleepers and other equipment. Then, a few hours later, at the height of the heat, which regularly reached 40^{0} C, a second train would arrive with more rail and accessories but also, crucially for the morale of the white engineers, goodies such as jam, sausages, whisky, cigarettes and even newspapers, "which enable the Briton to conquer the world without discomfort". The railway was laid with a Fordian division of labour, with separate teams preparing the ground, laying the rails and spiking them in.

By 20 July 1897, 130 miles had been completed, a remarkable rate of progress, but then work had to be stopped through fear that the advancing railhead was coming within range of the enemy. Progress only resumed after the capture by the British of the next village, Abu Hamed, some hundred miles away on the banks of the Nile, which was reached by November. It was then discovered that the intelligence which had suggested that the river was navigable from there all the way upstream was mistaken and therefore work on the railway had to continue. The discovery of water at two points on the line speeded up progress and greatly lightened the load on the trains, which had to carry their own water for the locomotives, using up a significant part of their capacity.

The line kept on advancing at a rapid pace until a year later, on 3 July 1898, it reached Atbara, giving the army, as Churchill puts it, the ability "to dominate the river and command the banks" all the way to Khartoum. With the completion of the railway, "though the battle was not yet fought, the victory was won . . . It remained only to pluck the fruit in the most convenient hour, with the least trouble and at the smallest cost." Indeed, new gunboats were ordered and broken up into sections that could be accommodated on the railway, rebuilt and relaunched on the navigable section of the Nile. Having overcome resistance and conquered the intermediate towns, the final battle took place at Omdurman, fifteen miles from Khartoum, where Churchill was proved correct: the might of the well-supplied British Army easily overcame the enemy despite being hugely outnumbered. The British lost just fifty men, compared with about 10,000 enemy casualties, and Gordon was richly avenged.

It was, of course, not only the railway but the whole logistical operation which ensured victory. Churchill described what it took for one box of biscuits to reach the front line from Cairo, involving a dozen changes of mode, including camel as well as boat and train, to cover some 1,150 miles. He was full of admiration for the transport officers who maintained a regular supply of food, equipment and ammunition over this lengthy supply chain, and had a far better appreciation of the challenges and importance of logistics than many military leaders. In a long section in the book, he concludes that while bravery and discipline may often result in unexpected victories, "in savage warfare in a flat country the power of modern machinery is such that flesh and blood can scarcely prevail and the chances of battle are reduced to a minimum. Fighting the Dervishes was primarily a matter of transport. The Khalifa was conquered on the railway."

At the other end of the putative but never completed Cape to Cairo, the railways were also about to play a major, if very different, part in a war. The Boer War was another eminently preventable clash which started off with patriotic cheers, and ended with much soul searching about the state of the British Empire. At the turn of the century, the current Republic of South Africa was divided into four territories: Natal and the Cape Colony, which were British colonies, and two Boer republics, the Transvaal and Orange Free State. To the north, Rhodes had created the British South Africa Company, which became Rhodesia. South Africa had been initially colonized by the Dutch and

Germans, but the British arrived in the early nineteenth century and tensions between the two groups were at the root of the Boer wars. In the first Boer War, which was small and was little more than a few skirmishes ending in one major battle where the Boers triumphed during the winter of 1880–81, the Boers had established their right to autonomy in the Transvaal, but the British refused to accept that the Boer republics could be fully independent states. Prior to the second Boer War the discovery of great mineral wealth — especially gold — in the Transvaal, which was largely exploited by British capital, had exacerbated tensions and the large British mining companies were concerned that Boer intransigence might threaten their interests.

The immediate *casus belli* was the British demand for voting rights for their citizens living in the Transvaal but the President, Paul Kruger, had prevaricated, postponing their eligibility for the franchise. A solution might have been found but for the bellicose nature of Sir Alfred Milner, the British High Commissioner in South Africa, who effectively sabotaged the peace negotiations. In truth, though, the long-standing hostility between the two colonizing forces in the country had been bubbling away for many years and it would have taken a concerted peace initiative on both sides to have prevented a war. Britain had long sought the establishment of control over the two Dutch colonies and saw Boer intransigence over the franchise as an opportunity to unify the whole of South Africa under the British flag. In fact, preparations for war had started early in 1899 with measures such as the

149

establishment of the Department of Military Railways and the construction of ambulance and armoured trains in the railway yards of both Natal and Cape Town.

Girouard, now a major, was appointed as the head of the Department of Military Railways and, having read the numerous reports on the performance of the railways in the Franco-Prussian War, he was aware that the Germans had gained an advantage by having a clear administrative structure in contrast to the French muddle. The old question arose: who should be in charge of the railways, the military or the railway managers? Girouard knew the answer. He was aware that, left to their own devices, military commanders would, for example, insist on having trains steamed up and ready "just in case", or require wagons to be unloaded while still on the main line, blocking it for other traffic. The military, in other words, had to be trained to understand the scope and limitations of the railways, and could not be allowed to be their master. Girouard immediately appointed a group of officers who would act as liaison between the military and the railway authorities, and, as Pratt puts it, "protect the civil railway administration from interference by military commanders and commandants of posts". At the station level, officers were appointed who would be the sole liaison between the railway administration, the stationmasters, and the military, in order to prevent senior army personnel commandeering trains for their own purposes.

This structure was all the more important because the railways in South Africa were fairly basic affairs, all built to the narrow 3ft 6in Cape gauge and designed to accommodate light goods and passenger trains, rather than heavy military traffic. Moreover, the distances were huge. From Cape Town, the principal British base, to Pretoria, the Boer HQ which would be the ultimate objective, was over 1,000 miles and the roads were poor and unusable at times of heavy rain. A single-track railway line stretched from Cape Town on the southern coast through Kimberley and Bloemfontein through to Johannesburg and Pretoria, while a branch headed off from Mafeking towards Rhodesia. From Durban on the east coast there was another line through to Ladysmith which also eventually reached Johannesburg. These lines became the vital supply route for the Army as supplies to the forces at the front were sent from seaports, sometimes quite long distances, along the railway to a railhead and picked up by horse transport, and consequently the shape of the railway network in southern Africa determined the course of the war. For the British in particular — the Boers all had horses — the railway was the major means of transport for long distances, although there were times when the soldiers would march or ride while their supplies were taken by rail. It was inevitable, therefore, that the key battles took place in railway towns or in countryside easily accessible from the line. The British could only maintain their army using railway resupply and the various towns whose names reside in the memory through the prolonged sieges they suffered were

151

important precisely because they were on the railway line. Many of the same cast of characters as in Sudan turned up in the Boer War: Churchill, Kitchener and Girouard, who was to prove to be a crucial figure, all played significant parts.

The war finally broke out in October 1899 and in its first phase the Boers captured large swathes of land in the two British colonies, including long stretches of the railway, and besieged three British garrisons at Ladysmith, Kimberley and Mafeking. Attempts by the British Army to relieve the sieges ended in a series of humiliating defeats and early in 1900 reinforcements had to be brought from Britain, creating a force totalling 180,000 men. The takeover of much of the railway in the British colonies by the Boers resulted in a shortage of stock, prompting the military to send immediate requests to Britain for extra locomotives and wagons. For their part, in the early stages, the Boers themselves rather ignored the railways, preferring to keep to their horses but proving adept at sabotaging lines used by the British.

In the second phase of the war, the British staged a fightback with expanded forces and here the railway was crucial as the army headed northwards to re-establish control over its own territory and then advance into the Boer states. The arrangements made in anticipation of the conflict came into play. Every day, all the Army's requirements were collated through Girouard's Department of Military Railways, which decided whether requests should be accepted or rejected. The number of wagons allocated for each department, such as hospital, ordnance or engineering, was calculated in great detail and nothing could move without a permit from Girouard's department. A small group of soldiers carrying out a specific duty might be exempted but they would have to travel sitting higgeldy-piggeldy on the supplies. As Ernest Carter, a railway historian, concludes, this disciplined allocation of railway resources in the Boer War "proved conclusively that even a single line passing through enemy territory could be maintained in a serviceable condition sufficiently reliable to allow of a campaign being conducted at a point many hundreds of miles from a supply base".

As the Boers retreated, they invariably destroyed railway facilities, making heavy use of dynamite, still a relatively new explosive first patented in 1867 and little used in intervening wars. It was the usual catalogue of mayhem, except that dynamite made the job of destruction far easier: bridges and long sections of track were blown up, railside equipment such as pumps and water tanks was destroyed, stations were flattened and huge obstructions were brought down by triggering explosions on the sides of railway cuttings. In response, the British created an organization of 20,000 men, a tenth of their overall strength, composed of a motley mix of soldiers, former railwaymen and local natives, to ensure the continued operation of the railways.

When the British Army began to invade the Boer republics, the Department of Military Railways spawned a separate organization, the Imperial Military Railways, both to repair and maintain captured lines in

153

the two republics, and to operate them. The Afrikaners employed by these railways were unwilling to stay in their jobs under the British and therefore had to be replaced by soldiers and railwaymen from the Cape Colony and, later, also by local black workers.

As the British troops headed northwards, elaborate patrols were devised using armoured trains to protect the line, which was absolutely vital for the British advance. It was the first time that armoured trains were extensively and successfully operated in any conflict. The British had deployed them in Egypt, Sudan and India in the 1880s, using conventional rolling stock that was reinforced with steel plating and equipped with a few machine guns and sandbags for protection, and often pushing a light wagon at the front to detonate mines or limit the damage from obstacles left on the line. They were little more than armoured patrol vehicles, but during the Boer War far more sophisticated versions were developed.

Several had been built in anticipation of the war and ultimately twenty saw action on the South African railways. Their reputation was initially rather tarnished by the capture on 15 November 1899 of an early model carrying 120 men including, famously, Winston Churchill, who yet again had made sure that he was in the right place at the right time to see action. This time, he was a mere reporter, sending despatches to the *Morning Post* although at times he behaved as if he were still an officer in the British Army. Churchill recounts an early sortie with the train, which he describes as a strange machine, ridiculing it as "a locomotive disguised in the habiliments of chivalry. Mr Morley [John Morley, the leading opponent of the war] attired as Sir Lancelot would seem scarcely more incongruous." His first foray with the train passes off without serious incident but his second leads to his capture and a series of brushes with death.

Churchill's train had consisted of a couple of sets of four vans, three of which were armoured, including one with a 7-pounder gun so old-fashioned that it was still loaded through the muzzle ("an antiquated toy", as Churchill described it), an ordinary wagon with a breakdown gang and a locomotive which, for protection, was in the middle of the train between the two sets of wagons. The patrol's mission was to try to obtain information about the siege at Ladysmith and the state of the railway. At 5.30 a.m., the train crept out of Estcourt, thirty miles south of Ladysmith, and had reached Chieveley, about halfway to their destination, when Boer horsemen were spotted. Captain Haldane, the commander of the train, decided to beat a retreat but the train had fallen into an ambush. Round a curve, they saw a large troop of 600 Boers above them and bullets and shells started raining down on the wagons. The engine driver opened the regulator to accelerate out of trouble, which was precisely what the Boers had sought, as the train then ploughed at speed into a boulder they had laid on the tracks round a bend. Even though the train was notionally in the command of Haldane, it was Churchill who assumed control of the situation, or at least he did according to his account written for the Morning Post. He reports how he told

155

the driver, who was a civilian and therefore anxious just to escape, that "if he continued to stay at his post, he would be mentioned for distinguished gallantry in action", not an honour that was Churchill's to bestow. Nevertheless, with such encouragement, the fellow "pulled himself together, wiped the blood off his face [and] climbed back into the cab of his engine". Leaving Haldane to sort out the defence, Churchill organized the removal of the debris and the stone from the tracks, and ordered a group of men to push the broken wagon off the track. Despite being still under fire, they succeeded and the engine, minus the front group of trucks, which had become detached, gradually pulled away. All these efforts to escape proved, however, to be in vain because, as Churchill describes it, "a private soldier who was wounded, in direct disobedience of the positive orders that no surrender was to be made, took it upon himself to wave a pocket handkerchief." As a result, the men around him began to surrender and Churchill tried to run away. While Churchill criticizes the hapless fellow, the humble soldier's action most likely changed history by ensuring the great man's survival. Churchill had already run down the track with two Boers shooting at him, fortunately missing him on either side ("two bullets passed, both within a foot, one on either side . . . again two soft kisses sucked in the air, but nothing struck me"), and had fortuitously, too, forgotten his Mauser pistol in the cab of the locomotive, and was therefore unable to shoot his pursuers. Without the private's white handkerchief, it was probably only a matter of minutes before

Churchill, who was behaving as a combatant rather than a newspaper reporter, would have been shot. After his capture, however, anxious to be released, he stressed his civilian role but to no avail and he was imprisoned in Pretoria, from where he escaped, regaining British territory by jumping goods trains like an American hobo.

Churchill's armoured train was an early version, more lightly armed than its successors. Later types would be far more heavily protected and were successfully used on several occasions against the Boers. The armoured train became a far more sophisticated weapon, consisting of a locomotive in the middle, pushing armoured vans and wagons with various pieces of equipment for repairing lines. At the front, there was an open wagon fitted with a cow catcher — like US locomotives — both to sweep obstructions off the rails but also to explode mines, thereby saving the rest of the train, particularly the locomotive, from further damage. Behind the locomotive there was a heavily armoured wagon with usually a 12-pounder quick-firing gun or a couple of smaller ones. Each end of the train would be protected by armoured trucks containing soldiers armed with rifles and a machine gun. It proved a useful weapon. In one skirmish, the legendary Boer leader Christiaan de Wet, who had been instrumental in developing successful guerrilla tactics, often focussed on sabotaging the railway and disrupting communications by wrecking the telegraph wires, was for once caught napping when

157

four armoured trains managed to cut him off from his wagons and he lost all his ammunition and explosives.

While armoured trains were occasionally used in offensives against entrenched Boer positions, for the most part they were deployed to patrol lines in an effort to prevent sabotage. They were also used rather like the cavalry to make reconnaissance trips and escort conventional trains. Nevertheless, as Churchill's mishap showed, they were vulnerable to ambush and could not be deployed without their own protection force, usually in the form of cavalry reconnaissance teams who would check the line and the surrounding area but at times bicycles were used, too. These were remarkable contraptions developed in a Cape Town workshop by Donald Menzies, who experimented with various types. The basic version, which did see regular active service, involved two men sitting side by side, with the great advantage that they could ride and shoot at the same time, since, obviously, no steering was required as the wheels were flanged like those of all railway rolling stock. It could travel at up to 30 mph but was not stable at such high speeds and generally cruised at about 10 mph. Menzies also produced a huge eight-man version with four pairs of men pedalling side by side, but it was beset with difficulties as it was too heavy — 1,500lb with eight men aboard — and consequently was difficult to brake, made too much noise and caused violent shaking, and there is no evidence that it was actually used in combat situations.

The official report published after the war recommended that in the operation of armoured trains "it was important that the officer commanding the train should be a man of judgment and strong nerve . . . he had to be ever alert that the enemy did not cut the line behind him . . . and had to keep his head even among the roar which followed the passage of his leading truck over a charge of dynamite, and then to deal with the attack which almost certainly ensued". Inevitably, having such strong-minded officers in charge of the trains led to clashes with the railway authorities as the armoured trains transcended the boundary between the military and railway. Girouard later complained that the officers commanding the trains frequently rode roughshod over the railway's needs: "Armoured trains were constantly rushing out, against orders of the Traffic department, sometimes without a 'line clear' message, and this caused serious delays to traffic." One can almost feel Girouard's frustration as he continues: "In fact, instead of assisting traffic by preventing the enemy from interrupting it, they caused more interruptions than the enemy themselves." As Pratt put it, "civil railway officials were heard to say that attacks by the enemy are not nearly so disturbing to traffic as the arrival of a friendly General with his force". Regulations were subsequently issued to ensure that the armoured trains, like all other traffic, deferred to the army officers whose job was to liaise with the railway authorities to ensure efficient use of the lines.

The armoured trains proved popular with the British and were a formidable weapon, causing panic among the enemy, as stressed by an officer who had served in them: "There is no doubt that the enemy disliked them

159

intensely and that the presence of an armoured train had a great morale effect." The post-war report rather optimistically outlined seven uses for armoured trains, including obvious aspects such as reconnoitring, patrolling and protecting the rail lines, along with more adventurous ideas like "serving as flank protection to infantry" and "attempting to intercept the enemy". While for the most part this analysis overemphasized their usefulness, since armoured trains would play little role on the Western Front in the First World War, they would assume much greater importance on the more fluid Eastern Front and, in particular, would be crucial to the Bolsheviks' victory in the subsequent Russian civil war. In the Boer War, they were used to best effect to counter guerrilla attacks, a role they would play numerous times again.

The armoured train was a natural development of the basic idea of mounting guns on trains, which, as we have seen, was first used in battle in the American Civil War. Such trains were a railway weapon, likely to be deployed in an offensive action, in contrast to armoured trains whose main purpose was to patrol an unstable area. The concept of using the railways to deploy large artillery guns had made considerable progress since the days of General Lee. In particular, the problem of aiming the guns had been solved to some extent by incorporating a turntable on the car, which enabled the gun to be rotated easily, and methods of dispersing the force of the recoil, using a specially constructed chamber, had also been developed, enabling guns to be fired broadside without toppling over or damaging the

160

track. The French had used a couple of rail-mounted guns to defend Paris during the siege in 1871 and a unit of the Sussex Army Volunteers had experimented with putting a 40-pounder on a rail wagon. As a result of these developments, the British Army tried to make use of a pair of mobile guns built in the workshops of the Cape Government Railway during the Boer War. In the event they were little used in anger, principally because of the difficulties of bringing such unwieldy and slow vehicles within range of a battle site on a single railway track already heavily used by conventional traffic.

Once the advance into the Boer republics had started, the British expected to win the war within months as the superiority of their forces told — and back home the Tories won an election on this basis. The fighting was, however, prolonged for two years by the ability of the Boers to wage a destructive and effective guerrilla war with a small force, frequently targeting the railway and other transport links. The Boers' guerrilla tactics were extremely difficult to counter since they were operating in their home terrain against an enemy unaccustomed to this style of fighting. The Boers, who were mostly farmers, were all experienced riders and excellent shots, with the result that even a small group of men could prove difficult for the less skilled British to defeat. In response the British became more and more ruthless, with a scorched-earth policy of astonishing cruelty that involved destroying the Boer farms and forcing the destitute women — the *vrouewen* who were at the centre of the Boer rural lifestyle — and

161

children into camps. To force the Boers' families off the land, livestock was slaughtered and crops destroyed, giving them no alternative but to leave their homes. The treatment meted out by the British to these refugees in what became the world's first concentration camps was the cruellest aspect of the war, and, inevitably, to transport them they were herded into trains, prefiguring the similar German atrocity by forty years. The mortality rate in the camps was appalling, with 26,000 deaths, a quarter of those interned, and, most horribly, no fewer than half of those under sixteen perished. Women whose husbands were still fighting were singled out for harsh treatment by being given smaller rations. There was a series of separate camps in which 107,000 Africans were interned, but an accurate assessment of the death rate was never made. The terrible conditions endured by the Boer women and children caused a scandal back home which greatly increased opposition to the war.

Clearing the farms in this way was designed to break the will of the Boers and prevent them living off the land. Protecting the supply line, most importantly the railway, became the key strategy for the British. While the Boers continued to attack the railway lines during this third phase, the British engineers became increasingly adept at repairing such breaches. They would boast that a routine break in the tracks discovered by the dawn patrol would be repaired in general by 9 a.m. Of course, they had far more difficulty repairing the damage wreaked by the retreating Boers in their own territory, which caused long delays to the cumbrous British Army moving into the republics. However, the engineers became adept at restoring at least a limited service very quickly. During the course of their retreat northwards, the Boers destroyed more than 200 bridges, several more than a hundred feet in length. Yet for the most part services were restored within days by putting in a temporary line, often with steep gradients and sharp curves, over hastily constructed low-level bridges cobbled together with sleepers and rails. While these jerry-built constructions were at times washed away in wet weather or collapsed under the weight of heavy trains, they were vital in keeping the British line of communication intact.

As territory was won by the British, the railway lines had to be protected and land defended through a process of attrition. The railway was crucial to this strategy. Once the British established control over a section of track or a bridge, a chain of blockhouses was built alongside them to prevent attacks by Boer squads. Connected to each other by telephone and telegraph, they were sited so that one could be seen from the next, a maximum of three-quarters of a mile away. Huge quantities of barbed wire, a recent invention, were strung up between them and trenches and trip wires provided an additional obstacle to any Boers attempting to reach the railway. While proving very successful, the blockhouses required huge numbers of soldiers to man and protect them. By the end of the war some 8,000 of these blockhouses had been built next to the railways, along other key supply routes and across the veldt, demanding the services of 50,000

British soldiers and 16,000 Africans, probably twice the total number of Boers who were fighting in the final guerrilla phase of the war. The blockhouses were expensive, too — costing up to £1,000 each — and difficult to construct, taking about three months, but proved remarkably effective as in conjunction with the armoured trains they all but guaranteed the security of the railway line.

This tactic of containment and harassment worked, albeit slowly. The Boers eventually surrendered in May 1902, ground down by the gradual progress of the British through their territory, and with little room to manoeuvre as the soldiers in the ever lengthening strings of blockhouses provided increasingly detailed intelligence on the whereabouts of the enemy. The Boers were harried and, unable to fight, forced into finally accepting peace terms which the British had offered several times previously. After lengthy negotiations, the Boer republics were incorporated into the British Empire a few years later, but the cost of dragooning the Boers into Britain's fold had been high. Far from being the short conflict which the politicians expected, it turned out to be the bloodiest and most costly of Britain's wars between 1815 and 1914.

In railway terms the Boer War was a dress rehearsal for the forthcoming world war, even though the nature of the conflict was quite different, but in the intervening period another war was fought alongside a single long stretch of track in which the railway played an even more central part. The Russo-Japanese War of 1904–5 was, however, a very different type of war, involving massive battles on a scale that resulted from the ability of the railways to deliver huge numbers of troops and supplies rapidly to the theatre of war. As all the fighting took place in Manchuria and Korea, it was the first major war to be conducted entirely on the territory of nations not involved directly in the conflict, a feature that, of course, was only made possible by the efficiency of the lines of communication created by the railways.

Of all the wars discussed in this book, the Russo-Japanese is the only one in which not only did the railways play a central role in the way that it was conducted, but the construction of a line actually triggered the war itself: "Russia's eastward expansion had brought with it a great railway which the equally expansive Japan had seen as a threat to its own territorial ambitions. The result was the Russo-Japanese War which *would* not have been fought on the scale it was, had the railway not been built, and indeed *could* not have been fought at all in the railway's absence."

The Trans-Siberian, at more than 5,700 miles by far the world's longest railway, was in effect two railways and had, right from the outset, been a military project undertaken in the final decade of the nineteenth century by the impoverished Russian state at vast expense, with the aim of uniting the two ends of the biggest nation in the world and imposing the rule of St Petersburg on its furthermost province. Siberia had always been a distant land, reachable only by the most arduous journey, taking two to three years on horseback from western Russia, whereas the railway made it possible to reach Vladivostok on the Pacific coast in under a month. The railway, built in the most difficult conditions through remote lands with terrible winters, was a remarkable achievement on behalf of a nation still struggling to leave behind its feudal past. The initial route of the railway, completed in 1903, used the newly constructed and shorter Chinese Eastern Railway which went through Manchuria to reach the Pacific coast, rather than the more northerly direct line crossing entirely Russian territory, which was not completed until 1916. The Russians had taken advantage of the weakness of the Chinese, who had been beaten in the Sino-Japanese War of 1894–5, to acquiesce to their demand to build the railway on Chinese soil. The Trans-Siberian had been started, from both ends, in 1891 and had mostly been completed, with a gap at Lake Baikal, the largest in Asia, by the turn of the century. The decision to go through Manchuria was partly practical, as the territory was easier than further north, but there was imperial intent, too. The Chinese Eastern Railway was in its own right a massive project, undertaken in just six years and requiring the construction of nearly 1,000 steel bridges alone. When completed in 1903, it employed 20,000 people, mainly Russian, and while notionally a private company, it received massive subsidies from the state. The headquarters was at Harbin in northern Manchuria, a town created by the Russians which became a centre of both commerce and learning, with a major polytechnic to train students in the skills of building and maintaining railways.

Russian imperial ambitions appeared to be confirmed by the construction of a branch line, the South Manchurian Railway, which went from Harbin through the Liandong peninsula to Port Arthur (Lüshun) and another port, Dalny (Dal'ny or Dalian), in which the Russians were investing huge sums to create a major harbour. Russia had long searched for a warm-water port that would allow round-the-year access to shipping, unlike Vladivostok, further north, which is closed by winter ice, and these two ports on the Liandong peninsula were seen as ideal for Russian trade with the United States. Following the Sino-Japanese War of 1894–5, Russia had signed a lease with China to obtain unrestricted access to the peninsula, but the investment in these ports was seen as a hostile act by the Japanese, who, coming out of their long period of isolation, had their own ambitions to establish themselves on the Asian mainland. They viewed the South Manchurian Railway as a "dagger pointing at the heart of Japan", giving Russia access to both Manchuria and Korea, but, in reality, it was unclear whether Russia's aims were purely commercial or whether there was military intent, as Russian imperial policy at the time was muddled and incoherent. The Russians were diplomatic *ingénus*, led by an arrogant backward-looking tsar who may well have been unaware of how the construction of this network of railways would appear to the outside world. The fact that 25,000 men were needed to guard the two railways did not support the notion that their purpose was solely peaceful and the construction of the branch line through the Liandong peninsula sufficiently convinced the Japanese of Russia's imperial ambitions for them to launch an attack on Port Arthur in early February 1904.

The precise timing was also railway-related. The single-track Trans-Siberian was still not fully functional as, hampered by poor construction standards and prone to derailments and other delays, it could provide at most three trains per day. The Japanese felt that this would hinder Russian efforts to despatch enough forces to defend Manchuria but realized that any delay might allow the Russians to improve the railway.

The attack on Port Arthur was inconclusive but the Japanese managed to blockade the harbour for several months. Meanwhile, a Japanese force landed in Korea and headed north towards Manchuria, while, in response, the Russian tactics were to try to delay any major offensive by the Japanese sufficiently to allow themselves time to bring in reinforcements by rail. It was now that the consequences of the primitive construction techniques employed on the Trans-Siberian made themselves felt. The line had been built with too few passing loops and the poor track conditions limited speeds on long stretches to just 15 mph, greatly restricting the capacity and prolonging the journey for the troops. There was a particular bottleneck on a section through Manchuria where a tunnel had not been completed, entailing trains having to make a lengthy haul up a mountain range and having to be broken up to facilitate the climb. During 1904, improvements to the railway were prioritized: extra loops were hastily built, the vital tunnel was completed, the worst sections of track were improved, and trains were regulated so that they went at the same speed, thereby increasing throughput.

The worst constraint, however, was Lake Baikal, where the line had not yet been built. Although construction of the Circum-Baikal railway around the southern edge of the lake had started in late 1899, it was not scheduled to be completed until 1906. In the meantime, passengers and freight had to be carried across the lake — a long thin strip of water 400 miles long and 35 miles wide at the crossing point — by ship and, in winter, transported on the ice, creating an inevitable logjam. The Japanese had taken this into account when deciding when to launch the war as they expected the Russians would not be able to complete that section in time to use it during the conflict. As the Japanese predicted, at Baikal station on the west side of the lake there was, according to a contemporary observer, a build-up of "mountains of cases, pyramids of bales, containing articles and provisions of which the troops already in Manchuria are in sore need. Russian officialdom is not seen at its best in such circumstances, and the absence of all grip in the situation becomes daily more deplorable."

In order to convey goods and men to the railway on the other side of the lake, three separate tracks were laid across the ice: a sledge route marked by poles, mostly for officers; a foot track, over which whole battalions marched; and eventually a temporary rail line, once the ice had become sufficiently thick to support the weight of the wagons and the men and horses hauling them across the ice. In order to speed up the flow of goods, an attempt was made to use a locomotive on this track but even though the line had been laid on extra-wide sleepers to spread the load, the ice could not support the weight and the engine sank, taking several men with it. Consequently, the tracks across the lake proved insufficient to transport all the build-up of supplies and equipment across it and the backlog at Baikal was not cleared until the summer. Without locomotives to haul them, all the soldiers had to cross the ice on foot and suffered greatly as their uniforms were not weatherproof and recruits were not even issued greatcoats to protect them against the Russian winter. Their only solace was the series of wood and felt rest houses sited every four miles, where they were given soup, tea and stale bread and where, if they were lucky, they could get treated for their frostbite.

The logistics were made worse by a huge stream of refugees fleeing in the other direction who also suffered indescribable deprivations. A journalist reporting on the conditions wrote that the trains contained "no lavatories, no food to be got along the line, hardly any water, no milk and [there were] six hundred children of all ages huddled together for warmth . . . it was one of the pitiful sights of warfare, and a mere forerunner to the woes behind." This episode showed up all the failings of the Trans-Siberian during its early years, highlighting the contrast between the brilliance of the technological achievement in constructing the railway and the terrible conditions endured by those who travelled on the line.

Midway through the war a ferry, transported in pieces on the railway, was reconstructed at Lake Baikal under the instructions of three British engineers from Newcastle and was able to transport matériel and men over the lake during part of the winter as the stern was fitted with icebreaking equipment. However, the ship soon became redundant as the Japanese calculation in respect of the construction of the Circum-Baikal railway proved wrong. Once war broke out, the Russians set about completing the line round the lake with alacrity, boosting the workforce by half to 13,500. It was a heroic effort. Both the geology and the weather were hostile in the extreme and the high cliffs and mountains overlooking much of the lake necessitated the construction of countless tunnels and bridges. The route was so circuitous that the line eventually proved to be 163 miles long to progress eastwards a mere forty miles and it is today a great tourist attraction. The first engineering works train travelled on the line in October 1904, and while it took another year for the railway to be brought into full operation, it ensured that supplies and men could be transported towards Manchuria far more quickly than the Japanese had anticipated.

Eventually, from a maximum of only three trains in each direction per day, by the end of the war the Trans-Siberian could cater for up to sixteen pairs, still fewer than one per hour. Moreover, there was the added problem of finding sufficient locomotives and rolling stock to operate this level of service. A train would routinely consist of twenty-eight troop-carrying freight cars, each with room for forty men (or eight horses, or, for the Cossacks unwilling to be parted from their steeds, a combination of both!). Little comfort was provided for the Russian soldiers: the cars were lined with felt and fitted with a stove, used both for heating and for making tea, essential when temperatures outside could reach -45°C at times. There were small windows allowing the men a glimpse of the endless steppes and forests, and while some cars had sleeping shelves, in others the only bed was the floor. There were a further six cars for ammunition and kit, and a comfortable upholstered passenger car for the officers, who, on some trains, also had use of a lavishly decorated Orthodox church car. In all, each train provided transport for 1,100 men and their officers. The long periods endured by the men in these conditions without supervision from the officers, who were comfortably ensconced in their separate coaches, were of concern to the military authorities, who were worried that the regular soldiers would pay heed to the talk of disaffected reservists, thereby stimulating revolutionary ideas.

Because of the onerous conditions, after every three days of travel the soldiers were allowed a rest day, and therefore the journey from Moscow would take at best thirty days, and at worst as many as fifty. Such lengthy journey times resulted in heavy demands on the amount of rolling stock: 400 locomotives (two per train) and 8,000 wagons were needed just to maintain a regular service of four trains per day, while for the desired target of fourteen per day, a staggering 1,400 locomotives and 28,000 cars were required. These, too, are probably underestimates, given the difficulties of repairing stricken engines anywhere in the wilds of Siberia, the lack of workshop facilities and spare parts and the widespread use of railway cars in sidings as temporary barracks and storage. Haupt's rules on the effective use of railways during wars were clearly still being ignored.

The Russians scoured Europe for extra stock, and despatched many locomotives from their other lines to the east, but still struggled to keep up with the demands of the longest railway route in the world. Therefore, even when the line had been improved, it could still not operate at full capacity because of the rolling stock shortage. Nor was the ability of the line to deliver vital supplies and troops helped by chronic mismanagement, with the usual conflicts between railway managers and the military, exacerbated by the tendency of senior officers to use the line for their own purposes regardless of the disruption that caused to the Army's main supply system. A British attaché noted that when the heads of the navy and the Army met, the journey of several hundred miles between the two headquarters at Mukden and Liaoyang was undertaken on a special train for the admiral. According to the diplomat: "This necessitated the line being kept clear for indefinite periods of time and dislocated all the other traffic arrangements, as the then chief of the railways declared." This habit of senior officers using the railways as their personal transportation system would, as we shall see, be repeated in future conflicts.

Once the war settled down into stable fronts in its later stages, the 11,000 Russian railway troops, with the help of numerous Chinese labourers, built a remarkable 350-mile network of narrow-gauge field railways with horses and mules hauling the trains. These hastily built lines were used both for carrying munitions and soldiers to the front from the railhead and to remove the sick and wounded to safety. In the period before the battle of Mukden, when the front became static and the troops entrenched, rather presaging the situation in the First World War, these light railways became a vital part of the line of communication. One section near Mukden was thirty miles long and its horse-drawn wagons were able to cover that distance in just five hours, far faster than the alternative road. For the wounded, too, these railways were a great boon since they were a far more comfortable way to travel for men in pain than in the back of a cart pulled slowly along bumpy roads.

While the Russians had improved their transport situation by completing the Circum-Baikal railway a year ahead of schedule, and setting up these field railways, the Japanese had also been working on their logistics by building a new railway and that was to give them a decisive advantage. Initially, they landed troops in Korea, which they controlled, and marched them north to Manchuria. There had been, though, plans for a network of railways which would connect Korea with Manchuria, and the Japanese set about accelerating

174

their construction, with a quite stupendous effort that would give them a decisive edge in the war. In particular, by the end of December 1904, the Japanese had completed the line from the southern Korean city of Fusan to Seoul a year earlier than scheduled. It was no simple task. A contemporary report in *The Times* says it was "a feat of engineering which reminds one of the railways of Switzerland. Two ridges have to be crossed, and in each case the line makes a wide curve gradually ascending the steep slopes and half-way up it enters a tunnel which pierces the mountain at a height of 2,000 feet." By linking this railway with another hastily completed line, between Seoul and Wi-Ju, it now became possible to travel by rail from Fusan (Busan) into Russia, a counterbalance to the construction of the Trans-Siberian, and a warning to the Russians that they were not the only imperial power which could also use the railways to impose itself on distant lands.

Crucially, the new railway could be used to transport troops up to Manchuria, rather than having to march along a primitive mountain road prone to closure. Moreover, after the Japanese finally took Port Arthur in January 1905, they could use the Russian-built South Manchurian Railway as a second supply route. However, the Russians had not left any locomotives behind, and the Japanese had to resort to using men to haul wagons along the line. They developed a system of combining sets of wagons (carrying only a quarter of their normal 20-ton cargo) using sixteen Chinese labourers, eight pushing and eight pulling on ropes. According to the historian John Westwood, "a forty car

175

train seems to have been the record, but after some disastrous if spectacular runaways down gradients, amid a scurry of entangled coolies, a ten car limit was imposed". Eventually, the line was converted to the Japanese 3ft 6in gauge from the normal Russian 5ft and operated with locomotives imported from Japan, relieving the poor coolies of their terrible task. The Japanese, like the Russians, also made heavy use of horse-drawn narrow-gauge railways to take supplies right up to the front.

Through the use of these two railways in the south and east, "Japan had in effect created a flanking strategy, whereby counter-attack into the heart of Russia was possible via the Manchurian or Korean system. Coupled with this, Japan had provided the one dimension it hitherto lacked: the ability to provide its Manchurian forces with the support of the railway." This trapped the Russians. Their forces were gradually chased out of the heartland of Manchuria, abandoning swathes of the southern part of the region: "At the same time, the flanking effect achieved by the completion of the Korean railway network applied still greater pressure on Russian forces. Having to divide their attention between confronting regular Japanese forces in the South and the spectre of a further front opening in the East, while supplies for the large Russian Army dwindled, the Russian military was faced with multifaceted threat and few options at its disposal."

The Japanese had learnt that the Russians were sending a naval squadron from the Baltic to reinforce its Pacific fleet but it had to travel all the way round the world, taking seven months to effect the 18,000-mile trip from the Baltic around the Cape of Good Hope and across the Indian Ocean — demonstrating why the Trans-Siberian had been built in the first place. The fleet had been despatched in October 1904 and clearly its destiny already seemed ill-fated since, passing near the United Kingdom, the Russians had fired on a group of thirty British trawlers which, because of a Chaplinesque series of blunders, they had mistaken for Japanese torpedo boats, even though they were thousands of miles from Asia on Dogger Bank. The incident, in which three sailors were killed, nearly brought Britain into the war on the side of the Japanese, with whom it had a treaty, and resulted in much anti-Russian coverage in the newspapers. The fleet never reached Russian waters in the Pacific. The Japanese simply lay in wait until the Russian navy had to sail through the straits between Japan and Korea, where they sank nearly all the ships, preventing the much-needed reinforcements from reaching the beleaguered Russians.

The final battle of the Russo-Japanese War at Mukden was, therefore, played out on Japanese terms. In a situation that would repeat itself on a much larger scale in the First World War, the two sides had become entrenched across an eighty-mile front south of Mukden.

The battle commenced on 20 February and raged for three weeks. By then the two forces virtually matched each other, with an enormous number of men, 620,000, taking part in the fighting. Despite the apparent logistical advantages, the Japanese were worried about continued reinforcements on the Trans-Siberian and their leader, Field Marshal Prince Oyama Iwao, wanted to use this battle to chase the Russians out of Manchuria finally. The Russian leader, General Alexei Kuropatkin, deployed his forces defensively, hoping as ever to gain sufficient time for the army to arrive in force. However, thanks to their newly arrived reinforcements, the Japanese were able to launch several suicidal but successful attacks against entrenched positions and machine-gun emplacements. Kuropatkin retreated, digging in further west and leaving the Japanese to take Mukden on 10 March. It was the last major land conflict of the war, though occasional skirmishes flared up and the Russians continued bringing in reinforcements from the west along the Trans-Siberian.

While the Japanese won both the land and the naval battles, the fact that the Russians had completed the line around Lake Baikal, and were building up capacity on the Trans-Siberian, theoretically gave them a stronger hand in the ultimate peace negotiations at Portsmouth in New Hampshire, brokered by the USA under the ebullient leadership of Teddy Roosevelt. By October 1905, when the war came to an end, the Russians, at last, greatly outnumbered the Japanese as a million men had been despatched by the now far more efficient railway. In fact, the Russian build-up of troops had come too late. The war was proving so unpopular in Russia that it had already prompted an unsuccessful revolution and the Tsar had realized that pursuing it would only add to the unrest. Therefore his hand was in reality weak as he entered the peace talks. However, thanks to the Russians' stronger military position the terms thrashed out after much behind-the-scenes negotiation by Roosevelt gave them far more than they might have expected given the clear nature of their defeat. The Japanese were greatly disconcerted by the fact that while they had unequivocally won the war, they were treated almost as the losers in the subsequent peace negotiations and they did not get the monetary compensation they had sought, nor all the territory of Sakhalin Island that had long been a source of dispute between the two nations. This discontent contributed to the growing militarism that would be expressed most vigorously in the country's involvement in the Second World War.

Despite its success at the negotiating table, Russia had not won a single battle in the war — some were draws rather than outright victories for either side — and had lost the bulk of two of its three fleets. Nevertheless, its military leaders basked in the misapprehension that having eventually delivered such a huge force to the front through the railway, Russia would probably have won a continued conflict. In his extensive post-war writings, General Kuropatkin did not doubt that the canny timing of the attack by the Japanese was the decisive factor, but he argued strongly that had he been able to deliver more troops quickly through the railway he would have won. This failed to recognize the fact that the Japanese, too, had improved their logistics thanks to the railways they had built and would have been able to respond in kind to any increase in numbers on the Russian side. Defeated generals are wont to blame logistics but it was not really the newly built railway's fault, since it had performed quite heroically in delivering an army of a million men and their supplies over more than 5,500 miles of largely barren wasteland. Kuropatkin ignored that it was his failure to exploit the potential that the railway had given him, and his enemy's ability to improve their lines of communication rapidly, that led to defeat.

Indeed, both sides had used the available railways to maximum intent and, as a result, never before had such vast numbers faced each other on the battlefield. Overall, the Russians had sent more than one million men to Manchuria, boosting their forces from 125,000 to 1,300,000 by the end of the war. The Japanese, for their part, had built a railway and adapted another to their needs, but crucially they were better able to exploit these assets. They started off with 300,000 men, and tripled the total to 900,000 during the same period.

Independent analysts contradict Kuropatkin's view that it was only a matter of timing that prevented Russia from winning, arguing that, as the war unfolded, the balance "shifted in the direction of Japan, and it was only a matter of how the denouement was to take shape in the ensuing months". The Japanese were better supplied with ammunition and better fed than their Russian counterparts. The difference between the two combatants was that the Japanese managed to improve their supply chain in the second half of the

180

conflict with the use of two extra railways, whereas the Russians, short of the ability to supply their troops from the ports on the Pacific, were entirely dependent on the Trans-Siberian, which, despite improvements, was still inadequate. The paradox was that the Russians had built an amazing railway — its inadequacies should not be used to detract from the fact that it was probably the most ambitious engineering project ever undertaken, even including the building of the pyramids — and yet had been unable to use it to bring about victory. That may have been because the military commanders were still rooted in the mores of feudal Russia, in sharp contrast to the modernizers who built the railway, led by the remarkable Sergei Witte, the driving force behind its construction and later Prime Minister of Russia. Witte, indeed, made sure that the dead hand of the military had been kept out of the construction process of the railway, which, as a result, was very advanced in its application of modern engineering skills. The disparity could be seen on every train heading east with its complement of peasant soldiers, mostly illiterate, travelling on the new iron road, probably for the first time — a potent symbol of the nation's attempt at modernity.

One example of the Russian military's lack of understanding of the railways' potential and their missed opportunity to blend the old with the new was the way they failed to combine their awesome Cossack cavalry with transport by train. The Japanese cavalry, which had feeble horses ill-suited to the local environment, was a weak point in their armoury and

181

had the Russians used the Cossacks as shock troops, transporting them by rail to the point of attack, they would have sown terror among the Japanese fighters. As it was, the fact that the Cossacks played little part in the war was a missed opportunity on the part of the Russians. Whereas the Russians viewed their railways in a passive way as merely a support facility and a means of transport, the Japanese recognized their value as a weapon of war: "The Japanese saw their railways as an element to be integrated into their overall strategy, using the lines as a support facility, but also integrating them into their broader plan of attack." Neither did the Russians understand the lessons learnt in previous wars on the relations between the military and railway managers: "lines of communication between Russian officers and railway officials were at all times based on the assumed superiority of the former". As we have seen numerous times, railway managers have to be left to operate the railways to reap the maximum benefit from them.

Because of its location and timing, the Russo-Japanese War is seen as an obscure conflict whose importance is often underestimated. Yet, in several respects, it was a prelude to the type of conflict which would engulf the world a decade later, as illustrated by the fact that at the battle of Mukden there were 620,000 combatants, probably more than at any previous battle in history. All the paraphernalia of modern warfare was on show: the telephone, the telegraph, the machine gun, barbed wire, torpedoes and, of course, the railways, both large and small.

Indeed, if any war showed that the railways completely changed the scale and nature of war, it was the Russo-Japanese War. It was not only made possible by the Trans-Siberian Railway, but, as we have seen, was a direct consequence of its construction. While the soldiers fought on the battlefield, another battle raged behind the scenes to improve railway connections to that distant front in order to mobilize sufficient forces and supplies to overwhelm the other side. It was the railway battle that was won decisively by the Japanese.

The lessons of the Boer and Russo-Japanese wars on the use of railways in wartime were not directly relevant to the forthcoming conflict that would envelop the whole of Europe because they were fought around single, very lengthy, lines rather than whole networks. Nevertheless, as the next chapter shows, these two wars were important in highlighting the central role of railways in future conflicts, a lesson that became universally understood as thereafter detailed plans for railways were included as a core part of every country's preparations for war. As the historians of the role of the Russo-Japanese railways conclude, "The strategic role of railways on a continental scale would henceforth be seen as crucially important for the transport of war." The First World War, which started less than a decade later, would certainly confirm that.

CHAPTER SIX

The War the World Anticipated

With hindsight, it is possible to view the period between 1870 and 1914 as one long preparation for a war that everyone saw coming. Of course, it is not that simple. The war might have been averted entirely if the right diplomatic decisions had been taken, or if a less bellicose set of political leaders had been in power. Or, alternatively, another type of war might have occurred with perhaps a different set of alliances and a different outcome had Archduke Ferdinand's driver not mistakenly gone down the street where the sickly student assassin happened to be waiting.

However, given the changes in Europe during this period and the tensions surrounding them, a canny futurologist of the late nineteenth century trying to guess when war was most likely would undoubtedly have plumped for the mid-1910s as odds-on favourite. It is, therefore, difficult to resile from the view taken by most historians that the First World War was inevitable. This was a period of rapid economic growth which destabilized the old power balances created by the

Congress of Vienna at the beginning of the nineteenth century. Instead of a structure of the five great powers — Britain, France, Austria-Hungary, Germany and Russia — with a wide range of interlocking interests, Europe had divided into two blocs — the two Germanic powers and the rest — with several explicit military commitments and alliances. The build-up of Germany's strength, its ambitions for expansion, the gradual collapse of the old order and the tensions caused by rapid technological developments all increased the likelihood of conflict. French resentment at the loss of Alsace-Lorraine after the Franco-Prussian War and the failure of the Russian ruling class to implement any significant reform of the tsarist absolute monarchy added to the unstable atmosphere throughout Europe. Indeed, the lengthy periods of peace in the nineteenth century, broken since Napoleon's day by relatively few conflicts — and short ones at that — could be seen as exceptional by historical standards. At the most prosaic level, the timing of the war was just right, too, in another respect. The generals on the European continent were, by then, too young to have fought in the 1870–71 conflict and perhaps harboured romantic views of the nature of battle.

Apart from these long-standing tensions, the theory that attackers had an inherent advantage over defenders, which as we have seen arose partly as a misinterpretation of the outcome of the Franco-Prussian War, pushed Europe towards war: "During the decades before the First World War, a phenomenon which may be called a 'cult of the offensive' swept through Europe. Militaries glorified the offensive and adopted offensive military doctrines, while civilian elites and publics assumed that the offense had the advantage in warfare", despite the counter-evidence, since the proponents of this idea "largely overlooked the lessons of the American Civil War, the Russo-Turkish War of 1877–8, the Boer War, and the Russo-Japanese War which had demonstrated the power of the new defensive technologies". And yet every European power adopted a military strategy based on the idea that a "quick win" could be achieved by the attacker and that there were windows of opportunity which had to be grasped to ensure victory with sufficient *cran et élan*, as the French put it. Nothing characterizes the sheer arrogance of this concept more than the French entering the war with their troops wearing bright blue uniforms with red trousers, an overt invitation to "shoot me".

The growth of the railways in the thirty years following the Franco-Prussian War further convinced the military leaders that attack was the best means of defence. This was a period of tremendous expansion on the railways, which still remained unchallenged from cars and lorries and yet had to cater for the demands of fast-growing economies. Existing lines were improved and capacity increased, while new ones were built to connect virtually every town and village with the railway network. The track mileage in Europe almost tripled between 1870 and 1914 to 180,000 miles and in the larger countries such as Germany and Russia the increase was proportionately even greater. The improvements in quality, speed and capacity were even more important. According to van Creveld, "at the time of the Franco-Prussian War, it was reckoned that a single line could carry eight trains a day, a double one twelve, whereas on the eve of World War 1, the figures were forty and sixty respectively". Dense networks had been built up throughout the Continent, ostensibly for peaceful purposes, but actually the construction of many lines made sense only if their value to the military was taken into account, since commercially, they were basket cases.

The growth of the railways had gone hand in hand with the huge changes in Europe in the decades after the Franco-Prussian War. The production of raw materials such as coal and pig iron trebled in the three leading powers, Britain, France and Germany, as industrialization swept through the Continent. Their populations also increased rapidly as people became more prosperous and, crucially, hygiene had at last begun to improve, cutting the death rate from infectious diseases, but more ominously the size of the armed forces grew proportionately far faster. France, the second-largest military power in Europe, had roughly 500,000 men available in 1870, while by 1914 the Army was able to mobilize 4 million, even though the population had risen by only 10 per cent. This increase in scale of the armies made it inevitable that the military would take a far greater interest in the main way of transporting them, the railways. Therefore, this rise in army personnel was more than matched by an increase in their complements of railway experts and

187

during this period all the major powers developed burgeoning specialist railway sections of their armies to operate, maintain and even build railways in wartime.

Periodic scare stories in newspapers and powerful jingoistic movements in several European countries added to an air of inevitability about the prospect of war. The Franco-Prussian War was seen as unfinished business on both sides. The French wanted Alsace-Lorraine back, while the Germans felt that even their triumphal march on the Champs-Elysées in 1871 was not enough to assert their permanent superiority over their western neighbour. In German eyes the bloody French remained respected in the arts and culture, their language was widely used in diplomatic circles and their economy was still buoyant. As an example of Germany's permanently bellicose attitude towards its neighbour, an official by the name of Steiber dreamt up a plan to place spies in key positions at junctions and strategic stations in the French railway workforce so that they could carry out sabotage missions in the event of the outbreak of war. The plan, conceived in 1880, was implemented with the approval of Bismarck but was discovered by the French three years later and 182 Germans were hastily repatriated.

Towards the end of the century, an added source of tension was the rush by the major powers — and minor ones, too, such as Belgium and Italy — to establish colonial empires. Railways became the means through which colonial powers could consolidate their dominance over a country. In addition to opening up markets and ensuring sources of supply of minerals and agricultural produce, railways unified political territories and made the job of policing an area far easier. Railways, it was recognized, were both the economic lifeline of remote regions and the physical demonstration of military domination by the colonial power. The Russo-Japanese War had grown precisely out of a struggle between competing powers and in Africa the efforts by Rhodes to build a Cape to Cairo railway had almost resulted in a war with the French over their rival plans in the immediate sub-Saharan area. As a historian of the Middle East in the pre-war period suggests, "railways having become so important, it was soon merely sufficient for one nation to announce the preliminary plans for a new railway to engender suspicion, hostility and jealousy in other powers".

The collapse of the Ottoman Empire offered a country such as Germany, which had come rather too late to establish direct control of huge swathes of land, the opportunity to carve out an area where it could exert economic domination. Railways were seen as the instrument through which Germany could establish its dominance with the nicely alliterative Berlin — Baghdad railway as the centrepiece. The railway was conceived by the Germans as a way of giving them access to a port on the Persian Gulf — the plan was for the railway eventually to reach Basra — and allowing them to trade with the Far East without having to go through the British-controlled Suez Canal. This was a direct threat to long-standing British interests. The British had been a powerful force in the Gulf since the early nineteenth century and had agreed with Russia spheres of interest in Persia while all the coastal sheikhdoms had treaty relationships with India. The Germans had already financed the Anatolian Railway from the coast through to Ankara, which would be part of a Berlin — Baghdad railway. Significantly, rather than taking the easiest route along the sea, the railway had been built inland, despite the extra cost, since it required the construction of a five-mile-long tunnel in order to shield the line from the guns of the British navy, which patrolled the Mediterranean. While the German involvement in the Anatolian Railway attracted little interest, let alone opposition, from the other Great Powers, once the crumbling Ottoman administration sought to get a concession to extend the line to Baghdad, Britain, France and Russia all put in proposals to build the railway. The Turks eventually chose an Ottoman corporation which was actually a front for German interests which had a majority holding and were funded by the Deutsche Bank. The labour force was to be Turkish and, oddly, it was set out in the contract that all would be required to wear a fez, while the managers would be German, as would all the construction materials, which were to be imported duty-free. Initially, even though the concession effectively precluded the construction of any other lines, the British appeared relaxed about the idea and there was even a lengthy article in *The Times* lauding the proposal.

However, as the implications for control of the region and the supply of oil, which was quickly assuming great importance, became apparent, the British, French and

Russians all started to object and make interventions to block the construction of the railway. While the Anatolian Railway had been a modest effort, the scope and potential of a Constantinople — Baghdad and Basra line, which would be 1,500 miles long, were clearly on a different scale, comparable to the construction of the Trans-Siberian, which, as we have seen, already had one war to its name. The British, in particular, were obstructive, which was hardly surprising given that the railway threatened their efforts to establish dominance in the Persian Gulf and gave Germany direct access to India and the Far East. Worse, there was a more direct threat to British interests. The concession for the railway allowed the establishment of a German naval base in the Persian Gulf and navigation rights through the Shatt el Arab waterway fed by the railway, which was likened in the press to a 42cm gun pointed at the heart of India. If nothing else, the agreement to build the railway showed the level of German intent in its colonial ambitions: "The railway was a manifestation of a dramatic and alarming growth of German economic power. It played a role in the British-German trade rivalry, in their strategic manoeuvrings, and in the German-English press controversies. The railway helped unite the Entente powers against Germany . . . The railway involved a major conflict of national interests; failure to estimate the sources of this conflict correctly on both German and Entente sides definitely helped bring on World War 1."

The British effectively ensured that the project would be stalled when in 1911 they prevailed upon the cash-strapped Ottoman government not to raise tariffs to finance the railway. Although several sections had been completed, construction was stalled by this manoeuvre, as well as by engineering difficulties, and the line was nowhere near completion in 1914. While superficially the differences over the railway appear to have been resolved following much diplomatic negotiation before the outbreak of the war, there is no doubt that the planned railway contributed to the growing hostility between Britain and Germany. As the historian F. Lee Benns suggests: "Although before the outbreak of the war in 1914, understandings were eventually reached regarding the Baghdad railway by Germany, Russia, France and Great Britain, the project had already done much to poison the international atmosphere. Germany had come to believe that the opposition of the *entente* powers was only part of their general policy of encirclement." Indeed, another author, Morris Jastrow, writing before the end of the war, went further, suggesting that the railway was *the* major cause of the instability in Europe and consequently the war: "No step [apart from the concession to build the railway] ever taken by any European power anywhere has caused so much trouble, given rise to so many complications and has been such a constant menace to the peace of the world . . . the Baghdad railway will be found to be the largest single contributing factor in bringing on the war because through it more than through any other cause, the mutual distrust among European powers has been nurtured . . . A railway which as a medium of exchange of merchandise and of ideas ordinarily fulfils the function of binding nations together, in this instance has been the primary cause of pulling them apart."

While Jastrow may be exaggerating the railway's importance, there is no doubt that it played a significant role in cementing relations between Germany and the Ottoman Empire. Indeed, the immediate signing of an accord between the two nations as soon as war broke out, followed by Turkey joining the war in 1915, gives credibility to the notion that the Germans were buying military support through their investment in the railway. The line itself had only reached the current Turkish — Syrian border by the outbreak of war and was actually not completed until 1940, when the first train ran between Istanbul and Baghdad using British locomotives. The line, however, was to play a significant part in the Middle East theatre of the Second World War. By contrast, the Hejaz Railway from Damascus to Medina was completed and proved much more successful, mainly because a railway to assist the hajj made it deeply attractive to devout Muslims, and, as we shall see in Chapter Eight, was the focus of a guerrilla campaign during the First World War by Arabs at the instigation of T. E. Lawrence.

Back in Europe the railways were becoming the centrepiece of plans to mobilize for war. Much effort was expended by all sides — except, for the most part, the British — on schemes to use the railways to the best effect in the early stages of a conflict. Indeed, the railways, and specifically the rigidity of railway timetables, have been blamed for the timing — and by some for the very fact — of the outbreak of war, but, as we shall see below, this is based on flimsy evidence. The truth is more complex and perhaps more mundane. The railways were essential to the way the war was waged and were an integral part of preparations. In Germany, the Chancellor, Bismarck, expended considerable energy after the 1870–71 war in trying to gain state control of the railways as he was convinced that only nationalization would enable the military to control them in the event of war. The constitution of the new *Kaiserreich* created as a result of the war gave the state power over the railways "in the interest of national defence and general transportation" and a central government railway organization was created. The problem for Bismarck was that the structure of the new Germany as a federal country meant that much power remained with the states, and they were reluctant to bow to Prussian pressure over anything very much, let alone their precious railways. In the decade following unification, Bismarck tried desperately to use this clause in the constitution to impose the rule of central government — essentially Prussia — over the railways of the other states. However, as Allan Mitchell concludes in his book on French and German railways of the period, "throughout the 1870s, Bismarck actively sought to create a uniform national railway system for the new Reich — and he failed".

Eventually, at the end of the decade, Bismarck managed to push through legislation in the Prussian parliament to empower the state to purchase private rail companies throughout northern Germany, effectively bringing much of the system under state control. That gave him the ability to direct investment to a large section of the railways in the north and the mileage of Prussia's railways consequently increased by 50 per cent between 1870 and 1885, but in the south he still had to rely on the goodwill of individual states to provide the capacity which would be needed for military purposes. In the 1890s, officers from the central railway administration in Berlin began covertly to inspect railway installations in the states to assess their military readiness, a measure of the Prussians' fear that their war mobilization would be disrupted by the unwillingness of the states' railways to accept control from Berlin. While Bismarck's central railway administration managed to ensure that the states applied national standards to the operation of their railways, such as the rule that the stationmaster should blow two long blasts of his whistle to indicate the train could depart, and more importantly that technical requirements for signalling and braking systems were unified throughout Germany, he had great difficulty persuading them to double the tracks on single lines where there was no obvious commercial imperative. The southern states, Bavaria, Baden and Württemberg, understandably felt that if Berlin wanted these extra tracks for military purposes, the federal government should pay. Eventually a compromise was reached whereby most of the cost of the investment — ranging from 75 per cent in Bavaria to 95 per cent in the vicinity of the French border — fell on the Reich. However, the development of a strategy of invading Belgium on the way to France reduced the need to rely on these railways.

This was not a trivial matter. It is difficult to overstate the importance of the railways in the Bismarckian view of Germany's place in the world. Germany saw itself as the powerful peacemaker of Europe, maintaining that its superiority was necessary to prevent the outbreak of wars. That required being able to resist attacks from either side, and, as Mitchell puts it, "only the railways could render German aspirations possible. Only they could connect the two fronts and bring the weight of the Reich's military machine victoriously to bear." Interestingly, while generally France was dismissed as a competing power by Germany's rulers, who suggested it was in decline both militarily and demographically, the military would simultaneously use the spectre of French strength and resilience as an argument to pour ever-increasing resources into strengthening railway lines leading to France.

Throughout the period between the 1870 and 1914 wars, the German military asked repeatedly for more money to pay for new railway bridges and tracks. Apart from the construction of battleships, investing in the railways, particularly the construction of more bridges over the Rhine, took precedence in military thinking over all other spending and the military ensured that the investment was carried out in line with their needs. For example, large junctions were laid out to take extra traffic and through-stations replaced termini where trains had to reverse out to facilitate the flow of supplies. Stations close to the border were, as the French secret service had noticed, expanded with huge sidings and extended platforms, far in excess of any conceivable need in peacetime, and operating methods were slowly standardized so that the whole railway system could be put on a war footing at short notice. Military, rather than commercial, imperatives were even allowed to intrude on operating policies such as electrification. By the turn of the century, electric railways were already becoming recognized as more efficient and faster, but the German military was adamantly opposed to the introduction of electrification. Apart from the cost — installing electric equipment is expensive, though it saves money in the long run as the trains are cheaper to run — the military was worried about the difficulty of co-ordinating electric and steam operations in wartime on a partly electrified network and, in particular, they feared that the system would be far more vulnerable since an attack on the electricity supply could result in all trains on the line being stopped. Therefore any lines that were electrified had to be capable of reverting to steam use in the event of war. Another military requirement was for the Prussian railways to build their locomotives with a demountable top section that could be removed when the engine ran on French tracks. This was the result of a series of embarrassing and damaging episodes during the Franco-Prussian War (see Chapter Four), when the chimneys of Prussian locomotives venturing onto French tracks for the first time smashed into bridges on

French railways because they were lower than their Prussian counterparts, which the military authorities did not want repeated. Rather suspiciously, this adaptation continued to be a requirement of German locomotive design long after the end of the war.

On the personnel level, the German military also ensured that in wartime they would establish direct control over the railways. Peacetime railway administration was in the hands of regional directorates to which were attached military officers (*Bevollmächtigten*) who would take over in case of war. However, whether these officers would assume command during the preparations for war or only when it was officially declared was not made clear.

The railways, incidentally, had another side effect on military strategy: they also rebalanced the equation between the importance of navies and land forces. Since the invention of the ocean-going ship in the middle of the fifteenth century, seaways had become much more flexible carriers of trade and projectors of military power than their land-based competitors. But the coming of the railways changed this fundamentally, as demonstrated by the Russo-Japanese War conducted at the end of a long railway line and supplied from distant parts, demonstrating that far-off armies were no longer dependent on the vagaries of sea transport by the navy. Armies, therefore, assumed greater importance than the senior service, and this was reflected in military planning, with the massive increase in the size of the fighting forces. This, in turn, placed yet more burden on the railways.

As the new century dawned, Germany's military plans became more and more sophisticated and at their core was the notion of a rapid mobilization through the railways. German military intentions had first been set out by Alfred von Schlieffen, the chief of staff, in 1899 and were revised annually in a lengthy process involving both the military and the railway authorities. The key idea was to prepare a scheme whereby Germany could win a war waged on two fronts — against France in the west and Russia in the east. It was assumed that since Russia would take a long time to mobilize, and did not have sufficient railways to deliver large numbers of troops to its western border quickly enough, France had to be overcome before the Russians were in a position to attack. The idea was that once victory had been achieved in the west, troops could be transferred quickly to the Russian front.

Schlieffen was obsessed by the strategy of Hannibal at the battle of Cannae, where he defeated the Roman army by launching an attack in 216 BC around the enemy's flanks and annihilating them from the rear. Unfortunately for Schlieffen, he knew that he would not be able to muster sufficient forces to envelop the French from both sides — and in any case the common border with Lorraine was well protected by fortresses and hills. Therefore he envisaged an attack around the northern flank through Belgium at the cost of perhaps ceding some territory, temporarily, to the French in the south as he anticipated that they would concentrate forces there in their anxiety to reclaim Lorraine. This would suck their resources into an area which was

199

easier for the Germans to defend with relatively few troops because of the hilly topography. The fact that the plan violated Belgian neutrality, which was protected by treaties with, amongst others, Britain, was completely ignored by Schlieffen. He calculated, wrongly as it turned out, that the treaty was merely a piece of paper which the British would happily quietly forget about. The plan became grander with every annual iteration and by the start of 1906, when Schlieffen was replaced by the younger Moltke (the nephew of the elder Moltke and rather burdened by his uncle's reputation), it envisaged a huge enveloping right-wing sweep from Liège to Brussels, before turning southward to march through Flanders and Paris. Liège was the key as it was a major railway junction for the lines stretching into France. It was crucial to the success of the plan, therefore, that it was taken quickly before the Belgians could mount sufficient resistance to protect it for any length of time. After Liège, the whole of northern Belgium would open up so that the German lines would stretch so far to the right that the last man would, Schlieffen suggested, "brush the Channel with his sleeve". Moltke scrapped the idea of invading the equally neutral Netherlands as well as Belgium and reduced the size of the sweep, recognizing that those on the right would have to march a far longer distance than the troops further south, but otherwise the Schlieffen Plan remained at the core of German military strategy for the early stages of the war, even though Schlieffen himself died the year before it started.

The Schlieffen Plan was, of course, utterly dependent on the railways. More than that, it was in effect a railway timetable. The need for speed was paramount as the plan was based on the notion that there would be a window of just six weeks in which to overwhelm France before the troops had to be relocated eastwards to the Russian front. The plans for the advance were fixed beforehand, based on two notions that proved to be mistaken: that the small Belgian Army would not fight, and that they would not sabotage their railways. Liège was to be overrun by the twelfth day, the French frontier crossed on the twenty-second and the decisive victory, with the conquest of Paris, on the thirty-ninth day. It sounded all so straightforward and was "as rigid and complete as the blueprint for a battleship", but it was an elaborate fantasy.

In the decade before the war, annual revision of the plan took into account recent improvements to the rail network and these were set out in ever more complex detail. The first four days of mobilization were to be taken up with, first, the despatch of frontier defence troops and then experienced covering troops to protect the regions of deployment. It was only on the fifth day that mobilization of the bulk of the Army was envisaged and this would be carried out through a series of frequent railway movements between a limited number of embarkation and arrival points which all had a standard capacity of fifty trains per day each way, including a window of four hours with no scheduled services in order to allow for mishaps and mistakes.

Schlieffen envisaged one double pair of tracks for each army of around 200,000 men. An army corps (about 50,000 men) was allocated 140 trains, spread over seven days in order to allow an orderly entrainment. The breakdown of numbers and equipment shows the extent to which horses took up a large proportion of the overall capacity: of the 6,000 carriages which made up these trains, nearly half (2,965) were required for cavalry and a further 1,915 for artillery and supplies, with the rest for the infantry. Extensive rehearsals of these operations were carried out annually with war-game scenarios that tested the ability of the officers to improvise in the face of a damaged bridge or a broken-down train blocking the line.

Stations had long been prepared for the rapid loading and unloading of military trains and it was in this that the Germans excelled. The capacity of a railway is often determined not by the number of trains, but the ability to ensure they can be loaded and unloaded efficiently. Even small stations had special unloading bays that could be used by artillery and most were provided with a hard-surfaced road alongside the track which could be used for unloading in an emergency. The plan allowed an hour to disembark a trainload of infantry and double that for an artillery battery. There was no on-board catering, which meant that the trains stopped for meals at predetermined stations for an hour while at smaller stations soldiers were allowed up to twenty minutes to buy produce from local pedlars. As soon as mobilization started, normal passenger services were to be greatly curtailed, though not, as the military had sought, scrapped entirely, since the government recognized that this would be impractical and liable to lead to civil unrest as it would result in shortages of food and fuel in towns.

To ensure that railways could be repaired and small extra sections of line built speedily, Prussia created a railway regiment out of the disparate companies that emerged from the 1870 war, comprising a total of just under 5,000 officers and men. To support this initiative, the Army compiled a detailed list of all reservists possessing railway experience and still eligible for military service who could be called upon quickly as reinforcements. A staff officer was allocated to every line and, far from being considered as a backwater for unambitious officers, the railway section of the general staff was a highly regarded placement. According to Barbara Tuchman: "The best brains produced by the War College, it was said, went into the railway section and ended up in lunatic asylums", presumably because ensuring the smooth operation of the railways needed a particularly meticulous but quite narrowly focussed mind.

Physically, the lines were in place. The nine main routes leading towards France dating from 1870 had been improved and increased: by 1911, there were no fewer than nineteen rail crossings over the Rhine, sixteen of which were double-tracked. There were, too, a series of lines leading towards Belgium. Several had initially been built as single-tracked light railways but were converted into double-track heavy rail lines by

203

1909 when sidings "out of all proportion to the local traffic" were also constructed. This had not escaped the notice of the French secret services (the *Deuxième Bureau*, loosely equivalent to MI5), who, observing the pattern of rail-line construction, were able to anticipate that it was highly likely that Belgian neutrality would be violated. Edwin Pratt, the historian, is in no doubt that German intent was clear from its construction of railways heading into Belgium on a scale that far exceeded actual demand: "The German War Department has arranged for a simultaneous advance by fourteen separate routes across Holland, Belgium and the Grand Duchy. In view of all these facts, there is no possible room for doubt as to the prolonged and extensive nature of the preparations made by Germany for the war she instigated in 1914." According to Allan Mitchell, "it was the study of rail patterns that led the *Deuxième Bureau* to a near certainty that a German attack could be expected north of the Moselle river through Luxemburg and a southern portion of Belgium". The lack of similar activity in the east, towards Russia, also allowed the French to assume that the Germans were intending to adopt a defensive posture towards Russia, rather than trying to invade it. Therefore, from the study of the railways, the French had sufficient evidence to know the German plans and yet, because of disagreements among the generals, they only partially acted on it.

The French, of course, had their own plans for mobilization and for the military takeover of the railways at the outbreak of war. As with the German plan, there was no hesitation about who would take control of the railways in the advent of war, but the details of the organization were not as comprehensive or focussed as those of their eastern neighbour. Like the Germans, there was a shadow military organization ready to take control of the railways at the outbreak of war. The railways, most of which were owned by six major companies, remained private concerns, which caused much handwringing among the military about the potential difficulties this would cause in wartime, but an agreement worked out in 1903 ensured that the railways would be requisitioned for military purposes as soon as it became necessary. Once war broke out, the railways were to be divided into two: control of the Interior Zone would remain with the railway authorities while the Army Zone would be run by the military. The military had, as in Germany, pressed for greater standardization of equipment between the private companies, to make it easier for rolling stock to move between them, but this had largely fallen on deaf ears.

The lessons of 1870–71 had been understood, and, indeed, any resistance by the railways to military proposals was routinely met with references to that humiliating conflict. In the 1880s, the French war ministry had created a *Commission Supérieure* on which generals, civil servants from *Ponts et Chaussées* and senior railway managers sat to devise a wartime rail policy. A plethora of laws — no fewer than seventeen were passed within a decade of the Franco-Prussian War — emerged from this committee dealing with everything from the technical instruction of railway

205

troops to the systematic destruction of railways which were likely to fall into the hands of the enemy. The French do not do bureaucracy by halves and these rules were codified into a massive 700-page volume in 1902 which remained largely unaltered until the outbreak of war in 1914. A railway regiment of around 3,000 men was formed and a line commission was established for each of the main railway systems consisting of both railway and military staff. The legislation drawn up to cover the eventuality of war proved to be useful in peacetime during the 1910 railway strike which the war ministry broke by using emergency laws to instruct the strikers that they were conscripted to undertake "army exercises" and failure to carry out these orders would result in punishment for desertion — a potentially capital offence.

The French, like the Germans, had built railways that would be invaluable for mobilization, with the same squabbles between the military and railway companies over who should pay for them. In 1870, France had only six direct lines to the German frontier but by 1888 there were fifteen main arteries of mobilization, nearly one for each army corps, and all of them were double-tracked. The military not only pressed for the construction of lines and the addition of tracks, which they funded in cases where the lines had no commercial value, but also imposed a veto on the construction of lines that might be prejudicial to defence, particularly in the region covered by the Est company, which was always going to be in the front line. In particular, several lines that went too close to

206

fortresses were vetoed, although modern artillery had pretty much made the very idea of hilltop redoubts redundant.

The French equivalent of the Schlieffen Plan was Plan XVII, which, as its numbering suggests, had gone through many iterations and the latest version had been finalized a year before the outbreak of the war. Despite its name, Plan XVII, finalized in 1911 by Général Joseph Joffre, was not a plan of military operations, but merely a scheme for delivering large numbers of troops to whatever front might emerge. It established in great detail the role that each line and each station was to play according to various scenarios depending on the provenance of the attack. It had started out life as Plan XIV in 1898, taking into account the weaker forces that France was likely to have at its disposal. While initially the plan was based on the expectation that a German attack would come directly from the border, later versions did place some emphasis on the notion that Germany might attack through Belgium. As Barbara Tuchman puts it: "Unlike the Schlieffen Plan, Plan XVII contained no stated overall objective and no explicit schedule of operations." It was a defensive plan that was designed to respond to an attack from the Germans rather than to launch an offensive, although it provided for a continued advance into Germany once the initial attacks had been repelled.

The Russians, too, were making preparations. Despite their poor record in recent conflicts — defeat in the Crimea and Manchuria and difficulty in overcoming the Turks at Plevna — the rest of Europe was terrified of the Great Bear, largely because of its sheer size and ability to put more men into battle than any other nation. The prospect of a battle against the Russians instilled terror. Barbara Tuchman is again eloquent: "The savage cavalry charge of yelling Cossacks was such a fixture in European minds that newspaper artists in August 1914 were able to draw it in stirring detail without having been within a thousand miles of the Russian front." For the French and British, the massive Russian steamroller was seen as a source of comfort, while in Germany there was a permanent dread of the Slav hordes in the east. And hordes there were. Including reservists, the Russians had a potential available force of 6.5 million men. The problem, of course, would be getting them to the front fast enough, although in the event this proved easier than envisaged. The French were desperate for the Russians to be an effective force and through a series of loans and the offer of military advisers improved both the Russian Army and the railways. Throughout the early 1910s, the French worked hard to cement their alliance with the Russians through regular meetings between the top military on each side and these negotiations bore fruit in 1912, when they secured the commitment from General Gilinsky, the chief of the Russian general staff, that within two weeks of the outbreak of war the Russians would have 800,000 men at the front.

This was fanciful. In any mobilization, the Russian soldiers not only had to travel much further to reach their regiments — the average was 700 miles compared with fewer than 200 miles for the German troops —

but also their journeys would be on a railway system that was inadequate to the task because, compared with the German railways, it had only one-tenth of the length of track per square kilometre. There was, too, the difficulty of the incompatibility in gauge, that brilliant defensive measure which, as we have already seen in the previous chapter, had proved to be a major barrier to launching successful attacks. Barbara Tuchman highlights the problem succinctly: "To send an army into modern battle on enemy territory, especially under the disadvantage of different railway gauges, is a hazardous and complicated undertaking requiring prodigies of careful organization. Systematic attention to detail was not a notable characteristic of the Russian Army."

Russian preparation for the war had indeed been chaotic. The war minister for the five years running up to the outbreak of war was an old-fashioned, idle womanizer, General Vladimir Sukhomlinov, typical of the aristocracy who ran the country: "clinging stubbornly to obsolete theories and ancient glories, he claimed that Russia's past defeats had been due to mistakes of commanding officers rather than to any inadequacy of training, preparation or supply".

His proudest boast was that he had not read an army manual for a quarter of a century. It showed. Sukhomlinov, a veteran of the Turkish campaign of the late 1870s, stopped the process of modernization that had been proceeding gradually since the defeat at the hands of the Japanese, and he sacked a chief of staff every year during his tenure. His preparations — or rather lack of them — left the Russian Army perilously short of equipment, notably guns and shells, and the plans were predicated on the basis that the war would be conducted with hordes of soldiers wielding bayonets rather than guns.

However, as we shall see in the next chapter, in the event Russia mobilized surprisingly efficiently thanks to the efficacy of its railways. The improvements introduced thanks to the support of the French had not been incorporated into the Russian military's plans, possibly because the railway authorities feared that impossible demands would be placed on them if the extent of the facilities had been known. Russia's preparations for war were embodied in Plan 19, which had first been drawn up in 1910 and had not been significantly amended to take into account the subsequent improvements. The scheme envisaged the curtailing of all civilian traffic apart from a daily mail train, a measure that was rather easier to impose in what was an authoritarian monarchist police state than in the other combatant countries, which had more democratic political cultures, and a traffic of thirty-six trains per day, still quite ambitious given the state of the railways, travelling around 250 miles in a day. There were roughly ten lines pointing westward, which therefore gave the Russians the potential to mobilize rather more effectively and quickly than the Germans envisaged. In fact, the Russians had a further programme of railway improvements which would have made mobilization even more effective. By 1917, the general staff were expecting to be able to deliver 560 trains daily to the front, suggesting perhaps that it was fears about this extensive upcoming investment in the railways, which would soon have exposed the Schlieffen Plan as totally unworkable, that determined the timing of the war. According to one source, "shortly before Sarajevo, the Kaiser reportedly believed that 'the big Russian railway constructions were preparations for a great war which could start in 1916' . . . and 'wondered whether it might not be better to attack rather than to wait' ".

The Russian government as ever was as much terrified by the enemy within, the growing movement against the tsarist regime, as any external threat. In order to cope with militant workers and revolutionaries who might be tempted to strike or take to the streets when war was declared, the secret police arranged for armoured trains to patrol lines that might be affected by civil disorder. This precaution proved unnecessary because, just as in Berlin, London, Paris and Vienna, patriotic feeling for the war overrode long-standing feelings of discontent.

The British planned for war, too, but, sensibly, on the assumption that it would not take place on their soil. Their preparations, therefore, were focussed principally on how to organize the railways to facilitate the despatch of troops to ports and the creation of a railway corps which would be able to maintain and repair railways both in Britain and, should a force be sent overseas, in other countries. Previous planning had actually been directed at how to mobilize the railways against an invasion but had been carried out in a typically British amateurish approach. In 1865 the

Engineer and Railway Volunteer Staff Corps was created, gathering together army officers with railway managers who were made honorary colonels or majors. The Corps, which was a voluntary body with no official backing from the War Office, was an officer-only body which created a fantastically elaborate 311-page book of timetables covering six different concentrations of troops against invasion. Given that the military was reluctant to provide information to the civilians in the Corps, "these timetables had had to be compiled largely by guesswork" and consequently "the result may well have been a shambles". Fortunately these plans were never put to the test, but it was not long, however, before the government realized that the outbreak of war would require special measures in relation to the railways and wanted to ensure there would be no doubt as to who would be in charge of them in wartime. Consequently legislation covering the nationalization of the railways in the event of war was passed in 1871 but it was not until 1896 that a War Railway Council, composed of both railway and military members, was created to advise the military on railway matters in the event of a war.

The one major test for these wartime arrangements prior to 1914 had been the Boer War, when nearly a quarter of a million men and 30,000 horses, along with guns, ammunition and other supplies, were sent to Southampton on their way to the Cape. According to Pratt, "the operations were conducted with perfect smoothness, there being no overtaxing either of the railway facilities or of the dock accommodation". He put this down to the appointment of a railway transport officer at Southampton who acted as an intermediary between the railway company, the military and the docks and co-ordinated their requirements. Most crucially, the railway transport officer, irrespective of his rank, had the final say over the train schedule and under the regulations not even a general could countermand his decision. This ensured that the railway managers only had to deal with one source of military authority. Similar railway transport officers were appointed at other key stations used for the despatch of troops to South Africa and this innovation proved vital in the organization of rail transport in the First World War. Following the Boer War, the railway branch of the Royal Engineers became firmly established and two permanent railway companies were created and trained on a specially created military railway.

In 1912, as tension mounted in Europe, the British government, conscious that the implications of the legislation on railways in wartime had not really been properly thought through, created the Railway Executive Committee to replace the purely advisory War Railway Council, consisting of managers of the biggest railway companies, who, it was envisaged, would take complete control of the railways during wartime. As a result, later in the year there were extensive army manoeuvres designed to test how fast troops could be deployed and assess how easily the railways could absorb the extra traffic. Oddly, the exercise, which involved 200 trains, took place in East Anglia, the territory of the Great Eastern, an unlikely setting for

213

any actual troop movements, which were always likely to be focussed on the seaports of the south coast served by the London & South Western. Nevertheless, they passed off successfully, with King George V remarking on how it seemed possible for the railways to cope with both the extra troop trains as well as the normal traffic. The satirical magazine *Punch* could not resist lampooning these efforts, by commenting that "one of the chief objections to hostilities in this country disappears now that it has been shown that our golfers would be able to get to their courses without interference". However, as we shall see in the next chapter, British mobilization would prove remarkably effective.

The Austro-Hungarian Empire also had a detailed mobilization plan on similar lines to the German scheme, but with the added complication that the Austrians did not know who their enemy was going to be. Therefore, the whole of Europe had plans to mobilize their armies based on the correct premise that it was only the railways which could deliver the enormous numbers of men to the front. This was, though, uncharted territory given that the scale of preparation was far greater than for any other previous war. Not only were more countries involved, but, as already mentioned, there had been a huge increase in the size of the armies since Napoleon's time. In total, across Europe, there were 20 million men in varying degrees of readiness who could be mobilized quickly at the outbreak of the war, more than at any time in history. Moreover, the requirements of these vast bodies of men had increased by an even greater proportion than the numbers of troops since the *impedimenta*, as van Creveld calls it, carried by armies into the field had become vastly more complex. Each man needed more equipment and, on average, fired more bullets and shells — which were mostly larger than before — and used artillery that was heavier and less manoeuvrable: "The wagons constituting the train (field bakeries, hospitals, engineering equipment etc) of a German army corps [50,000 men] numbered thirty in 1870 but had more than doubled forty years later." Moreover, not only were there more guns requiring a constant supply of shells, but the damage they would inflict created extra demands. Whereas previously heavy artillery was almost indestructible, now it could be destroyed by enemy action and consequently need to be replaced.

The railways were a key component in an arms race that seemed almost bound to lead to conflict. In a famous essay, the historian A. J. P. Taylor went as far as to suggest that the very existence of these plans based on railway timetables made war inevitable. Taylor argued that the lengthy elaboration of these plans was not a signal of intent but rather an attempt by each one of the various continental powers to develop a deterrent that would persuade their rivals that it was too risky to embark on an invasion by signalling that they were the most powerful regional power. Instead, Taylor suggested, the logic of the process led them into a war none of them expected to have to fight, because when the crisis began in the summer of 1914, the need to mobilize faster than their potential opponents made the leaders prisoners of their own logistics. Specifically, Taylor says that the fact that mobilization plans were entirely dependent on railways since the automobile was hardly used (except by the odd general speeding to his headquarters) meant that a point of no return was quickly reached. Constrained by the limitations of the railway, every country had to try to mobilize faster than its rivals and consequently it was the strictures of the railway timetables that forced them into conflict: "All the European powers had built up vast armies of conscripts. The plans for mobilising these millions rested on railways; and railway timetables cannot be improvised. Once started, the wagons and carriages must roll remorselessly and inevitably forward to their predestined goal." Mobilization, he suggests, should not have been the trigger for war because it takes place within a country's own borders and there had, in fact, been previous such call-ups of men in the years running up to the war which had not resulted in conflict.

This misses the point. The notion that it was all down to the railway timetable is fundamentally flawed, resulting from Taylor's failure to understand railway operations. He was, in fact, using his theory about the railways to back up his wider argument that, at the time the war broke out, tensions in Europe were receding and the war was therefore the result of an unfortunate series of events rather than an inevitable outcome of the geopolitical situation. While the railway timetables were, obviously, a vital component of the mobilization, they were not as inflexible as he suggests. He argues that they had been timed to the minute, months or even years previously, and therefore could not be changed. However, the German plans, for example, had, as mentioned above, a four-hour period every day when no trains were scheduled. Moreover, previous experience stretching back to the days of Haupt and the American Civil War had shown that skilled rail operators can work miracles on a railway route provided they are given total control of the workings, as had indeed been granted to the military in most of these countries.

The inevitability of war once the process of mobilizing these 20 million men had commenced was more the result of the inflexibility of the military mind than any predetermined logistics resulting from the railway system. If anything was the deciding factor, it was the attitude of the younger Moltke, the central character in this drama. Moltke was a reluctant chief of staff. A lugubrious character who wore such a permanently downbeat expression that the Kaiser, Wilhelm II, called him "the sad Julius" (unaccountably since he bore the same name as his illustrious uncle Helmuth), he responded to his appointment by asking the Kaiser whether he expected "to win the big prize twice in the same lottery", a suggestion that he was only offered the post thanks to his name. According to Barbara Tuchman, he undertook the task only on condition that "the Kaiser stopped winning all the war games, which was making a nonsense of manoeuvres." Amazingly, the Kaiser obeyed.

After the assassination on 28 June 1914 of Franz Ferdinand, the heir to the throne of the Habsburg Austro-Hungarian Empire, by a Serbian nationalist, Gavrilo Princip, in Sarajevo, the capital of Bosnia-Herzegovina, a series of diplomatic manoeuvres and threats brought Europe to a crisis. The Serbians wanted Bosnia-Herzegovina, which the Austrians had administered since 1878, to be part of the then autonomous Kingdom of Serbia, while the rulers of the Austro-Hungarian Empire, suspecting that the ever-troublesome Serbian government had been involved in the murder, decided to take a strong line. They consulted with Germany, which promised to back them should Russia, Serbia's traditional ally, threaten to intervene. Strangely, both Moltke and the Chancellor, Wilhelm II, went off on holiday during this growing diplomatic imbroglio. An Austro-Hungarian ultimatum was finally sent on 23 July and pretty much accepted by the Serbians "with just enough reservations to save a scrap of prestige", according to Taylor. Too many, though, for the Habsburgs, who promptly declared war, which was something of a gesture since the empire was not ready to call up its troops.

It was enough to trigger off a chain reaction. Russia began mobilizing, hesitated and stopped, and then resumed. The Germans demanded that the Russians desist but were met with a refusal, and so began calling up troops themselves. It was at this stage that the issue of the railway timetable came into play, but not in the way that Taylor suggests. A conversation between Prince Lichnowsky, the German ambassador in

London, and the British Foreign Secretary, Sir Edward Grey, on 1 August was misinterpreted by the ambassador as an offer by Britain to stay out of a war between Russia and Germany. The Kaiser leapt on this as a possible solution to the concerns about fighting simultaneously on two fronts and rushed to see Moltke. Time was pressing. The first act of war was to be the seizure of a railway junction in Luxembourg, which was a vital through-route to France for the Germans. It was scheduled to take place at 7p.m. and the Kaiser went to ask Moltke to stop the action. It was not that the Kaiser wanted to prevent the outbreak of war but rather, at this very late stage, he wanted the troops to go east rather than west. Moltke was not being asked to stop the trains, but merely to reverse them. He was unequivocal. Moltke had spent eleven years working towards this day, first as Schlieffen's assistant and then as his successor, and he was not going to bow to the Kaiser's impulse with the vain hope of a one-front war. In an image redolent of the French chaos in the early stages of the Franco-Prussian War, "he saw a vision of the deployment crumbling apart in confusion, supplies here, soldiers there, ammunition lost in the middle, companies without officers, divisions without staffs, and those 11,000 trains, each exquisitely scheduled to click over specified tracks at specified intervals of ten minutes, tangled in a grotesque ruin of the most perfectly planned military movement in history". It was not to be. Moltke refused, telling the Kaiser: "Your Majesty, it cannot be done. The deployment of millions cannot be improvised . . ." and fatefully added the

219

words, "and once settled, it cannot be altered." Therefore it wasn't stopping the trains that Moltke felt was impossible — it was reversing the thrust of the attack. He was, in any case, intent on beating the French, indeed had lived for that moment. He was not going to turn back on the advice of a mercurial Kaiser. Germany that day declared war on Russia, a move which has later been considered unnecessary but which clearly had nothing to do with railway timetables. The decision was not a result of logistics, but of politics. Russia, for its part, was well aware that its mobilization would be taken as an act of aggression by the Germans, triggering a whole series of responses. Contrary to what Taylor suggested, mere mobilization by Russia, feared so much by Germany, was in itself a *casus belli*.

That was not quite the end of the matter. The Kaiser sent a telegram to King George seeking clarification and, as the deadline for the attack on defenceless Luxembourg approached, his Chancellor, Bethmann, insisted that no military action should take place before they received a reply. The Kaiser's telegram was an attempt to stop the invasion, which was to be carried out by an infantry company of the 69th Regiment under command of a Lieutenant Feldmann. It was too late. The First World War had started, not by the rumbling of trains but with a small convoy of cars led by the lieutenant entering the small town of Ulflingen, known locally as Trois Vierges, where the Germans seized the station and telegraph office. It was undoubtedly a coincidence that the Germans had launched the bloodiest war in history by violating a place whose name represented Faith, Hope and Charity, but was later perceived in the public mind as connoting Luxembourg, Belgium and France. Hastily, once the Kaiser's telegram had been received, a second convoy was sent to call back the lieutenant and his men, but finally, once King George's reply made clear no such deal was on the table, the Kaiser acquiesced to the Luxembourg invasion. Soon after midnight, an armoured train was sent across the frontier, followed by a trainful of Feldmann's men, and by the end of the day, 2 August, the whole of the small Grand Duchy had been occupied.

Would it have been possible to refocus the direction of attack at such a late stage? The Schlieffen Plan, which was regularly revised, certainly included a contingency for an alternative plan against Russia with all the trains running eastward. General von Staab, the chief of the German railway division, upon reading Moltke's memoirs published after the war, which said that it could not have been done, responded with a book to prove that it could have been. In pages of charts and graphs, Staab explained how, given notice on 1 August, within two weeks he could have deployed four out of seven armies to the Eastern Front. However, there would have been no question of a quick victory in the east, unlike the rapid takeover of France envisaged by Schlieffen. The paucity of railways and the sheer size of Russia would have held up the Germans for far longer than a few weeks. It would have been a different war, but probably one that was just as prolonged and which in all likelihood would have

221

spread to a second front given the various alliances across Europe.

There are other good grounds to dismiss the Taylor thesis, most notably that the numerous other factors leading to conflict make the rigidity of railway timetables an unlikely catalyst. Historians list twenty or more possible causes, and while the debate over the weight that should be attached to each of them has never been resolved, there are compelling reasons to suggest war was inevitable given the political situation in Europe in 1914. German military ambitions were not a passing whim and the strengthening of its navy over the past twenty years was a threat to the other Great Powers, apart from the Austro-Hungarian Empire. The continued weakening of the Habsburg empire created an air of instability in central Europe and there were continuing arguments over the colonial ambitions of the various European nations. The diplomatic failings in the immediate run-up to the war had a long history and these disputes were always likely to boil over into something far more serious. Europe was a ferment of possible conflict, and it would not take much to light the blue touchpaper, particularly since all sides, their trains bedecked with signs bearing the jingoistic slogans "*Nach Paris*" or "*Á Berlin*", thought it would all be over by Christmas or even before the leaves fell off the trees.

Taylor's analysis is probably best thought of as an allegory on the nuclear arms race which was raging at the time he was writing and which, as a prominent member of the Campaign for Nuclear Disarmament, he strenuously opposed. In a broader sense, if Taylor had merely emphasized that the build-up of railway strength in the Great Powers during the run-up to the conflict was significant, then his argument would have been irrefutable. But to place the blame for the outbreak of war on the rigidity of timetables is a step too far.

Taylor was on firmer territory when he stressed, as we have seen, that the military on all sides were convinced that attack was the best form of defence. The disaster of the First World War was that the Great Powers all had offensive military doctrines, which encouraged them to attack first while the new technology — barbed wire, machine guns and, especially, railway networks — all favoured defence. All the major powers had commissioned reports on the experiences from previous wars, notably the American Civil War and the Russo-Japanese War, where there had been clear demonstrations of the effectiveness of defensive firepower and the advantages of holding positions against attackers. Yet, thanks to Clausewitz, whose doctrine had ordained a quick victory through a decisive battle — such as at Königgrätz — the military establishments across the whole of Europe believed that the advantage was with the attackers. Clausewitz, though, had written his thesis almost a hundred years previously, long before the railways had been invented, and yet, as Barbara Tuchman notes acidly, "his works had been accepted as the bible of strategy ever since." As the next chapter shows, it was the defenders, helped by the railways, who had the advantage for most of the war and military strategy needed rewriting.

CHAPTER
SEVEN

The Great Railway War on the Western Front

The Germans did not get to Paris in thirty-nine days. Or in fact ever. The Schlieffen Plan did not work and generations of historians have subsequently analysed its shortcomings. Moltke took the rap and soon resigned but it was the inherent failings of the plan, not his tinkering, which led to its undoing. Neither can blame for its failure be laid at the door of the German railways. They had been taken over, as envisaged, by the military authorities, who, despite being at times "overzealous and overbearing", carried out the task of mobilization remarkably efficiently. On 4 August, the long-prepared war timetables were introduced, which greatly limited any traffic other than military. The first trains to be despatched carried infantry brigades destined for the capture of Liège, the vital Belgian railway junction in the Meuse Valley, and over the following two weeks 3 million soldiers were carried by the railways in more than 11,000 trains. Yet, according to John Westwood, "nevertheless, the German railways were never extended to their full capacity during this period; they could have carried even more traffic." There were, though, enormous bottlenecks on the Belgian railways, notably in Liège, through which much of the attack was funnelled.

The plan failed because of its strategic and logistical flaws. Not only was it based on the mistaken assumption that the Belgians would surrender without a fight and keep their railways intact, but it expected too much of the troops on the right flank, who were supposed to march much further than was realistic if they were to be in a fit state to fight. In fact, after the failure of German diplomatic negotiations — which had all the subtlety of an armed bank robber demanding the money from a terrified teller — Albert, the Belgian king, ordered the destruction of railway tunnels and bridges even before the first German troops had set foot in his country. Consequently, the Belgians set about disabling their railway system with ruthless efficiency, concentrating on blowing up the tunnels to prevent any hope of rapid repair. After the invasion, the Germans deployed large numbers of men, a force of 26,000 workers, to try to sort out the broken railways but to little avail. Even a month after the German occupation of Belgium at the onset of the crucial battle of the Marne in early September, only a sixth of the 2,400-mile Belgian rail network was functioning. Moreover, the surviving lines were in a poor state. Most of the rolling stock had been destroyed or taken to France by the Belgians, and even where the track had been left intact, signalling equipment was sabotaged. The Belgians also indulged in the kinds of tricks deployed the world over by reluctant railway workers, such as routing trains onto the wrong lines at junctions or "mistakenly" sending them into sidings.

The destruction of the Belgian railways delayed the progress of the German troops but did not entirely put paid to the Schlieffen Plan. Neither did the fierce, albeit brief, resistance of the Belgian Army. Instead, the plan was ultimately defeated by its own incoherence and the absence of a clear logistical framework, especially in relation to what was intended to happen once the troops and their horses had advanced beyond their railheads. The early German invasion swept all before it, with the result that the forward troops were soon much further ahead of their rail supply line than had been originally envisaged. At times parts of the German army were seventy or eighty miles from the railhead, which made it impossible to furnish them with food and ammunition from the rear. Consequently, it was back to the old Napoleonic practices of the troops having to live off the land. There was no problem feeding the men since the advance crossed rich agricultural land and — as with the start of most wars — it was harvest time. As ever, however, obtaining food for the horses was a much greater burden, necessitating foraging ever further afield and in several cases there were extreme shortages. Many horses were fed green corn, which can weaken or even kill the beasts, and the lack of horse transport was to prove damaging — especially, as we shall see later, at the battle of the Marne — since there were few railways available to the Germans. The cavalry was still deployed as an advance guard during the marches, but by the time the battle commenced they had been mostly immobilized as a consequence of the horses' exhaustion. Most importantly, the animals' poor condition was instrumental in limiting the mobility of the artillery, which was all horse-drawn. In some cases, a whole gun team had perished before crossing the border as a result of the shortage of fodder and by the time the Germans reached France on 24 August all the mounted forces were suffering from exhaustion. Ammunition, too, was in short supply. As mentioned in the last chapter, modern weapons used far more bullets and shells — which also tended to be heavier — than those in Napoleonic times, and it was no longer possible to keep up the supply to the guns from a couple of horse-drawn trucks ambling behind the front line.

The Germans' advance was hampered, too, by their mismanagement of the railways. So effective on their home territory, they forgot the vital rules that Haupt had set out in the American Civil War once they crossed their border. Understandably, it was more difficult running trains on another country's network but that did not excuse the lack of discipline which characterized their operation of the Belgian lines. The railways were already in a bad shape thanks to the Belgians' sabotage, but according to van Creveld the military authorities "reduced their efficiency still further by rushing through the greatest number of trains", irrespective of the congestion that was caused and failing to allow time for the empty wagons to be returned. Worse, "impatient field commanders often interfered with the traffic, either 'hijacking' trains destined for other units or putting wagons out of operation by using them as convenient magazines". It was familiar stuff, the same mistakes that had been made by local military commanders ever since the railways had first been employed in warfare. Although van Creveld suggests that these were "temporary shortcomings which time and experience would cure", by then the battle of the Marne had been fought and lost.

By the end of August, the right flank of the German army was in a parlous state and its weakness was to prove fatal to the notion of the quick victory envisaged in the Schlieffen Plan. The German First Army was on the right wing of the sweep across Belgium, and the plan was dependent on those troops covering a huge distance in order not to get separated from the rest of the forces further south. Moltke had modified the Schlieffen Plan so that soldiers passed by Brussels rather than going further north with their "shoulders brushing the Channel", but that still involved the German First Army covering a much greater distance than the forces further south. A diversionary attack by British forces on Antwerp, initiated by Churchill, though always doomed to defeat, was a cause of additional difficulties to the right flank. By early September, these troops, who had been covering distances of twenty to twenty-five miles a day, were exhausted, but it was impossible to give them even a day's rest before throwing them into the battle of the Marne, where their role was to encircle the French from the rear. Their supply lines were over-extended and for most of their advance they were at least sixty miles in front of their railhead, which inevitably led to shortages of ammunition and food. Van Creveld estimates that whereas in the wars of the 1860s and 1870s it was possible for an army to operate a hundred miles in front of its railhead, by the start of the First World War the distance was around half that, depending on variables such as the weather, the state of the roads and the proximity of the enemy, because of an army's increasing logistical requirements. Once in France, most of the Germans were rarely within fifty miles of their railhead during this initial phase of the war.

The battle of the Marne was the first turning point of the war as it stopped the progress of the German invasion and initiated the process of entrenchment that was to last nearly four years. The Germans had advanced well into France by the end of August and Paris was braced for their arrival, with the government making preparations for its move to the safety of Bordeaux in the south-west. The French had all but given up, while the Germans were expecting to be able to walk into the capital with little resistance. At that point the flaws in the Schlieffen Plan became bitterly exposed. The troops on the right flank were simply too exhausted to be able to march further to the west and encircle Paris from the rear. Instead, the order came on 4 September for them to pursue the retreating French forces by turning south and passing Paris from the east to try to envelop them. By then the British

Expeditionary Force, men of the regular army who had been despatched hastily over the Channel since there had been no time to organize conscription, was fighting alongside the French. The rapid arrival of the British in France had surprised the Germans, who had not expected them to intervene in their march through France and it had been made possible by the efficient use of the railways. Southampton had been chosen as the port of embarkation and a detailed timetable had been devised by railway and military planners that entailed special trains arriving at the port every twelve minutes, sixteen hours a day. The operation had been conducted remarkably well and by the end of August 670 trains had carried just under 120,000 men to the port for embarkation to France. The smoothness of the movement of troops had even attracted compliments from Lord Kitchener, a man not known to be generous with praise but who fancied himself as something of a logistics expert. And, more importantly, the Germans had not been aware of the BEF's arrival until the two armies literally bumped into each other at Mons on 22 August, the day before the battle there.

The battle of the Marne took place two weeks later, when the Allies realized that the German advance was stuttering and decided that a counter-attack was the best opportunity to stop the retreat and prevent any further invasion. They launched a massive attack on the German flank, splitting the enemy forces into two. The crucial figures in that decision were Maréchal Joseph Joffre, the head of the French Army, and the military governor of Paris, Général Joseph-Simon Gallieni.

Joffre had always envisaged a counter-attack around Paris but it was Gallieni who had persuaded him of its precise nature when he spotted that the German flank had decided to pass to the east of the city.

The decision to attack the Germans' flank changed the course of the war — and indeed of history — at the cost of huge numbers of lives on both sides. The attack was launched on 6 September by the newly created French Sixth Army, made up of reservists and troops of the First and Second armies hastily redeployed from the abortive attack in Lorraine and supported, reluctantly, by the exhausted remnants of the BEF. Led by Général Michel-Joseph Maunoury, the French soon opened up a thirty-mile gap in the German lines and overcame fierce resistance to push the enemy into retreating for the first time in the war.

At one point 6,000 reinforcements were sent to battle in a fleet of 600 taxicabs, a story that has become legendary but was probably more important for morale than for its military value: "the last gallantry of 1914, the last crusade of the old world," as Barbara Tuchman suggested. In fact, as A. J. P. Taylor explained, it was the French Army's ability to use the railways to good effect that was to prove the decisive factor: "[the Germans] had been moving round the outside of a circle [round Paris] on foot, while the French could send troops straight across the circle by train".

Indeed, the ability of the French to move troops by rail was not happenstance, but rather the result of Joffre's understanding of how to make the best use of the railways. The lines emanated like the spokes of a bicycle wheel from Paris and there were few efficient cross-country routes (something which still pertains today, as anyone who has tried to take a train from, say, Bordeaux to Strasbourg can testify). The Schlieffen Plan had envisaged a flanking movement at a considerable distance from Paris, on routes that were ill-served by railways because they went round Paris and therefore were only served, at best, by minor lines. Nearer Paris there were better circular routes — including *La Grande Ceinture*, a kind of railway *Périphérique* which connected all the radial routes — and therefore Joffre recognized that it was essential to resist the German attacks at the right distance from the capital to allow the French to move easily along the front by rail on the radial lines while denying the Germans access to the *Ceinture*. According to Marc Ferro's acclaimed essay on the war, "the victory of the Marne appears to be as much a result of Joffre's strategic intelligence as of German blunders . . . Joffre soon came to see that, in the Paris region, the German plan would turn against Germany, and elected to fight there. From the beginning, he had demanded control of the railways; trained in technique, he had foreseen that his victory, the Marne, would be won on the French railways."

Moreover, what French railways might have been available to the Germans had been blown up by the retreating forces. For the most part this destruction had been carried out thoroughly, but it was a difficult juggling act. The decision on when to demolish a railway line or bridge involved tough calculations and precise timing: "torn between the need to delay the enemy and the thought that tomorrow they might require bridges and railways themselves for a return to the offensive, the French left destruction of communications to the latest possible moment, sometimes too late". at other times the French erred on the side of caution, blowing up bridges too soon and thus hindering their own logistics. The order for destruction could be given by relatively lowly officials and on occasion this resulted in blowing up bridges which were still needed: "nine local bridges were ordered to be destroyed by one prefect [the *préfet*, the chief of the local *département*] 'as a simple measure of strategic prudence'; a few days later sappers were studying their reconstruction." The same delicate balancing act was required for removing rolling stock from threatened lines. If coaches and locomotives were withdrawn too soon, it hampered the retreat but delaying too long ran the risk of leaving them in enemy hands. Fortunately for the French, on the Nord railway, the network most affected by the invasion, they got it right: while the company lost more than half its 2,400-mile network to the Germans it managed to retain the bulk of its stock.

The battle of the Marne was decisive in that it halted the German advance, although van Creveld argues that the logistics would have told against the Germans anyway: "Had that battle [of the Marne] gone in their favour . . . there is every reason to believe that the state of the railway network would have prevented the Germans from following up their victory and penetrating further into France." The Marne could

233

have been even more decisive, resulting in an early end to the war, had not the victorious Allies' pursuit of the fleeing enemy been so slow, hampered ironically by the damage to the railway carried out a couple of weeks previously by the retreating French. By 11 September, the British Expeditionary Force was forty miles ahead of its railhead, and had to pause to await resupply. The consequent delay allowed the Germans to regroup and dig themselves in along the Aisne river, where they were to remain until 1918. Therefore rather than ending the war, the battle of the Marne resulted in the prolonged stalemate.

At the same time, the two sides began a series of encounters known as the "Race to the Sea" but which were really a succession of abortive attempts to outflank each other. The route taken by each army during these clashes was determined by the location of two north-south railways: the French and British controlled the line through Amiens, while the Germans were able to use the railways through Lille. During the Race to the Sea, one last chance of keeping the war mobile presented itself. A month after the battle of the Marne, the British and Germans clashed at Ypres, rather by accident, when two intended offensive operations bumped into each other. The Germans proved stronger and at one point could have advanced through the British lines, which were protected only by "cooks and batmen", but hesitated and, as Taylor explains, "as always happened, the defence brought in new men by rail faster than the attackers could move forward on foot. Once more the line thickened and settled down."

In a way, while both the German and French railway-based plans had failed, paradoxically each had proved worthwhile. The Schlieffen Plan did not get the German troops to Paris but ensured they were ensconced in the north-east corner of France. As a consequence France had lost much of its industrial capacity and the front ran along physical features that largely gave the Germans the advantage of height. As for Plan XVII, it had helped prevent the invasion of France but it was too defensive and consequently had allowed the enemy forces to penetrate so far into France that they could not be dislodged once the French counter-attacked. The failings of the two plans set the course for the terrible stalemate on the Western Front that, as Barbara Tuchman says, "suck[ed] up lives at a rate of 5,000, sometimes 50,000 a day, absorbing munitions, energy, money, brains and trained men". It is actually impossible to overestimate the impact of the events of this first month and the subsequent entrenchment: "The deadlock, fixed by the failure of the first month, determined the future course of the war, and, as a result, the terms of the peace, the shape of the inter-war period and the conditions of the Second Round."

With the ending of the Race to the Sea in November 1914 and the establishment of a front line that stretched 200 miles from the Channel through eastern France to Switzerland, a different task for the railways emerged. On one matter, all sides were agreed. Supplies and men would principally be transported on the railways rather than on motor vehicles — mechanical transport (MT), as it was called — or by foot. Supply routes and railway lines were synonymous. There was no choice because neither the roads nor the available trucks were up to the task of moving millions of men. According to A. J. P. Taylor, at the beginning of the war, "no army had any mechanical transport. There were a few motor cars in which generals and staff officers travelled when they condescended to get off their horses. The men slogged along on foot once they reached the railhead." Taylor is somewhat exaggerating as the French Army had 600 vehicles at the outbreak of war and the British Army 1,200, mostly requisitioned, which admittedly was insufficient for any major movements. Moreover, road transport was only really feasible as long as the weather was dry because the lorries kept to the roads and the horse transport went alongside in the fields. When it rained, the whole supply chain almost ground to a halt because the horses had to use the roads, slowing everything down to walking pace. There were indeed few lorries, though later in the war they became an integral part of the logistics despite their progress often being hampered by poor roads. In 1914, lorries were still remarkably primitive affairs. German army regulations stipulated that trucks were limited to being driven a mere sixty miles per day, six days a week, to allow for maintenance and repair. This was a wise precaution which the men disobeyed at their peril. This was demonstrated in the run-up to the battle of the Marne in early September when German attempts to use their lorries more intensively resulted in only 40 per cent being available for service because of accidents and breakdowns. The roads, too, were appalling, with few of them, other than major thoroughfares, being tarmacked. The location of fronts was determined by topography rather than accessibility and therefore they were not necessarily well served by road and, as we shall see later, another type of railway, running on rails just 60cm apart, became a vital part of the supply line.

Neither side had anticipated a stalemate. While the Germans had planned for a quick decisive attack that would then allow them to focus their efforts solely on the Eastern Front, the British expected a mobile war that ebbed and flowed as in the days of Napoleon. Therefore neither side had prepared for the entrenched battle lines that developed by November 1914. Yet that was always going to be a likely result given the primitive state of military transport technology in 1914 with railways supplying both sides of the Western Front, which happened to be in an area well served by several lines, unlike, as we shall see in the next chapter, the Eastern Front, which had a much sparser railway network. The fact that the railway systems were highly developed but motor transport was still in its infancy gave defensive forces a key advantage and they were further helped by their ability to make use of local undamaged and familiar lines while the enemy, in hostile territory, only had unknown and frequently sabotaged railways at their disposal.

The methods of transport available to the armies at the outbreak of the war explain the paradox which the railways created. They allowed for much faster movement — until the tracks ran out. As A. J. P. Taylor puts it: "Hence the extraordinary contrast of the war: fast in delivering men to the battlefield; slow once they got there." When the soldiers disembarked from the trains, they were in the same position as Napoleon's troops or even Roman centurions. Or actually, as he explains, it was worse: because armies in the twentieth century were so much bigger and carried so many more supplies, they were far more unwieldy. Horses were, as usual, the trouble: "In every army, forage for the horses took up more space than ammunition or food. They had to be fed from their homeland. In this way, the very size which had been designed to bring victory made it impossible for the armies to win or even to move." An entrenched army well served by a railhead was therefore at a huge advantage in repelling an invader because "reinforcements could always arrive by rail to a threatened position before the attacking side could break through on foot. Railway trains go faster than men walking." Taylor stressed that it was the railways, together with the machine gun, that gave defenders the advantage: "This is the strategic reason why the defence was stronger than the attack throughout the First World War. Defence was mechanised, attack was not." Yet, as we have seen, all the participants in the First World War had been under the impression that they had to hurtle headlong into war in order to gain the initiative. They were not just proved wrong: it was one of the great mistakes of history.

During the brief mobile war, the French railways had performed heroically and they now settled into a routine. As in Germany and Britain, the military had taken over their operation as soon as war broke out. Vast numbers of freight wagons were prepared for troop transport with the installation of benches and were marked "*8 chevaux, 40 hommes*", which fortunately for the soldiers were alternatives, not totals. (Strangely, a couple of thousand miles to the east, Russian wagons were emblazoned with the same instruction.) As planned, the major French railway companies were each handed over to a *commission du réseau* run by a four-person team composed of a senior officer from the general staff, a regional army commander, the head of the railway company and one of his technical advisers. This balance of two military and two civilian members should not be taken to suggest there was parity between the two sides. The Ministry of War made all the strategic decisions and "authority over the railroads now resided in the hands of the central state and military officials". The lessons of 1870 had sunk in and the mobilization saw none of the scenes of chaos that had effectively cost the French that war.

Soldiers were expected to report to a depot and were then transported with the rest of their regiment to the front. The call-up had started on 31 July 1914 and took up the first week of the war, and the deployment was carried out in the two weeks starting 6 August, during which a million men and 400,000 horses were transported to the border. The French standardized their trains to have one passenger coach for officers, thirty covered trucks (for the men and horses), seventeen flat wagons for equipment and two brake vans, far longer and consequently slower than their British equivalents: thus in England, an infantry battalion was carried in two trains scheduled to run at an average 25 mph, while in France they would be squeezed into one that travelled at half that speed.

Military traffic was prioritized with clear allocations for troop movements and other military requirements. The *commissions* determined the track capacity and generally allowed for twenty-four troop trains per day on single-track lines and double that on those with twin tracks. In addition there would be the military *trains journaliers*, which were mixed trains of troops, government officials, small consignments of goods and so on. The rest of the capacity would be allocated to supply trains and the mail service, which frequently resulted in the routine commercial traffic being squeezed out. Typically, a double-track route on the Nord network would be scheduled to take a train every ten minutes, or 144 a day, but this theoretical maximum allowed for no mishaps, errors or breakdowns, and, in the early days, was therefore rarely attained. Later, towards the end of the war, improvements, both technical and operational, sometimes enabled a throughput of more than 150 daily trains. Throughout the war, however, the limiting factor for troop movements was frequently not so much the shortage of track capacity but the lack of stations that could handle the arrival of a fifty-car train.

The French railways did not only have to cope with the deployment of their own troops but were also responsible for carrying the 115,000 troops of the

British Expeditionary Force to a very narrow area of the front. Amazingly, the British accepted without demur that the entire railway system be manned and controlled by the French. This unity of command prevailed throughout the war, although, as we shall see below, from 1916 the British took an increasing share of the work of construction and operation.

The British started arriving in France just three days after the declaration of war and were immediately deployed by rail from the disembarkation ports at Boulogne, Rouen and Le Havre through Amiens to fight the Germans invading through Belgium. Just as the railways had worked effectively in bringing them to Southampton, the movement of troops to the front on the French railways was carried out with surprisingly little difficulty. There were practical issues for soldiers, most of whom had never been abroad, such as the fact that French platforms are at a much lower level than in Britain, making getting on trains with heavy kit difficult, and instructions were being shouted in a foreign language few could understand. As a whole, though, the operation was successful, with barely 10 per cent of the 343 trains arriving half an hour or more late, showing that the railways could adapt quickly to sudden flows since the French had not expected the British to join the war so early.

The key to the success of the operation was the idea of appointing railway transport officers at principal stations which had been so effective in the transport of troops to the ports in the Boer War, as mentioned in Chapter Five. These officers headed teams of men, mostly with railway experience, and were crucial to the smooth running of the railway. Where possible, French-speaking officers were selected and they were widely deployed by the British through the French railway system. During the first couple of years of the war, they were carefully selected not just for their railway knowledge, but their ability to deal diplomatically with all kinds of demands and to liaise with the French railways. According to J. A. B. Hamilton, who served in the war and later wrote a book about railways during the conflict, initially the railway transport officers had been selected by the Royal Engineers but later, when the War Office took over the process, the rail service suffered badly because "the R.T.O.'s job became a dumping ground for the dimmer sort of officer or a bolt-hole for the one who could 'wangle' himself a 'cushy' billet". Even though they were not always officers — sometimes even lowly lance corporals were allocated the task if they were experienced railwaymen — they had the final say over all traffic movements. That was crucial, as Hamilton recalls: "in those early days, it was not uncommon for some newly-appointed military jack-in-office to ring up the local stationmaster and demand a special train, sometimes for a single officer".

As well as being the British advanced base, Amiens was a *gare régulatrice*, the key to the way that the French successfully operated their railways. These regulating stations, sited safely away from the front to ensure they were not in the range of enemy fire, were the crucial railway junctions from which the military

242

controllers ran the supply operation and were provided with all the requirements needed for the enormous logistical operation, such as vast sidings, a base for railway troops and their repair trains, and depots for artillery. These stations would act as depots where trains full of, say, fuel or food would unload and then new mixed trains would be formed carrying a mixed array of goods and personnel, and despatched towards the front line.

The importance of Amiens made its evacuation particularly difficult after the retreat from Mons, the British Expeditionary Force's first major engagement. Even the official report on the supply operation in the war emphasizes that the process tested the logistical skills of the Army to the extreme: "The lines were congested with a rearward flow of civilians, railway establishments from the north, military material and evacuated Belgian locomotives and rolling stock. Only by putting French-speaking officers on the trains were supplies and other requirements got through to the troops to ever varying railheads, often with the loss of a few trucks *en route*." For the most part, however, thanks to the static nature of the subsequent war, the location of the *gares régulatrices* remained the same for the duration of the conflict, obviating this kind of chaotic scene. After the battle of the Marne, Amiens was safely back behind Allied lines and remained the key junction for the despatch of British troops for the duration of the war.

The end of the short war of movement left the railways with a different but equally daunting logistical brief: supplying the front-line troops in their trenches. The scale of the operation was extraordinary, and far from offering an easier task for the railways, their difficulties were compounded. In fact, while the prospect of delivering millions of troops to the front may seem to offer insuperable problems, it is actually an easier job than providing those troops with regular supplies once they are entrenched in static lines, especially given the conditions and the proximity of the enemy. The official history of the supply operation is unequivocal on this point: "Experience showed that the maintenance of a force in the field was a more complicated traffic problem than a strategic troop movement. Besides the daily despatch of food for men and animals to the force at the front, new depots were constantly being established or shifted from place to place on the line of communication — supply, ordnance and remount depots, reinforcement camps, hospitals for men and animals in each of them required daily supplies of food . . . every day produces a new crop of demands." That last point was crucial: each day was different and the system had to be adapted. Railways are inherently inflexible, and new stations had to be created, extra sections of line built and a series of important cross-country links strengthened on a network which, as mentioned above, spread out like a bicycle wheel from Paris. According to the official account, "no one base was capable of supplying an army with all its needs. Railway traffic began to increase far beyond the maximum needs of peace time and placed an ever increasing strain on the French rolling stock and personnel."

The end of the war of movement and the arbitrary nature of the front line which emerged — at one point it split an abandoned brickyard down the middle — left the Allies with a truncated railway system. The front was served by two north-south routes. One was the Calais-Paris main line, which was a well-equipped double-track railway, while the eastern one, running perhaps ten to fifteen miles behind the front, was far less satisfactory as it was in effect a hotchpotch of cross-country branches, mostly single track, running from Dunkerque on the coast through Hazebrouck and Béthune to Amiens. There were various east-west lines connecting the two, notably the heavily used route from Boulogne through to Hazebrouck, and most of these, too, were single track and not built to carry the level of traffic required in wartime.

The demands placed on the system were now far more complex than a simple one-way flow and the requirements of troops, except of rations and forage, were irregular. The overall figures of the thousands of tons of supplies required and millions of mouths to feed are impressive enough but it is the detail that shows the enormity of the task. The official French report on the performance of the French railways during the war stated, for example, that because the entrenchment, which had started in the autumn, had not been anticipated, supplies of warm clothing had to be issued to all the troops as a matter of urgency. Two blankets, two sweaters, three flannel shirts, two pairs of gloves, socks, a pair of waterproof boots and much else for each soldier had to be sent to the front. Troops who were at listening posts near the front, where it was impossible to heat any food because of the proximity of the enemy, required extra sustenance, which was either 200 grammes of cold sausage, 150 grammes of sardines or 250 grammes of tuna. For all the French soldiers, there was one essential that could not be neglected: on average every *poilu* (squaddie) consumed 750 litres of wine — three whole barrels each — during the course of the war and, as the report emphasizes, there were millions of soldiers. The British did not, of course, share this taste of the fruits of the vine, but had other demands such as the need to brew up tea or have a fry-up as often as possible.

As the entrenched armies grew bigger, the demands from both the relief and replacement of tired troops and the equipment requirements meant the railway was over-extended. It was not only that the numbers of soldiers at the front increased, peaking at 6 million, but that their needs became ever greater. The authors of the French official report calculated that whereas in 1914 a French division (around 12,000 men) required around 70–140 tonnes per day to "meet all its needs", which could be provided by ten to twenty wagons, by 1918 that had grown around tenfold to 1,000 tonnes, necessitating two full supply trains of fifty wagons each. Even the 1914 figure was, as van Creveld points out, around double the requirements of the wars of the mid-1800s, demonstrating an almost exponential growth in the logistics of war which resulted from the construction of the railways and placed a near intolerable burden on them. Partly, of course, that was due to the very existence of the railways, since they offered a remarkable increase in the scale of the transport capability of a nation. For example, the two frontline railways, the Nord and the Est, both of which had lost sections of their networks to the invasion, had to cater for around eighty supply trains daily in 1914, a total which soared nearly threefold to 230 a day by 1916.

A logistical exercise of this scale inevitably created idiocies. Trying to sort out the problem of small parcels and deliveries took up a disproportionate amount of thinking at headquarters. There was a tendency for officers to mark all their particular consignments as "urgent" and even to despatch a man with them to ensure they arrived because such small packages had a tendency to get lost. Whole wagons were on occasion taken up with just one parcel. The official report on transport on the Western Front cites the discovery of a sealed wagon labelled "urgent" with no clue as to its contents. When forced open, the wagon was found to contain "one small package on which was seated a convoyman with his blankets and rations for three days". The hapless fellow was removed to the brake van with his precious package and his wagon replaced by a fully loaded one.

The year 1915 saw a series of failed offensives which were undermined by the absence of a surprise element. The railways were both hero and villain. They were essential for the logistics of any attack but that very

247

dependence on the railways ensured that none of these attacks ever took the enemy by surprise. The activity on the railways necessary to prepare the attacks could not fail to be seen by scouts from the air or balloons or even from nearby vantage points on hilltops. For example, the Champagne offensive scheduled for September 1915 required preparations on the railways behind the lines starting in July. It was to be an attack broadly aimed northwards and a new line was built parallel to a crucial single track running east-west between the villages of Saint-Hilaire and Sainte-Menehould which was within range of the enemy. Both lines, too, were fitted with signalling equipment to increase capacity. Several extensive platforms, 400 metres long, were built along this new section to trans-ship goods to the smaller 60cm-gauge railways which themselves were extended throughout the area. Signalling on various other sections of line was improved and, further back, storage tracks were laid for artillery and hospital trains, and to accommodate the large rail-mounted guns that would launch the offensive.

Not surprisingly, all this activity came to the notice of the Germans, who, in response, reinforced their defences. Like many attacks during the long stalemate on the Western Front, there was an initial break-through, with some units advancing two miles on the first day, but soon the breach was blocked, the Germans successfully defended their territory and by mid-October it was clear that the offensive had failed to make a significant breakthrough. The railways themselves, centred around the *gare régulatrice* of Troyes, had again carried out their duties efficiently and the absence of success of the attack could not be ascribed to any logistical failure.

The Germans were better prepared for the stalemate, having anticipated fighting on two fronts and perhaps expecting a siege of Paris, as had happened in their last war with France. There is no doubt that they had planned more efficiently for any eventuality. They had anticipated the problem of connecting fronts with railheads and equipped themselves with portable 60cm-gauge field railways. Edwin Pratt suggested that this was the result of the thoroughness of the Germans' planning for war: "*Feldeisenbahnabteilung*, the Field Railway Section, developed into a comprehensive scheme of preparation for war by organising every possible phase of military rail-transport and leaving nothing to chance that could be foreseen. Acting along these lines with her characteristic thoroughness, and profiting by some unsatisfactory experiences at the outset, Prussia gradually perfected a system for the efficient utilisation of railways in war which became no less complete in itself than the actual network of her strategical railways." These field railways used a tiny 60cm gauge and were designed to supply the front line from railheads without the need for road or animal transport. As a result of this diligence, the Germans had stockpiled vast quantities of equipment for the construction of a network of these light railways. They had gained knowledge of building this type of railway to establish military control over their African colonies, notably in South-West Africa (now Namibia), where over the previous decade they had built the Otavi Railway. It was the longest 60cm railway in the world, stretching an impressive 350 miles across a vast emptiness of savannah and hills to serve the massive Tsumeb minefields of copper, lead and zinc. This experience gave the Germans an edge in the use of such technology, even though the main manufacturer was a French firm called Décauville, and they entered the war already prepared to make use of these *Feldbahnen*. Within a few days of the start of the war, the Germans were laying light-railway track to help in their successful attack on Liège. Although they looked like oversized Hornby sets, the 60cm railways were eventually to play a major part in the conflict on both sides, especially in the later stages of the war.

These light railways provided an efficient — and often the only — link between railheads and the front line, and the contrast in their exploitation by the three main participants on the Western Front highlighted a deeper difference in the combatants' respective attitudes towards the war. The Germans had anticipated that field railways would be extremely useful, and the French had made some preparations and rapidly expanded their stock of narrow-gauge material once the war started. The British, however, had rejected the idea of building any such light railways because, they argued, they would serve no purpose in a war of movement. Even before the war, when the British High Command had been told of a German stockpile of military light-railway equipment by many authoritative visitors, including senior field officers, the view of Whitehall had not been changed. The official report on transport on the Western Front confirms this: "For the first two years of the war, the British transport arrangements were dominated by the idea that the war would soon revert to one of movement, that it was useless to embark on any large scheme which might be left far in the rear and become valueless before it had materialised and become of use. For two years, the British relied on Mechanical Transport which proved inadequate when masses of troops and great numbers of heavy guns were crowded into a limited area." This suggests that the British opposition to light railways was part of a wider hostility to rail because it was perceived as so inflexible. The British Army consequently put a lot more energy than either the Germans or the French into mechanizing road transport during the course of the war.

Meanwhile the French, although hampered by the fact that much of their manufacturing capability was in areas now occupied by the Germans, started stockpiling material for light railways as soon as the trenches were dug. The advantage of light railways was that in the conditions of the front line they were more flexible and efficient than any other form of transport, as the official report later explained: "The use of light railways was mainly due to the difficulties of road maintenance. With the coming of trench warfare, the roads from the constant traffic of heavy lorries suffered severely, especially in bad weather, the horsed transport owing to shell fire and the bad roads was unable to reach troops in the trenches, and supplies had to be transported over the last stage of their journey from the railhead to the trenches by manual labour." Railheads had to be at least seven miles behind the front line to be safe from enemy fire and there were only two ways of carrying supplies through this gap, men or mules, neither of which were particularly suitable as both required an extraordinary amount of effort and manpower.

Carrying supplies through the last few miles from the railhead was not only onerous but could be deadly. The rural French roads, never designed for military traffic, rapidly degenerated into rutted tracks under the weight of carts, lorries and horse-drawn artillery. Large sections of the army were diverted from their military roles into road maintenance but it was never enough, especially in the autumn and winter. Once the roads ran out it was worse: "Beyond the roads lay a nightmare quagmire of pulverised fields, ruined ditches and flooded shell-holes, threaded by temporary duckboard tracks and communications trenches. Through this muddy wasteland every single item needed by the troops — food, water, clothing, medical supplies, tools, timber, barbed wire, mortars, machine guns, rifles, ammunition and yet more ammunition — had to be carried on the backs of men and horses. Thousands of men died as they wandered off the tracks into flooded shell craters, or tripped and fell in the waterlogged trenches and were trampled by the men behind, or were picked off by artillery fire."

The track for light railways could be laid very easily with little ballast needed to support it and the equipment could be lifted up and used elsewhere if the front line moved, which is why they were sometimes called "portable" railways. In fact the advantages of using these railways between railheads and the front line had become clear to many British troops on the ground for some time after they saw the French operating them and there were all kinds of remarkable experiments: one division near Ypres laid wooden rails to deaden the sound, with the pointwork protected with metal sheets cut from biscuit tins. Haulage on these early British lines was principally by manpower although occasionally mules were used, and in a couple of cases strange petrol-driven machines fashioned from cars and any other available material were put on the crude rails. The French had not gone into the war with sufficient light-railway equipment but cottoned on faster than the British to their benefits. Shocked by the supply difficulties encountered in the first winter, they laid networks in the rear of most of their army positions and placed large orders for new material both in Britain and in America.

Gradually, two types of these narrow-gauge railways developed. The first, broadly, ran from railheads to depots near the front line and were normally hauled by petrol and petrol-electric tractors or steam engines; the second, often of an even smaller gauge than 60cm, were far cruder affairs, generally called tramways and invariably using men or mules for traction. In some parts of the battlefield, the light railways reached almost the front line, whereas, in others, transfer to the crude tramways was needed. The two systems were supposed to be kept independent of each other because the tramways were built to much lower specifications and were not able to take the weight of the locomotives or even most of the wagons running on the light-railway system. Later in the war, though, at some points the two were linked because rolling stock and supplies were accumulating at the transfer point, which was often in sight of the enemy, but connecting them sometimes resulted in derailments as heavier types of vehicle were allowed onto the fragile tramways.

Only after the success of the early experiments by officers on the ground with these temporary light-railway tracks did the top brass consider the worth of these light railways. As W. J. K. Davies, their historian, so aptly put it, "there are, alas, none so blind as those who will not see, and the reports made no impact on British military thinking". Despite the obvious necessity for these networks and the success of these experiments on the front line, it was not until September 1915 that the British HQ gave any official support to their introduction and it was only in February of the following year that the idea was fully endorsed. The takeover by the British of a French sector with three full-scale 60cm light railways finally convinced the military commanders of the usefulness of this innovation and led to the creation of a Directorate of Light Railways. It was not, though, until a few months later that the failure of the Somme offensive resulted in a U-turn by the army generals, when it became apparent that not only were light railways crucial during static periods but they were also vital during attacks when troops were moving forward into enemy territory.

Since the light railways ran at slow speeds, and required frequent repair, they were of necessity short, mostly between five and fifteen miles long. With a greater length much of the capacity of the line would have been taken up with the maintenance needs of the railway itself. Petrol tractors were the more useful means of traction, since they made less noise and could function more safely near enemy lines than the steam engines, which were noisy and too visible. Even the trains on the longer light railways were on occasion hauled by men or mules and contemporary accounts suggest the animals did not always take easily to the task. According to one driver, who recalls that his wagons were usually pulled by teams of six mules, "you can imagine what it was like at night, pitch dark, getting smothered with mud kicked up by the hind legs of the mule, straining your eyes continually at the rope in case it slackened and you were unable to stop the truck before it ran over the mule's legs; this in the army was a worse crime than killing a man because mules cost money!"

The great advantage of these toytown railways was the ease of repair and their flexibility. It was a simple job to replace tracks damaged by shelling or to reroute a line which ran through an area that became impassable. According to one account, derailments were so frequent that on the lines nearest the front "it was not unusual to have three or four [derailments] in one section in one night". Mostly, however, these mishaps presented little problem, solved by a bit of manhandling from any passing soldiers, or left for the next day, when manpower could be found. It was this adaptability that allowed these tiny railways to reach areas which would be unthinkable for standard-gauge trains to enter and made them increasingly indispensable. The system may seem crude but in the latter stages of the war light railways played an enormous part in the line of communication

Most traffic ran at night with, at best, a tiny light, and, since there was no signalling or timetable, trains were controlled from telephone posts next to the line. The train crew consisted of a driver and a guard who operated the wagon brakes, with the addition of a fireman on steam trains. Virtually all the lines were single track and if two trains in opposite directions met, the decision as to which would reverse to the nearest siding or loop was decided by the relative obduracy of the drivers. Usually trains were operated on the tramway line-of-sight principle with each driver being responsible for driving his train so that it did not collide with the one in front. It was not only goods that were transported on these lines. Wherever possible, men moving to and from the front were carried on the railways, saving them hours of plodding through the mud. As Hamilton recalls, "nothing better illustrates the universal role of railways in World War One than the pictures of troops and supplies being moved up through shell-scarred country along one of these light railways".

Even large guns, often straddling more than one wagon, were carried and towards the end of the war these railways were also used to support field guns, which were mounted on light railways and moved after firing off a few shells, denying the enemy the opportunity to respond.

Despite their size, these little trains had a heavy workload, as described by a Captain W. S. Burge, who was in charge of the 31st Light Railway Company, based in Arras until the German offensive of March 1918. Between 100 and 150 trains were sent out each night: "During the day the traffic for the night was organised, and after dusk it went in a swarm of small trains, sometimes in convoys, sometimes in single truck units. They had no lights, no signals but just crept out on crazy little rails weighing only 15lb per yard [about a sixth of the weight of track on standard-gauge railways] and with a gauge of only 60cm. On this line, laid mostly on mud and light metal sleepers, our little army of trains set forth at an average speed of six to eight miles per hour, with ten tons of ammo or material in each truck." Breakdowns and derailments were quickly dealt with: teams of men "trained in the gentle art of lifting a loco out of a shell-hole in thirty minutes with not even a sky-hook to pull them, were sent out at a moment's notice wherever needed". Ultimately, according to Westwood, "all the belligerents, even the Germans, made greater use of narrow-gauge field railways than they had expected. Partly this was because of the static character of the war, but partly because these railways had an increasing range of uses."

The crude nature of the light railways, however, was at times a severe disadvantage as they needed constant repair and disruptive derailments were frequent. They could carry a maximum of 30 tons and, consequently, for each standard-gauge train delivering to a transfer station, ten narrow-gauge ones were required. And, of course, they were slow. Not all the problems were the fault of the railways. Since the routes of these railways were laid on the most even available ground and the roads were so poor or often non-existent, their tracks tended to be used by everything from marching troops and pack mules to cars and even tanks, none of which was conducive to smooth running. Consequently, a remarkable fifth of traffic on the light railways consisted of the transportation of material for maintaining and building them. Probably nothing summed up their lack of sophistication and the improvised nature of their operation more than the fact that drivers often resorted to finding water for their steam locomotives from the nearest shell hole because of the lack of any consistent supply. Another example of improvisation on these light railways was the use of Ford Model T cars mounted on a rail chassis. The idea according to legend came from a Miss Bowen Cooke, the daughter of Charles Bowen Cooke, the Chief Mechanical Engineer of the London & North Western Railway, while listening to an officer on leave in Paris complaining about the inadequacy of front-line transport. The sparky girl apparently suggested a vehicle that could be used for both road and rail, and the idea was taken up by her father, whose works in Crewe produced no fewer than 132 of these strange vehicles. Unfortunately, though, according to the historian of the light railways, they proved something of a failure because "a chronic lack of adhesion sadly reduced the tractors' usefulness". Nevertheless, they must have made a handsome sight — and an entertaining distraction for the troops.

For the crew, operating the little trains might not have been as dangerous as fighting on the front but it was still perilous and difficult, as described by Captain Burge: "Every tractor driver or guard when they set out went on a very real adventure with no body of men to 'carry them through' — they were launched on their own with the full knowledge that anything might happen at any moment, but whatever did happen they nearly always delivered the goods one way or other."

The more efficient delivery of men and matériel to the front occasioned by these light railways did nothing to relieve the strain on standard-gauge French railways, which, towards the end of 1915, were showing signs of being unable to cope with the workload. The huge increase in passenger numbers and freight being carried compared to peacetime had to be handled by a greatly reduced workforce since many men had left to serve in the forces. The rolling stock of wagons and, especially, locomotives, over half of which dated back to the nineteenth century, was deteriorating, too. Trains were being cancelled and the civilian traffic was hit particularly hard since military trains took precedence. Yet many of the non-military services were equally important, carrying food and basic supplies to the population, as well as soldiers on leave to and from their home towns, and consequently the cancellation of all civilian services was not an option. By the beginning of 1916 the situation on the railways had reached crisis point, with even the military traffic beginning to suffer from shortage of wagons and delays caused by overcrowding, and it began to cause severe anxiety to the military leaders.

The two major battles of 1916, Verdun and the Somme, highlighted the crucial position of the supply chain, and in particular the role of the railways for the war's outcome. The battle of Verdun, which started in February 1916 and lasted for much of that year, was not only the longest battle of the First World War but also one of the bloodiest in the history of warfare and, according to A. J. P. Taylor, "the most senseless episode in a war not distinguished for sense anywhere". The Germans, led by the Crown Prince, who took personal control of the attack, became increasingly convinced that the capture of Verdun would signal their ultimate victory.

Legend has it that it was the lorry, using a network of small country roads, that saved the day at Verdun. In fact, railways played an equally important, and probably decisive, role in the logistical operation. It was actually the perceived weakness of the French line of communication to Verdun which had convinced the Germans to focus their attack there rather than on Belfort, which was probably a more vulnerable and easier target. Verdun, which had a historically strategic position on the Meuse river, was a salient cut off on three sides without effective railway communications and the Germans were convinced that it would be a trap into which they could strike a fatal blow against the French Army. There was the added incentive, too, of Verdun's symbolic significance as it had been the last fortress town to fall to the Prussians in 1871. The fortresses — there were several other hilltop forts in the area — themselves had more emblematic than strategic value as they were seen as being irrelevant to modern warfare, although they had been reinforced with huge amounts of concrete in the 1900s to resist all but the heaviest shells.

Verdun's eight-mile-long front, established in 1914, was, indeed, served by a precarious supply route. The railway line from the south into the town had been severed at Saint-Mihiel by the original German occupation while the other route from Paris was impassable because the tracks were within range of the enemy's guns. That left a small metre-gauge railway, the Chemin de Fer Meusien, which ran from the standard-gauge railhead at Bar Le Duc, and the parallel road, which was little more than a series of country lanes, a *route départmentale* rather than a *route nationale*, through to Verdun, seventy-five miles away. The strategy of attacking Verdun, therefore, was based on the notion that the German attackers, well served by railways, would be able to take over the French positions because their defenders would soon run out of supplies, particularly artillery shells. The Germans, though, had reckoned without Maréchal Philippe Pétain, the commander of the French forces, who had realized as soon as the attack on Verdun was launched that the battle would be won or lost on the basis of logistics, and had, too, underestimated the value of the little Meusien railway. Pétain ensured that the road was kept in good condition by creating a special unit of 8,500 men and 300 officers to maintain it. To keep the Verdun front supplied, therefore, 3,000 trucks travelled daily in each direction along this meandering unpaved route of crushed stone, a frequency of one every fifteen seconds, which meant that soldiers using it had to march on the side in single file. Any truck that broke down was simply pushed off the road into a ditch to ensure there were no major hold-ups. After the war it was dubbed *La Voie Sacrée* by a novelist but the drivers struggling with the terrible conditions called it more prosaically *La Route*, probably with the odd adjectival curse thrown in.

The windy little Meusien railway, though, proved an essential adjunct to the road. The line had struggled to keep the front supplied even before the battle, and once it began an appeal was made around the country for metre-gauge locomotives and wagons. Fortunately, there were many other railways built to that gauge in France and sufficient stock was found to run about one train an hour, which meant the Meusien carried about a quarter of the total supplies for the front in the early stages of the battle. As more rolling stock arrived, and improvements to the line were made, the railway's capacity increased to one train every forty minutes, providing much relief to *La Route*. Such was the importance of the supply routes that at the numerous level crossings between the railway line and the road

Pétain stationed cavalry troops to regulate the traffic and reduce the risk of accidents.

Appreciating that *La Route* would always struggle to cope, as soon as the battle of Verdun began, in February 1916, Pétain had ordered the construction of the Nettancourt-Dugny line, a forty-five-mile-long standard-gauge railway line parallel to the road, and, remarkably, this was completed in June, just four months after work had started. The new railway was an enormous boon for the line of communication and largely took over the carriage of supplies, especially the heavy artillery shells, relegating *La Route* to the transport of light trucks and motor cars. A. J. P. Taylor's assertion that it was the lorries which made all the difference ("Without the automobile engine, Verdun could not have been saved") underestimates the role of the Meusien and of the parallel line built so successfully in haste. Moreover, he ignored the role of the light railways, which were essential for carrying supplies for the last few miles to the front, which was served by a six-track 60cm railway. Indeed, the commemorative monument to *La Voie Sacrée* recognizes the role of the railways by depicting a steam locomotive as well as three trucks.

Neither the intense trucking on the road, nor the opening of the Nettancourt-Dugny railway line, had been anticipated by the German military planners. The ultimate result of Verdun was a ghastly score draw, resulting in the staggering loss of a total of more than 300,000 lives. The French held on to Verdun but at tremendous cost, while the Germans almost succeeded in their aim of breaking French morale but also suffered enormous casualties.

The Germans had thought their better logistics would be decisive at Verdun but underestimated the adaptability of the French. Pétain saved Verdun by understanding the importance of his line of communication and ensuring it could cope with keeping the front supplied. In the event, not only did the French supply route stand the test but Pétain was so confident of its robustness that he rotated his troops every fifteen days in order to keep them fresh, which placed enormous additional burdens on both road and rail. This policy resulted in more than 2 million troops being taken to and from the front during the course of the ten months of the battle. Of course, many of those returning were wounded and both railway lines proved particularly useful for transporting them away from the front as they offered a far more comfortable ride than the bumpy road. These troops heading for a brief respite on leave, dubbed *permissionaires*, were not, incidentally, the easiest passengers for the railways to carry. Pétain had created a special *Guide du permissionaire* to regulate their behaviour and they were supposed to travel exclusively on special trains. In their rush to get home, however, they jumped onto any available service, sometimes ejecting any hapless civilians who happened to be travelling in the same direction, and their rowdy behaviour became an issue of great concern to the authorities. Groups of soldiers, claiming to be lost, would use their railway passes to travel around the system for days, as had happened in the Franco-Prussian War. In an effort to keep the soldiers separate from the general public, special exchange stations, furnished with canteens and even cinemas, were established, but the problem persisted throughout the war.

Verdun showed yet again that the particular state of transport technology in the First World War undoubtedly favoured defenders rather than attackers. The Somme offensive would provide another hard-won lesson, that in the muddy conditions of the Western Front light railways were necessary to consolidate an attack as well as to support an entrenched position. The Somme offensive was led by the British and, like all others, was supposed to be the decisive breakthrough, but it started badly. The attack began earlier than planned, at the instigation of the French, who were anxious to create a diversion from Verdun in order to maintain morale among the Allied troops. Partly because bringing forward the launch of the attack left much of the German artillery intact, and also because the same suicidal "going over the top" tactics as in previous campaigns were used, 1 July 1916, the first day of the battle, became the bloodiest ever in British military history with 57,470 killed and wounded. When, within weeks, the Somme attack foundered, matters came to a head. According to the official report published after the war, it only took a simple logistical calculation to understand why it failed: "without some means of rapidly establishing communications across the shell-pitted area, no breakthrough was possible. The experience of the Somme showed that during an offensive on a twelve-mile front the loads to be distributed daily beyond railheads amounted to over 20,000 tons. To deal with such quantities, corduroy roads and a few isolated lines here and there were totally inadequate." The authorities had thought that standard-gauge railways could be brought nearer the front but this proved impossible because they took too long to build and repair, and were vulnerable to attack.

The official report on logistics published after the war was unequivocal about the experience of the Somme and explained why field railways were better than other methods of transport: "Experience showed that neither standard-gauge railways nor metalled roads could be extended across the shell-pitted area quickly enough to keep pace with the advance. A very costly offensive might gain a mile or two but the time required to reconstruct communications across the ground won gave the enemy time to recover and to reorganize his defences so that the whole process of preparing for and launching another costly attack had to be gone through again."

In other words, after two years of war and numerous attempted "offensives" and "breakthroughs", the military authorities realized that they had failed to think through the logistical requirements of the army once the initial advance had been made. Hundreds of thousands of men had died in battles which never had a hope of success because the logistics had not been properly considered. Of course, improving the line of communication served by the railways would not have

been enough to win the war, but a failure to recognize the importance of such preparation ensured that any breakthrough would be transitory.

The Somme offensive lasted until mid-November but in effect petered out after a few weeks, by which time it had failed in its basic aims since no permanent breach of the German lines had been achieved. By early August, when it became clear that the attack had resulted in no significant advance, a circular from the Quartermaster General announced a reversal of policy, stressing the need for armies to find substitutes for motor transport and requiring light railways to be used throughout the front line for the carriage of ammunition, engineering stores and general supplies. Consequently, the Ministry of Munitions placed a massive order for sufficient equipment to build and operate 600 miles of track, including 120 "tractors" (petrol or petrol-electric engines) and steam locomotives, only to find that the capacity of British manufacturers had largely already been taken up by the French. After pressure from the Army, supplies were rerouted to the British and a large construction programme was initiated, resulting in the completion of over 200 miles of 60cm railways by the end of the year with the ultimate aim of creating a network of 1,000 miles.

If light railways were the key on the front line, further back the smooth operation of the standard-gauge railways remained essential and during 1916 the French system was beginning to break down. As previously mentioned, the French were operating more traffic than in peacetime, with fewer personnel and a rolling stock of worn locomotives and ramshackle wagons; from the autumn of 1915, the system began to deteriorate, as increasing demands were placed on the network. Both men and material suffered delays because of the shortage of wagons, and the ports were becoming bottlenecks, with ships spending up to seventeen days in the French docks because cargo could not be unloaded and removed quickly enough. Throughout 1916, the French were frantically requesting extra rolling stock from the British in order to cope with the ever-increasing demands on the railways. Until then, the British had relied on local locomotives and wagons, but in May 1916 the French suggested that the British provide all the wagons, a total of 22,500, required for the movement of British troops and supplies. This caused consternation in the War Office because the British could not possibly supply so much equipment at such short notice, and the initial response was the standard British one of creating a sub-committee to examine the matter. In fact, British equipment had been used on the French railways since the autumn of 1914, when the South Eastern & Chatham Railway sent over ten locomotives, along with the men to operate them, for the unloading of ships in Boulogne. Construction workers and maintenance engineers had been also despatched to help with the repair and upkeep of the lines serving the British Expeditionary Force. This arrangement was regularized the following year with the creation of the British Army's Railway Operating Division, which from late

1915 began to take over the operation and maintenance of lines used by the British troops, who were, for the most part, entrusted with the northern sections of the Western Front. This new division also started building branch lines to provide extra routes to the front with the agreement of the French authorities.

After some hesitation, the War Office acceded to the French request for stock, promising to take over progressively the running and provisioning of more lines, and a flow of British wagons and locomotives began arriving in France from the other side of the Channel. The Railway Operating Division assumed control of its first line, a section of the intensively used Hazebrouck-Ypres route, in the summer of 1916, but it was not until the end of that year that real impetus was given to British efforts to strengthen the capacity of the railways in France. Sir Eric Geddes, the former deputy manager of the North Eastern Railway who later became Britain's first Minister of Transport, was appointed to undertake a rapid study of the transport situation in France. On his arrival in France, Geddes noted: "the troops were fagged out because of lack of transport. The railheads were ten to fifteen miles back. The roads were blocked and the ammunition and guns were piling up in England." There was no central control of the transport operation: "The transport network was so heavily sectionalised that responsible officers had a narrow focus on problems which enabled them to make slight adjustments but not to tackle the larger problems."

Geddes's findings were devastating. In his report, sent to the new Prime Minister, David Lloyd George, at the end of November 1916, he confirmed that the railway system in France was at breaking point. More than two years of intensive use, a depleted workforce and insufficient maintenance had taken their toll. The forty-five British locomotives working there were plainly insufficient and Geddes argued that 300 locomotives and 10,000 wagons should be despatched as soon as possible if the line of communication for the British Army were not to collapse. He also said the British needed to supply the material to build 1,000 miles of line for both new sections and extra tracks on busy routes.

The Geddes report had an immediate impact. It was clear that there was no time to build new locomotives, and therefore the British railway companies, which in any case were under government control, would need to provide them. Spare locomotives and equipment for the permanent way were garnered from railways across the country and sent to France. While the rail companies responded well to these demands for spare equipment, its shipment across the Channel was hampered by Germany's new aggressive naval policy of using U-boats to sink any Allied ship on sight. Not only were some of the consignments sunk, but others suffered prolonged delays because of the presence of the German submarines. There were problems of compatibility, too. The first wagons sent over to France had grease axle boxes, rather than the oil-based ones universally used in France. Since the French had no use for grease, none was available, and the wagons soon seized up, leaving them in sidings until a supply of grease could be sent over from Britain.

Geddes, however, did more than just demand extra supplies of railway material from Britain. He reorganized the whole logistical operation, bringing together all the disparate parts under one directorate, which he headed as Director-General of Transportation. That had been a long time coming. Back in 1914, Lord Kitchener had asked Sir Percy Girouard, the builder of the Sudan railway, to produce a report on the railway situation in France, which had made precisely the same recommendation but had not been acted upon because of the usual squabbles over territory between the different sections of the military. Girouard had also wanted an officer to be appointed to take general charge of railway work on the Continent, and Geddes now took on that role, two years after the original recommendation. He set up a central office in France with more than a hundred officers and 600 clerks, all of whom were given military rank in order to confirm their status, and he created separate sections to cover docks, railways, roads and light railways. These offices, which were only three miles from HQ, even acquired the name "Geddesburg" as an ironic recognition of their importance. It was on his initiative that the major programme for light railways was developed and he also beefed up the Railway Operating Division by drafting in railwaymen from other divisions. Its manpower rose to 76,000, incorporating thirteen companies (with around 250 men each) of civilian platelayers from the home railways who were engaged on three-month contracts at a high rate of pay and worked under the orders of civilian engineers, to build sections of both mainline and light railway. The Army disliked the use of civilians, however, because they were not subject to military discipline and these volunteers were soon dispensed with, as the official report recalls in a typically understated way: "As in the Crimea in 1855 and the Sudan in 1885, the experiment of employing civilians in an overseas theatre of war did not prove altogether satisfactory and further offers of assistance of this kind were declined." Over the course of the war, the British built around 800 miles of railway, and the French around four times that length, more than 3,500 miles.

Geddes was also instrumental in persuading the military authorities of the urgency of the transportation system by making simple logistical calculations which should have been worked out at the outset of the war. He showed, for example, that a corps of 50,000 men on a four-mile front would get through a maximum of 2,300 tons of ammunition, and using such simple arithmetic worked out that the shortfall in the transportation supply route could be as much as 50 per cent. It was not only railways that needed to be improved. The ports of Dover and Folkestone had long been under strain, and Geddes recommended the massive expansion of the so-called "mystery port" at Richborough in Kent, which had been created uniquely for military purposes, and eventually became a massive — and largely secret — installation with sixty-five miles of railway line and sidings. To improve the flow of material through the port, a cross-Channel ferry service to Calais and Dunkirk was created to handle large pieces of equipment such as heavy guns and even tanks. It was the first to use the roll-on, roll-off (ro-ro) system, enabling trains to board and disembark the ships directly. Until then locomotives and wagons had to be loaded and unloaded one by one with a quayside or ship-mounted crane. Three ferries were specially built, each able to carry ten of the large Railway Operating Division standard locomotives or fifty-four wagons, and even though they had stern entry only (unlike today's ro-ro ferries, which have ramps and seaworthy doors at both stem and stern), the turnaround efficiency was greatly increased.

Following the Geddes initiative, British rail supplies and workers poured into France and the Railway Operating Division gradually took over lines previously run by the French. By the end of 1916, it controlled a hundred miles and at the end of the war more than 800 miles of standard-gauge line and 1,000 miles of light railway, and it had also built a further 800 miles of track during the conflict. This arrangement required the establishment of a clear division of responsibility between the British and French. The British were responsible for carrying troops and material from the ports to the *gare régulatrice*, where the French took over. In many cases, railwaymen from Britain were used to drive these locomotives and found themselves working alongside their French counterparts. Indeed, since locomotives were pooled, many French civilian

273

trains were hauled by British locomotives driven by "*les Rosbifs*". As many of the locomotives supplied to the French railways were old and the demand for extra ones became insatiable, it soon became clear that the British would have to recommence the production of new locomotives, which had stopped at the outbreak of war. By the winter of 1916–17, the number of trains on the French network had increased by 50 per cent from peacetime levels, but many of its stock of 14,000 locomotives were laid up owing to the lack of spare parts or manpower to fix them. An additional constraint on the network was the multiplicity of different types of locomotives as the French, unlike the Germans and Russians, did not have a standard freight locomotive that could be moved easily around the system. Consequently, when the British started producing new engines for use in France, a standard type based on a Great Central freight design was chosen and more than 300 of these were eventually supplied. As demand increased further, another 500 locomotives were brought over from America.

By the middle of 1917, when another major offensive was being prepared, this time in Flanders, the central role that light railways could play had been recognized and for the first time they were included as part of the central planning. The attack centred on the village of Passchendaele near Ypres, with the aim of enabling the British to reach the Belgian North Sea ports from where it was thought, wrongly, that the Germans were launching U-boat attacks on British shipping. A recent French offensive, further south and aimed at German positions on the Aisne, had failed badly, creating a mutinous air in the Army, and the Passchendaele attack (also known as the Third Battle of Ypres) was felt necessary to restore morale among the Allies. The offensive started in early June with the successful blowing up of a German-held strongpoint, the Messines Ridge above Ypres, but then there was a fatal delay until the end of July before the full attack was launched. Passchendaele has become the symbol of the worst conditions endured by the soldiers in the First World War as the Flanders fields, mostly reclaimed marshlands, were already prone to flooding, and the terrible weather of that summer turned the whole area into a quagmire. Soldiers, weighed down by their 45lb packs, had to pick their way carefully through the mud on duckboards, knowing that a slip could lead to death by drowning. In these conditions, the 60cm railways proved invaluable. Everywhere that the troops made gains, a light railway would soon be constructed to support them. For example, according to W. J. K. Davies, the historian of the light railways in the war, "it took only sixty hours after Passchendaele had been occupied for a light railway to be operating right into the village, bringing up stores and taking back wounded." While the plight of the forward units in the difficult conditions was dire, their difficulties were greatly alleviated by the ability of the railways to deliver supplies right to the front, since road transport could not reach most of their positions.

It was not the logistical shortcomings which resulted in the offensive failing, yet again, to achieve a significant breakthrough. The Germans had been given weeks to prepare for the expected assault following the blowing up of their positions on the Messines Ridge, and they had reinforced their lines further back by building a series of pillboxes, the marshy land being unsuitable for deep trenches. The Allied attack foundered in the muddy morass created by a particularly wet summer and by early November, when the attack was called off, the British had reached only the one-time village of Passchendaele, now completely wrecked, an advance of seven miles achieved at a cost of 300,000 lives.

Until then the network of light railways had remained largely isolated from one another as each one ran between railheads and individual supply dumps near the front line. The lack of links between the light rail systems of the 1st and 3rd armies during the Passchendaele attack had meant weapons and other material had to be transferred between the two by a roundabout route on the standard-gauge railways, an utterly inefficient manoeuvre. Consequently, towards the end of 1917, the military authorities decided to create a long north-south line connecting these disparate systems about four miles behind the lines. The idea was that this would allow the rapid transfer of material, especially light artillery, between different sections of the front to help resist the expected German offensive. A further plan to create a parallel line, eight miles behind the trenches, had not been completed by the time the attack came in March 1918. Another idea which never got off the ground, and which demonstrated how the military authorities occasionally took leave of their senses, was that of building 200 miles of electrified 60cm railway powered by overhead cables, which would not only have been dangerous, since the wires would have been at head height, but also have been unsuitable for operations anywhere near enemy lines since they would have been easily visible.

At their peak, in March 1918, there were more than 1,000 miles of these light railways and 150 miles of tramway on the Allied section of the front, matched by a network that was probably even larger on the German side. The Germans had an enormous pool of 60cm gauge locomotives, having built more than 2,500 steam engines alone, many of which were deployed on the Eastern Front, notably in Poland. On the Allied side, not only was there a connecting line running north-south, but there was a network of marshalling yards as well as countless stations where material could be transferred from standard gauge to light railways. Quite often, too, there were intermediary yards where the larger trains, hauled by steam engines, were broken down into smaller ones pulled by petrol engines, which could operate closer to enemy lines. The vast majority of the deliveries to depots near the front were carried out at night, with trains often being prepared in the marshalling yards during the day and waiting for the cover of darkness to proceed.

It was not only the existing French network that required extra stock. Further strain was put on the railway system at the beginning of 1917 when the Allies devised a 1,500-mile trans-European railway service linking Cherbourg with Taranto in southern Italy, by a roundabout route that took in Tours in western France and the Mont Cenis tunnel, in order to support the Allied forces in the eastern theatres of the war and for use by French and British troops sent there. This service required more than a hundred locomotives to provide six trains per day to supply the theatres of Macedonia, Palestine and Mesopotamia, and was designed to replace the vast amount of shipping on this route, which was in constant danger of attack. The service, however, was interrupted by the Italian defeat at Caporetto in October 1917 and the German offensive on Amiens the following year, and never reached its full potential, mustering at best two to three trains daily.

There were other demands stretching the resources of the French railway system. The most significant was the transport of the American troops who started arriving during the summer of 1917. The French Paris-Lyon-Méditerranée railway had already performed well in carrying more than 100,000 Indian, Gurkha and Anzac troops up to the front from the Mediterranean port of Marseille, but now a far bigger operation was required when the troops started arriving from the United States, which had joined the war after Germany started sinking its ships. The Channel ports could not take the strain as the numbers arriving grew rapidly in 1918 and American soldiers had to be landed at the Atlantic ports on the west coast, mostly Bordeaux and Saint-Nazaire, requiring trains to transport them across France to the front. By the end of the war, 2 million

Americans were serving in France, and major improvements had to be carried out on these new military routes, which had not been designed to carry such vast numbers. The Americans brought a lot of equipment with them, including a huge number of "Pershing" locomotives, and operations on these lines were carried out in great measure by the 50,000-strong US Transportation Corps, most of whom were former railwaymen, but nevertheless their arrival placed further strain on an already overloaded rail network. The level of service was not helped by tensions between the American and French railway workers, which occasionally flared up into full-scale fights.

The Americans, like the British, had initially promised to provide all the necessary transportation for their men but at best they only managed around four fifths. The British, too, remained reliant on French labour and equipment. Despite the promised influx of British men and material to the French railways, according to the official report on transportation, "it was not until the final few months of the war in 1918 that the British were actually providing all of the locomotives, wagons, personnel, repairs and works which they required".

None of these difficulties should mask the basic fact that the Western Front was a miracle of logistics. The way that both sides could keep huge numbers of soldiers and enormous amounts of equipment in place, feed and rotate troops, supply ammunition and fuel, and keep everyone reasonably healthy was only possible because of the transport infrastructure in which the railways played the key role. Viewed in a negative light, perhaps this was unfortunate since without the efficiency of the railways, the war might have finished much earlier.

It was only in the last few months of the war that the conflict took on a different complexion. As we shall see in the next chapter, after three and a half years of stalemate in the final stages it became a war of movement once again. It was only to last eight months but briefly forced the railways into a different role. Meanwhile, however, another type of war had been taking place on the Eastern Front between Russia and Germany, a conflict that was ultimately decided by letting one man through the lines on a train.

CHAPTER
EIGHT

Eastern Contrasts

On the Eastern Front and in other theatres which were brought into action in the later stages of the war, a very different type of conflict took place. The Schlieffen Plan had been devised in an effort to avoid the risk of fighting simultaneously on two fronts, but the failure of diplomacy and the rush into war guaranteed that Germany was plunged into this unwanted scenario. Unlike on the Western Front, where a stalemate emerged within weeks of the outbreak of war, in the East it was the absence of railways which resulted in a more mobile war. According to A. J. P. Taylor, "an attacking force could advance fifty miles or so if carefully reinforced. Then the impetus of advance gave out, through lack of railways. The defenders, falling back on their supplies, consolidated their position: the line formed anew."

The Russians rushed into the war, somewhat unprepared, on 17 August 1914 in order to support their Western allies. Despite German expectations, the Russian forces mobilized reasonably quickly, though not in sufficient numbers to give them a decisive advantage. Their mobilization plans included the requirement that freight trains should cease to run while the troops were deployed but, in the event, according to Westwood, "the Russian railways did so well that they found capacity to restore their freight trains to service, rather sheepishly reloading the freight that had been jettisoned at wayside stations a couple of weeks earlier". his episode is typical of the Russian performance in the whole war, which was patchy, with surprisingly efficient episodes interspersed with others that had all the hallmarks of the inefficient and corrupt tsarist regime and its total disregard for the fate of the foot soldiers. While Russian industrialization had not really taken off by 1914, ensuring its army was short of equipment, the sheer numbers the military could muster, together with the scale of the country, guaranteed that Russia was able to put up stern resistance to the Central Powers, especially as it mostly faced the weaker of the two, the Austro-Hungarian Empire, across the battlefield in the initial stages. Moreover, Russia was industrializing fast, which meant that by the middle of the war it was better able to supply its troops with sufficient guns and ammunition. Russian logistics were hampered, though, by the kind of muddle which had characterized the French handling of the Franco-Prussian War. The railways were split, as in France, between those near the front, which were under military control, and the lines in the interior, which remained the responsibility of the ministry of transport. The usual mistakes were made with railway and military authorities squabbling over what trains should have priority, and officers refusing to co-operate by holding on to wagons, once they had been unloaded, for use as warehouses, offices or even living quarters.

The war was launched when two Russian armies pushed, with little clear intent, into East Prussia. After some hesitation, and an initial retreat which led to the replacement of their commander, the Germans responded with a counter-attack at the decisive battle of Tannenberg in the last week of August 1914, which routed the Russians. Thanks to the network of railways behind their lines, and their ability to exploit them to the full, the Germans were able to regroup after their initial setbacks, while the Russians were greatly hampered, again, by the change of gauge at the frontier, which resulted in troops having to disembark and either march to the front or wait for one of the few standard-gauge trains captured from the Germans. Therefore the Russians were not able to profit from the huge numerical supremacy of their army, since the arrival of troops beyond the railhead in Russia was delayed by the lack of rail transport. In contrast, the Germans were able to nimbly move troops around by rail to focus their attack on the Russians' weak points. The crucial manoeuvre undertaken by the Germans was, after a couple of smaller battles, to re-engage their troops so quickly by rail that a single German army was able to hold off the rather disjointed attacks of two Russian ones. The Russians' misuse of another technology, the telegraph, along which they sent uncoded messages that were easily intercepted by the Germans, did not help their cause either, as their marching plans were, quite literally, telegraphed in advance to the enemy.

Further south in Galicia, the Russians and Austrians were engaged in what A. J. P. Taylor called "confused conflict": "The railway network of western Europe virtually gave out here" and "there were great empty spaces where armies, ill-equipped by Western standards, wandered in search of each other". The Russians eventually emerged victorious thanks to their superior numbers, reaching the Carpathians, where they came up against the Germans who, stiffening the resistance of the weak Austro-Hungarians, halted their advance. Although the Russians' attack on the Eastern Front was checked, their very presence forced the Germans to use up vast resources which otherwise they would have been able to deploy to good effect against the British and French. Although the Schlieffen Plan had, in a way, been unnecessary because the Germans showed they were able to wage war on two fronts, the theory behind it was correct: fighting on both simultaneously weakened the Germans' ability to make a decisive breakthrough on either side.

These early battles confirmed that the Eastern Front would be a different type of war to the stalemate that had quickly been established in the west. Overall, there was a far less developed network of railways as the armies moved east and there were even fewer lines to accommodate them. It was a vast theatre that stretched east-west from the Baltic through to Moscow, a distance of around 750 miles, and down to the Black Sea a thousand miles away. The battles raged through this huge area, rarely settling down to any fixed front and dependent on lines of communication that were much less established than on the Western Front.

In 1915, the Germans focussed much of their effort on the Eastern Front, seeking to push the Russians back over their frontier. The superior railways on the western side of this vast region gave the Germans an inherent advantage, but they were overstretched by having to fight on two fronts and still lacked manpower and weaponry despite the extra resources provided by HQ in an effort to bring about a decisive breakthrough. A series of successful battles during the year cleared the Russians out of what is now Poland, but then the front settled down, running from Riga near the Baltic coast down to Ternopil in Ukraine, and would not change substantially until the collapse of the Russian resistance in 1917. After their substantial losses of 1915, the following year the Russians launched what is widely accepted as the most effective and skilled offensive of the whole war by any of the combatants, the campaign against the Austro-Hungarians by General Alexei Brusilov in present-day Ukraine. The attack was made in response to French requests to relieve pressure on Verdun by forcing German troops to move to the Eastern Front and it is a testimony to the brilliance of the offensive that it was named after the general who led it.

Brusilov realized that although his railway supply lines were far inferior to those of his enemy, his troops were able, through the use of stormtrooper tactics, to break through the Austro-Hungarian lines at several points. Rather than the conventional tactics of long inaccurate bombardments, which always resulted in a muddy morass that made progress difficult for the invading infantry, followed by massive troop movements, which invariably were spotted by the enemy, he launched a short barrage on 4 June 1916 and followed that up with attacks by small groups of soldiers on enemy positions. While Brusilov deliberately did not mobilize his troops in the conventional way, avoiding massive concentrations that posed an easy target for the enemy, the sheer numbers on both sides ensured it was one of the bloodiest battles in history.

Brusilov used the inadequacy of his rail support to his advantage by being more flexible and mobile, in which he was helped by the fact that the Army was now better equipped after munitions production had been stepped up. According to Brusilov's memoirs, "knowing the limitation of our rail transport . . . I knew that while we were entraining and transporting one Army Corps, the Germans would manage to transport three or four". Ultimately that lack of transport cost Russia the advantage gained by Brusilov and his attack petered out at the end of September after the Germans brought in reinforcements in sufficient numbers to counter it. The offensive, which cost nearly 3 million killed, wounded or captured on all sides, had been, according to A. J. P. Taylor, fatally undermined by the fact that "since most Russian railways ran east to west, not north to south, the reserves could not be moved in time".

Brusilov's skills and the stronger than expected resistance by the Russians made it harder for the

Central Powers to push back the Russians through eastern Europe. With the Russians fighting rather better than the Germans had expected and the Austro-Hungarians proving mostly ineffective and weakened by mass desertions of their Slav troops, the conflict on the Eastern Front lasted far longer than predicted. There were never enough troops to create a Western Front-type scenario of continuous trench lines, but instead key strongpoints, especially railway junctions, became the focus of battles. In the main, in the east battles were fought along the axis of the few main railway lines that remained generally intact, while in the west, once the Germans had reached beyond the range of their artillery, they had to fight across a railway-less terrain made impassable by previous battles. As the Germans were to discover even more forcefully in the Second World War invasion of Russia, once they crossed the border, they would be greatly hampered by the change of gauge, and the further they advanced into Russia the wider the front became and the thinner the logistical infrastructure behind them.

While the Russians struggled to supply their lines, the Central Powers' front, on the other hand, enjoyed the support of numerous standard-gauge lines, including several that had been built by the Austrians after the Russian attacks of 1914 in Galicia which had cut off their supply lines. One notable line, for example, was the twenty-one-mile Benzino Electric Railway between Tiha Bargaului and Dornisoara in northern Romania, a windy and slow railway which ran along the side of a mountain pass and proved crucial in keeping a

287

section of the front supplied. There was also a series of *Feldbahnen* built in great haste behind the lines to serve the trenches once the front settled down. These were huge networks, at times stretching several hundreds of miles and used, as on the Western Front, to deliver supplies and troops the last few miles between the railhead and the trenches, and also to connect the various sections of the front with long lines running broadly north-south. The lack of conventional railways in central Europe meant that the light railways were even more important than on the Western Front and tended to run over longer distances. As just one example, the Germans opened their first 60cm railway in Bulgaria in 1915 and by the end of the war there were no fewer than 200 miles of such lines, some of which remained in use long after the war and in one case until 1969.

Elsewhere, Italy, which joined the war late in May 1915, launched a series of attacks on the Austrians in the hope of gaining territory that the Italians had long claimed as theirs. The resulting battles between the Austrians and Italians largely took place in the mountains separating the two countries and consequently the Austrians built several long and heavily engineered narrow-gauge lines, together with many lighter lines and cableways, to supply their armies in the South Tyrol.

Indeed, virtually everywhere there was a front, railway lines, ranging from standard to 60cm gauge, would quickly be laid down to serve them. However, while railways may have been necessary to win a battle, they were not a panacea, and by no means guaranteed the right result. One of the railway failures of the war was the attempt by the Russians to defend St Petersburg with a series of fortresses in the Baltic linked by a network of 75cm lines. This system had been constructed on the order of the Tsar during the immediate run-up to the war because Russia's military leaders, alarmed by memories of the heavy naval defeat in the Russo-Japanese War, suddenly became aware that their capital might be vulnerable to an attack from the sea. Two networks of lines extending over 150 miles, based around Tallinn (now the capital of Estonia) were built to provide the batteries with both men and ammunition. In the event the system proved useless. The Germans did not invade by sea, but by land, and many of the guns served by the railway never fired a shot in anger. The Germans proceeded to take over the batteries and even built a few new positions, which required extending the railway network, so that by the end of the war the system consisted of more than 200 miles of track. However, it again proved militarily useless as the Russians never attacked those positions and the lines were simply abandoned to the Estonians when the Germans departed after the end of the war.

Taking over the enemy's railway lines was a common characteristic of the battles on the Eastern Front and the Germans gained control and made good use of vast swathes of railway in the areas that they occupied in central Europe. After their gains of 1915, the well-organized German railway troops became adept not only at repairing the damage that the Russians inflicted on the tracks as they retreated, which was often carried out ineffectively, but also at regauging long sections of the 5ft line used by the Russians to the standard 4ft 8½in. By May 1916, the Germans had converted almost 5,000 miles of track in what is now Poland, Belarus and Lithuania with relative ease, since it was a matter of narrowing by just 3½in rather than widening, though the work still delayed progress, especially as it was virtually impossible to carry out in freezing conditions because of the difficulty of lifting iced-up rails.

For their part, the Russians were hampered throughout the conflict with Germany by their inability to manage their railways efficiently. It took until January 1917 for the Russians to bring the administration of the railways under the control of the Ministry of Transport, and by then it was too late. According to John Westwood, "transport failure, partly due to the shortage of empty cars, led to food shortages in the cities and so to internal unrest". Indeed, the Russian Revolution was triggered off by a bread shortage in Petrograd (St Petersburg) which was a result of the mismanagement of the transport system. The collapse was stimulated partly by the arrival of Lenin from his exile in Switzerland in April 1917, in a special train which the Germans allowed through the front because they were keen to sow chaos and disorder in Russia. The train, on which smoking was not allowed, much to the discomfort of Lenin and his retinue of thirty fellow travellers, took him to Petrograd, where, immediately on his arrival, he gave a speech that sparked off the Bolshevik Revolution. Once the Bolsheviks took over the government in October 1917, they quickly sued for peace, allowing several independent states such as Ukraine, the Baltics and Poland to emerge in central and eastern Europe. The Communists were keen to pull out of the conflict because they were too busy fighting their own civil war, another conflict in which the Trans-Siberian Railway would play a major role, as did armoured trains.

Armoured trains played a very limited role in the world war. Despite the success they had enjoyed in the Boer War and their use in the defence of Port Arthur in the Russo-Japanese War, none of the major combatants had envisaged a role for armoured trains in the detailed war plans they had made in the run-up to 1914. In the west, they were barely used. In Britain, in 1914, the War Office commissioned a couple of trains, which were hastily built and kept permanently in steam, on the Norfolk coast and north of Edinburgh respectively, ready to repel the invasion which never came. How two armoured trains would make a significant difference to an all-out attack from the sea by the Germans was a puzzle which only the War Office tacticians would be able to unravel. The Belgians, too, had a couple of armoured trains that briefly saw action during the British assault on Antwerp in late September, but once the front settled down, armoured trains were not considered by the military leaders of any of the combatants fighting on the Western Front to have any value.

In the east, however, there was more interest in them from the military authorities on both sides. In 1912, the Russians had launched a programme of building armoured trains, similar to those used by the British in the Boer War, and four of them were sent to Poland in the early stages of the fighting, where they enjoyed considerable success. One of them played a decisive role in repelling a German infantry attack near Lvov, allowing the Koluszki station to be captured. Following several other successful deployments, the Austro-Hungarian Army had also built up a stock of armoured trains by 1916 and ten of these trains "served with distinction on the Russian, Romanian and Italian fronts". The Russians, too, greatly expanded their fleet, which reached a total of fifteen, including the most famous, *Zaamurets*, and these saw considerable action until the end of the conflict with the Germans.

The Russian war effort began to be undermined when the Tsar was overthrown by the provisional government of Alexander Kerensky following the revolution of February 1917. Kerensky, a social democrat, could not, however, resist the Red tide and he was, in turn, overthrown by the Communists in October 1917 after Lenin's triumphant return in his special train to Petrograd. The Communists established control over much of the west of the country in the immediate aftermath of the October Revolution thanks to the use of the railways. Select bands of armed revolutionaries spread out on the railways from their headquarters in Petrograd to make contact with the 900 soviets — revolutionary groups of local citizens —

that had sprung up in towns and cities around the country to put down anti-Communist forces opposed to the October revolution. John Keegan, in his classic work on the war, argues that "the Russian railways, during this brief but brilliant revolutionary period, worked for Lenin as the railways had not for Moltke in 1914. Decisive force had been delivered to key points in the nick of time, and a succession of local successes had been achieved that, in sum, brought revolutionary triumph." The Bolsheviks, however, failed to press through their advantage as their peace agreement signed at Brest-Litovsk in March 1918 collapsed, which stimulated counter-revolution by White Russians in Ukraine and in the east, which remained an area in turmoil for several years. It was in the latter that armoured trains really came into their own, being deployed more extensively and to better effect than in any other conflict.

This was partly a result of the nature of this war and of a terrain, which lent itself to their use. Whereas the battles on the Western Front were fought in densely populated areas where massed armies faced each other, and even on the Eastern Front armies eventually became entrenched, the Civil War took place mostly in the lightly populated areas of Russia east of Moscow. With air power still limited and few roads or cars, mobile tactics combining armoured trains and cavalry were the most suitable. The newly formed Red Army managed to take over a few of the armoured trains used by the Tsar, and then embarked on a remarkable building programme, with the number rising from twenty-three at the end of 1918 to more than a hundred two years later: "the armoured trains were by far the most complicated and expensive weapons operated by the Red Army and undoubtedly the most effective". It was quite fitting that the villain in the famous railway scenes in David Lean's *Doctor Zhivago* should be the dogged pursuer, Strelnikov, and his terrifying-looking armoured train, based on Leon Trotsky, who for a time ran the civil war from his mobile nerve centre in an armoured train.

Armoured trains were used most intensively on the Trans-Siberian, on which much of the war was fought, including a key battle between the Communists and an amazing band of Czech soldiers who had found themselves marooned at the wrong end of the line and enlisted in the White, anti-revolutionary, cause. The Czech Legion, initially around 40,000 strong but eventually reaching more than 70,000, were prisoners of the Russians and deserters from the ranks of the Austro-Hungarian Army who had found themselves stranded in Russia by the cessation of hostilities between Germany and Russia. Unable to be guaranteed safe passage through European seaports, they were despatched east on the Trans-Siberian towards Vladivostok, where it was planned for them to board ships to return to Europe. While the Legion's troops were supposed not to take part in the fluid and dangerous political situation in Russia, an incident at a railway station in Chelyabinsk, at the foot of the Urals, brought them into the conflict. A Hungarian soldier, in a train passing in the opposite direction, was lynched after a fracas started by an insulting remark, and the incident soon escalated with Trotsky, the head of the Red Army, foolishly ordering that the Czechs be disarmed. Instead, in May 1918, they rose up against the Bolsheviks, taking over the whole 5,000-mile eastern section of the line. The Czechs were strung along the line in trains heading for Vladivostok and therefore were able to take over the whole railway with relative ease, helped by using improvised armoured trains, as the Reds had little presence at that stage in eastern Russia and Siberia. The Czechs supported the hastily cobbled together regime led by Admiral Alexander Kolchak and based in Omsk in south-western Siberia, 4,500 miles west of Vladivostok.

The leading Western powers, together with Japan, saw the Czech move as an opportunity to defeat the revolution but in reality, exhausted after the First World War, they did not have the capacity to mobilize the huge armies this would have required. Instead, token forces were sent to Vladivostok, including a small British detachment under Lieutenant-General Sir Brian Horrocks. A remarkable man who later competed in the 1924 Olympics and became Black Rod in the House of Lords, Horrocks was given the task of guarding a train carrying ammunition for the White Army in Omsk in the spring of 1919. The journey took more than a month, and Horrocks, a fluent Russian-speaker, had to negotiate at virtually every station to prevent the stationmasters stealing his cargo. At one point, in Manchuli, the British officer's presence provoked a duel between two Cossack officers and Horrocks even accepted an invitation to act as a second, but the pair were arrested before the duel could take place. The British forces were ordered home shortly afterwards.

The support of the war-weary Western governments was never more than half-hearted and consequently Kolchak's White regime collapsed in November 1919, undermined by the lack of support from the Allies and its growing reputation for being as bloodthirsty as its Bolshevik enemy. (My father, Boris Kougoulsky, a Russian officer who deserted when he realized that the Communists were taking over, had personal experience of this. He fled to Odessa, where the Whites asked him to join their fight. He went to Yekaterinburg, where one of Denikin's aides showed him around, proudly pointing to the dead Bolsheviks hanging from every telegraph pole. My father thought better of signing up and thankfully fled to Paris instead.)

The armoured train proved to be the decisive weapon in the Civil War. The Whites themselves gathered together a fleet of around eighty armoured trains but the Bolsheviks proved more adept at exploiting their advantages. While the mission of the armoured trains was not to engage in set pieces against each other, this did happen on several occasions, resulting in spectacular dogfights. They were the "shock and awe" weapon of the age, as a contemporary Polish account outlined: "Armoured trains were the most serious and terrible adversaries. They are well-designed, act shockingly, desperately and decisively, have large amounts of firepower and are the most serious means of our enemies' tactics." The Bolsheviks learnt to exploit them to the full by turning them into a kind of mini-army, with infantry and cavalry sections, not unlike the British methods in the Boer War. According to the history of these behemoths, "armoured train tactics reached their maturity during this conflict".

The 165-strong infantry section was used to carry out attacks on enemy trenches or provide protection for the train when travelling through hostile territory. The infantry section was supplemented by a fifty-strong cavalry troop who acted as reconnaissance teams, and, supported by machine-gunners, ensured the track ahead had not been sabotaged. When the train was stopped, they would protect it and at times men would be sent up in balloons attached to the train to spot any nearby artillery. This combination of men and machine proved highly effective both in offensive and in defensive actions and "the Red Army officers concluded that an armoured train with such a raiding party was five times more effective than a train without one". Indeed, a train on its own was vulnerable to attack — and woe betide the poor soldiers caught in a broken-down train who were sitting ducks for the enemy and invariably summarily despatched while the train itself would simply be taken over for use against its former owners. The story of *Zaamurets* is the most remarkable of these adventures, rather like a fantasy in a *Boys' Own* annual. The train, which first saw service against the Germans in Poland in 1916, was despatched to fight the Czechs, who promptly captured it, helping them to gain control of the line. They used the train, which they renamed *Orlik*, to protect the

297

railway against Bolshevik raids and, when they finally retreated, used it to bring up the rear, at which point it was briefly captured and then released by Japanese troops. Just before Vladivostok finally fell to the Red Army in 1922, *Orlik* was taken by the White Russians to Manchuria, where it was used by the Chinese in their wars against the Japanese until its eventual capture in 1931.

Churchill had been so excited by the Czech takeover of the line that he wrote later: "The pages of history recall scarcely any parallel episode at once so romantic in character and so extensive in scale." Indeed, there is often an element of romanticism about battles fought around railways such as the legendary Andrews Raid in the American Civil War and Churchill's own adventures, and which are epitomized in T. E. Lawrence's attacks mentioned later in this chapter. The brutal reality of Kolchak's war was rather different, especially once the White counter-revolution began to collapse. As Peter Fleming, the brother of the James Bond author Ian, points out in his book on Kolchak, "by the winter of the following year [1919], romance had ceased to be a leading characteristic of the Legion's activities". The retreat of Kolchak's beaten forces along the railway, pursued by Trotsky's armoured trains, was on a par with the ghastly events on the line at the time of the Russo-Japanese War described in Chapter Six, but on a far greater scale. It was a miserable retreat undertaken at the worst possible time of the year and resulted in countless deaths from exposure and disease, particularly typhus spread by the lice in the soldiers' clothes. The

White Russian administration had made the mistake of failing to pay the workers on the Trans-Siberian for the previous three months — although they had plenty of gold and other valuables looted from the old regime, reckoned at a conservative estimate to be worth £50m at the time and which was travelling in one of Kolchak's seven trains — and the condition of the line had consequently greatly deteriorated. Kolchak and his retinue were allowed to use the line normally used for Moscow-bound trains, as the Trans-Siberian was double-tracked on this section, because nothing was heading westwards while the Reds were advancing. On the other track, a nightmarish scenario was being played out as the badly maintained trains broke down because of insufficient coal and had to wait at remote stations until stocks arrived. Their occupants suffered untold misery in the intense cold, many perishing in the stalled trains, as the locomotives were put out of commission by the plunging temperatures. The water in the engines which had run out of fuel soon froze and burst the pipes, requiring lengthy repairs. Even then, the only available source of water was snow, which would be used to refill the boiler, no easy task. Alongside the railway, there was the *Trakt*, the old road to Siberia on which a stream of bedraggled humanity, both soldiers and civilians, flowed sluggishly eastward, sometimes progressing faster than the trains held up on the slow line. No one knows how many died in this retreat but the corpses, which froze rapidly, were stripped and piled up like logs, awaiting the spring for disposal. Fleming describes eloquently how the

Trans-Siberian, this mighty railway barely twenty years old and arguably the greatest engineering achievement of the nineteenth century, had deteriorated into a "*via dolorosa*, a long narrow stage on which countless tragedies were enacted . . . in the strange and terrible scene, spread out across hundreds of miles of desolate country, there were no redeeming features . . . only the crows, perched in unusual numbers on the trees along the track, their feathers fluffed against the frost, had cause for satisfaction as they watched the trucks jolt past".

Kolchak's trains took nine days to travel the 1,500 miles to Irkutsk, but after that he was forced onto the slow line by the Czechs, with whom he had fallen out, and consequently made little progress until the Reds caught up with him. He was arrested, briefly imprisoned and summarily executed. The Whites were defeated but the Czechs got away, leaving Siberia in the hands of a semi-independent republic which later Stalin managed to incorporate fully under his control. The Trans-Siberian's second war was over.

Another long railway line stretching into barren country played a rather different role in the closing stages of the First World War. The Hejaz railway connecting Damascus with the Holy Cities of what is now western Saudi Arabia had been built by the Ottoman rulers, and financed by subscriptions from Muslims, in the early years of the twentieth century to ease the difficult journey across the desert for the huge numbers of pilgrims on the annual hajj. Although originally intended to reach as far as Makkah (Mecca, the birthplace of Mohammed), opposition from local tribes — who made an excellent living transporting the pilgrims across the last section of desert — prevented the final leg from being built. Consequently, the line ran from Haifa, on a branch line on the Mediterranean coast, to Damascus, the capital of what is now Syria, and south through the desert to Madinah (Medina), nearly 1,000 miles away. The terminus was still 300 miles short of Makkah but nevertheless made it much easier for Muslims to reach their two holiest cities. The journey to Makkah took a couple of weeks using the railway rather than the arduous five- or six-week journey by caravan.

While the religious reasons for its construction were emphasized by the Ottoman ruler, Abdulhamid II, the railway, like so many others, also had both an imperial rationale, as it was a way of cementing together the disparate elements of the crumbling Ottoman Empire, and an economic one, since there was the hope that the desert would yield up valuable minerals. It was, therefore, vital for the Turks to protect and maintain the line after the outbreak of war, which they had joined on the German side in October 1914. In 1915, the British decided to open up a second front, in the Middle East, to take pressure off the Western Front, landing at the Dardanelles to force the Germans to divert resources there. It was a disastrous failure, with delays and uncertainty allowing the Turks to reinforce their positions over the beaches, resulting in the abandonment of the attack by the end of the year. Britain was left with two armies in the Middle East, in

Palestine and Mesopotamia (in what is now Iraq). In Palestine their main role was to guard the vital Suez Canal but in Mesopotamia the war against the Turks, which was primarily about protecting oil supplies from the Gulf, had initially resulted in a humiliating defeat for the British at Kut Al Amara in April 1916. The British had over-extended themselves by trying to occupy Baghdad, running too far ahead of their largely river-based supply lines, a problem which was eventually remedied through the construction of a large network of narrow-gauge railways. Kut was retaken from the Turks early the following year and Baghdad was seized in March 1917, finally giving the initiative to the British in the Mesopotamian campaign.

By the summer of 1916, the British saw that the best way of putting extra pressure on the Ottomans would be through encouraging the Arab tribes, led by Ali, Abdullah and Feisal, three sons of Sherif Hussein, the Emir of Makkah, to rise up against Turkish rule. With tacit encouragement from the British through diplomatic channels, the Arabs started harassing the Turks in June, targeting the Hejaz railway as the focus of their attacks. Initially their efforts were crude, involving "tearing off lengths of the metals with their bare hands and tossing them down the bank". Since the Turkish army had efficient repair teams and large reserves of track, these attacks did little to hinder their war effort.

The Arabs needed explosives and better organization. Enter T. E. Lawrence. Captain — he later became a colonel — Lawrence arrived on the Arabian Peninsula in October with no official mandate but his timing proved perfect. An Arab-speaker who had travelled extensively in the Middle East, Lawrence had only managed to take time off his desk job in Cairo (Egypt was a British colony at the time) by applying for leave. He never went back to the paperclips. Instead he was sent unofficially by the British military to meet Prince Feisal in the desert, because the Arabs' attacks had petered out, and came back convinced that with supplies, especially guns and ammunition, and support the Arabs could make a significant difference to the war in the Middle East. An overt all-out attack on the Turks was ruled out by the British high command, but the idea of a war conducted cheaply and with little direct British involvement by offering support to the Arabs proved appealing. The British Army was so taken with the suggestion that it funded Lawrence to the tune of £200,000 per month, which he used to buy supplies and camels and to enlist the support of the Bedouin tribes.

Lawrence returned to Cairo and, having persuaded his superiors of the value of supporting the Arabs, rejoined Feisal's irregular army as liaison officer in December 1916 to launch a series of attacks on the Hejaz Railway. In January 1917, the British seized Wejh, a port on the Red Sea, to use as their base for attacks further inland on the Arabian peninsula. The takeover of Wejh was crucial not only in ensuring that the anti-Turkish forces could be supplied, but also in thwarting any Turkish notion of further attacks on the Egyptian side of the Red Sea, and from this point their military ambitions were limited to retaining control of the Hejaz Railway in order to keep Madinah supplied.

The first attack on the railway was actually carried out not by Lawrence but by Herbert Garland, an eccentric major (*bimbashi*) attached to the Egyptian Army, and a party of fifty tribesmen, who blew up a troop train in February at Towaira. The gang had been fortunate as the guides had taken them close to a blockhouse protecting the line but they had not been overheard as they laid their charges. Indeed, the railway was well protected by a series of blockhouses at key structures such as bridges and tunnels, and therefore the attacks were focussed on remote areas of the line. Simply blowing up the track was futile as the repair work could be effected quickly, especially as there were plenty of spare rails in Madinah that had originally been intended for the extension of the line to Makkah which was never built. As he explains in his classic *Seven Pillars of Wisdom*, Lawrence instead devised tactics that were designed to cause maximum disruption to the Turks while avoiding an all-out confrontation and he deliberately targeted trains with specially devised mines that he normally laid himself.

By the time Lawrence arrived, the Arabs had already taken over several towns in the Hejaz, including Makkah, but the Turks still held Madinah at the end of the line which could only be supplied by the railway. Lawrence ruled out the idea of trying to take the town because the Arab irregular forces were no match for the well-organized Turks in set-piece battles. Instead, the tactic was to launch a series of raids along the length of the railway, similar guerrilla methods to those employed by the Boers against the British in South Africa: "Our idea was to keep his railway just working, but only just, with the maximum of loss and discomfort . . . The surest way to limit the line without killing it was by attacking trains." Lawrence led his first raid on the railway at Abu Na'am in March and there were some thirty more attacks in the following months, most carried out by Arab forces led by Prince Abdullah and supported by forces of the Egyptian Army and a small French contingent. They were supplemented by a few bombing raids by aeroplanes on the railway, which was at the limit of their range from their base in Egypt. Lawrence's attacks took a disproportionate toll on the Turkish forces. Very few of the attackers were killed in these engagements, while the Turks usually lost dozens, if not more, each time. The attacks kept the Turks on the defensive and prevented Fakhri Pasha, the commander of the Turkish garrison at Madinah, from launching an attack to try to regain Makkah. This was vital since the fact that the Turks had lost control of the holiest of cities, after 600 years of Ottoman rule, was a great spur to the continuation of the Arab Revolt. While the railway was rarely closed for more than a day or so by the attacks, the number of trains was reduced from the peacetime level of two daily to two every week, which created food and fuel shortages in Madinah, stimulating internal dissent. About half the population fled northwards on the railway — one train of such refugees, mainly women and children, would have been

305

blown up by Lawrence but for the good fortune that his mine did not go off.

Meanwhile Lawrence turned his attention to the Port of Aqaba. His little army left Wejh in July 1917 and cleverly attacked the railway on several occasions as he headed north to fool the Turks into thinking that was the purpose of his mission. The Turks expected that any attack on Aqaba would come from the sea. Instead, Lawrence and Feisal, with a force of 2,000 men, mostly on camels, for once took on a static army head on but triumphed easily thanks to the element of surprise and the lack of proper defences in what was then a small fishing village. The Turks put up little resistance and the bloody side of this desert war was exposed by the subsequent massacre of more than 300 Turkish soldiers by the vengeful Arabs, the kind of incident which, as Lawrence relates in his book, was repeated several times during this campaign. There were virtually no casualties on the Arab side, though Lawrence nearly killed himself by accidentally shooting his own camel in the head and being thrown off at full speed, but suffered only cuts and bruises.

Now the focus of the revolt turned north, with the idea of chasing the Turks out of what is now Jordan, Syria and Lebanon. The capture of Aqaba helped protect the British right flank in Palestine, where a different type of war was taking place, one which involved building a railway rather than destroying it. Having initially only sought to defend the Suez Canal, the British, led by Lawrence's hero, General Edmund Allenby, decided to go on the offensive across the Sinai towards Palestine but they needed a railway to supply them, just as Kitchener's army had when reconquering Sudan. The aim was to push through from Egypt to Palestine, and chase the Turks out of Gaza, and then Jerusalem, with the ultimate goal of Damascus. The railway was started at Kantara, on the eastern bank of the Suez Canal, and was gradually extended eastwards during 1916 and the early part of 1917. It made slow but steady progress, reaching the front at Gaza, 125 miles from its terminus, where the Turks were entrenched, supplied by their own railhead at Beersheba and later a specially built branch just out of range of the British guns. It would take Allenby three attempts to dislodge the Turks from Gaza, but when he finally did, and marched on to capture Jerusalem at the end of 1917, it was celebrated as one of the few genuine victories by British forces in the war.

Lawrence had used Aqaba as a base for repeated attacks on the Hejaz railway until the winter, when there was a lull in the fighting. Allenby's progress towards Damascus was delayed, too, as two of his divisions (around 25,000 men) were redeployed to the Western Front. In the spring, when the drive to Damascus finally began, the policy towards the railway changed. It was imperative to cut off the line up from the Hejaz so that the Turks could not use it to bring reinforcements from Madinah against Allenby's forces. Consequently, Lawrence's group attacked the railway in various places, having developed a more sophisticated type of mine inappropriately called "tulip". This was a much smaller charge, a mere 2lb of dynamite compared with the 40lb or 50lb ones used previously, and involved placing the charge underneath the sleepers, which would blow the metal upwards "into a tulip-like shape without breaking; by doing so it distorted the two rails to which its ends were attached", which was impossible to repair and consequently forced the Turks to replace the whole section of track. In early April 1918, the last train between Madinah and Damascus made it through but after that the line was blocked by successive attacks which left more Turkish troops stuck in the Hejaz protecting a line that was now of no strategic use than were facing Allenby in Palestine. In the decisive attack at Tel Shahm, led by General Dawnay, Lawrence showed his regard for the railway by claiming the station bell, a fine piece of Damascus brass work: "the next man took the ticket punch and the third the office stamp, while the bewildered Turks stared at us, with a growing indignation that their importance should be merely secondary". The Turks had clearly never met any British trainspotters with their obsession for railway memorabilia.

Attacks against the northern part of the railway continued, and the line was cut off in several other places, either by Lawrence or the British forces coming from Palestine. The attacks on the Hejaz railway had been an exemplary case history of guerrilla warfare. It was not all about Lawrence, as he readily admits in the *Seven Pillars*, but without his ability to stimulate the Arab revolt, General Allenby's task in sweeping through Palestine would undoubtedly have been harder. Although in the later stages some armoured vehicles and even air support became available, the basic tactics remained the same throughout: "The campaign remained dependent on the speed and mobility of the irregular Bedouin forces, and on the inability of the better trained, well-equipped Turkish troops to follow the raiding parties into the desert . . . As Glubb Pasha (of later Trans-Jordanian Arab League fame) remarked: 'the whole Arab campaign provides a remarkable illustration of the extraordinary results which can be achieved by mobile guerrilla tactics. For the Arabs detained tens of thousands of regular Turkish troops with a force scarcely capable of engaging a brigade of infantry in pitched battle'."

The Turks, too, were equally courageous and in their stubborn defence of the line there is another side to the more famous Lawrence story, which is the difficulty of putting a railway permanently out of action. There was no shortage of difficulties for railway operations. Fuel was a constant worry and by the end of the war the houses in Madinah had been stripped of all timber and even the city gates and wooden sleepers from the track had been removed to keep the locomotives running, which required constant improvisation in the face of the constant attacks. While even today a few wrecked locomotives can still be seen in the desert, for the most part the Turks rescued damaged engines and repaired them in their works yards. The historian of the lines, James Nicholson, remarks that the foot soldiers were genuinely heroic: "Confined to their stations and a narrow strip of land, they were cast adrift in a vast and hostile country, far from the main centres of command." They were dependent on the railway for all their needs and therefore by 1918 "many were close to starvation, clothed in rags and ravaged by scurvy". And yet, despite that, they managed to keep the railway operating until nearly the end of the war.

It was fitting that the Arab irregular forces under Feisal and Lawrence should join up with Allenby for the final assault on Damascus. The task for Prince Feisal's army, which included Lawrence and several other British liaison officers, inevitably centred around the railway. He was asked to cut off the vital junction town of Deraa to prevent Turkish reinforcements coming up from Amman, a task that Lawrence, now in an armoured car rather than on a camel, and his explosives expert, Major Peake, achieved with the loss of only one Arab fighter on 17 September, two days before the launch of Allenby's final offensive. The Turks, desperate to bring up reinforcements from the south, took ten days to repair the line, but then Lawrence blew up a two-mile section of track, using his cunning tulip-mines, and the Arab forces followed up his attack by capturing a train and the station at Ghazala. This was Lawrence's final railway attack and he reached Damascus a few days later, where the fleeing Turks had blown up the railway which they had constructed with such pride barely a decade before, burning down Damascus Qadem station. Allenby's forces had marched along a series of railway lines in order to move quickly across Palestine and he had made heavy use of his cavalry, which at one stage outflanked the Turks with a charge consisting of both horses and camels. The railway he had built as a supply route from Egypt eventually stretched more than 250 miles from the Suez Canal across the Sinai and along the coast through Palestine to the port of Haifa, and after the war a bridge over the canal connected the line with Egyptian railways. For a time, the line even boasted a couple of bizarre petrol-driven armoured trains. These were deployed on patrols whose personnel were issued with a strange set of orders, including: "no one except officers and Royal Engineers are allowed on the roof of the train when it is moving" and "men sleeping under the train [presumably to keep cool at night] and standing on the buffers when the train is in motion, or displaying culpable ignorance of the other dangers of a railway, will have no claim on the government for compensation". Clearly, these trains were not being operated by experienced railway personnel.

The seizure of Damascus has an almost legendary status among military historians as a tactical masterpiece by Allenby because of the speed with which the Allied forces overwhelmed the well-entrenched Turkish defences. Prince Feisal was allowed to take control of the town, overturning the centuries-long Ottoman rule, and become King of Syria, while Lawrence, after organizing the clean-up of the hospital where the dying and sick had been left without food for several days, returned to Britain. Oddly, in what was arguably the last remaining combat in the First World War, the Fakhri Pasha, the commander of the Madinah garrison, refused to surrender to the Egyptian Army and held out until 10 January 1919, when his officers mutinied and handed him over to the British. It marked the end of the Ottoman Empire, with the result that the lands through which the railway ran were formed into three new states: Syria, a French-mandated territory, Trans-Jordan, a British-mandated territory with Abdullah as Emir, and Saudi Arabia. The Hejaz was an imperial railway that, ironically, contributed to the destruction of the empire which had created it. However, while the Ottoman Empire was no more, the Arabs did not obtain the promised independence for which they had fought. Lawrence had only been able to attract support among the desert tribes because he told them that the British had informed him that the Arabs would obtain the freedom to rule their own land. In fact, Lawrence's superiors were lying and he was betrayed. A carve-up between the British and the French, enshrined in an agreement signed secretly back in 1916, had created a series of dependencies with Britain given responsibility for Jordan, Palestine and Iraq, while Syria and Lebanon went to the French. It was a shabby deal that sowed the seeds for today's conflicts in the Middle East.

The Lawrence episode demonstrates the extent to which what had started as a European conflict in 1914 gradually developed into a genuine world war. There were numerous theatres of the war which have attracted far less attention than the Western Front, and in virtually every one of these the railways played a significant part. Light railways, in particular, were found to be almost universally useful. The most substantial example was on the Macedonian front after

Allied troops landed in Salonika in November 1915. Originally the Allies had promised to provide protection for Serbia but this proved impossible because of the lack of available forces and the Germans invaded the country. The Allies subsequently sent a substantial force to try to reclaim Serbia but the offensive soon became bogged down in the winter conditions and the difficult terrain, which was rocky and largely impassable for motor vehicles, leaving mules as the mainstay of the line of communication. In the spring of 1916, some progress was made but the campaign had settled down to a Western Front-type stalemate by the summer and remained stable for the next two years. Given the lack of roads, a huge network of 60cm railways was built, with lines that were far longer than its equivalent on the Western Front. Most served the front lines by running through the hills from a railhead and the longest, stretching fifty-five miles from Thessaloniki to the battle zone, was built in great haste by a force of 4,000 Turkish prisoners just in time for the final assault against the Central Powers in September 1918. Unlike the light railways on the Western Front, the line was operated as a conventional railway with a signalling system, proper stations and copious sidings.

This was part of the process of innovation that had been stimulated by the First World War, the apogee of the use of railways in warfare. They were not only the principal means of long-distance transport, and with the development of networks of 60cm railways ubiquitous, but the war stimulated the use of rail for all

313

kinds of purposes, ranging from carrying huge guns to ambulance trains. Nevertheless, the key problem with railways was that, obviously, they could only go where there were tracks and while the far more flexible 60cm railways could be laid down in great haste, they could not carry the huge artillery. The military love big guns and it was always something of an ambition to fit them to a railway in order to make them mobile. Before the 1914 war, there had been limited use of this type of artillery, notably by the French when trying to regain control of the capital during the Paris Commune, and early in the war it was again the French who tried hardest to exploit the potential of the combination of trains and artillery by mounting huge 320mm guns on rails. The guns had a range of seventeen miles but, like other such massive guns mounted on rails, the barrel could only be elevated and not moved sideways, and thus the whole weapon had to be on a curved section of rail track to enable it to be aimed with precision, greatly limiting its potential. Towards the end of the war, the Germans devised a far bigger gun with the aim of creating panic in Paris. The Paris Gun, the *Kaiser Wilhelm Geschütz*, had a 34-metre-long barrel based on naval technology and was rail-mounted on a special carriage, which was shunted into a special turntable from which the gun was fired. Operated by navy personnel from a forest seventy-five miles from Paris, it was first used in March 1918 and over the next few months fired around 350 shells, killing 256 people — eighty-eight of whom were in a church congregation on Good Friday — and causing many Parisians to flee the city. Its shells were the first man-made objects to reach the stratosphere, but despite the panic they caused the gun was not a great success as it required constant maintenance, limiting its daily capacity to just twenty shells, which had a relatively small payload of explosives. Mystery surrounds the precise details of the gun because the Germans took it with them when they retreated and destroyed it, leaving no working drawings behind. On the Eastern Front, two 380mm rail-mounted guns were built by Skoda in 1916 and used by the Germans. Again, they enjoyed little success and one was captured by Romanian forces (and can now be found in the Military Museum in Bucharest). As we shall see in the next chapter, it was Hitler who would have the biggest ambition for such guns.

Another universal use of available railways during the First World War was to transport the wounded. As with many aspects of the military use of the railways, the lessons on the provision of ambulance trains had to be relearnt, despite the experience and progress made in previous wars. Despite the fact that ambulance trains had been widely used in the American Civil War and had become quite sophisticated, with treatment facilities available on the trains, in the subsequent conflicts in Europe it was mostly back to dumping wounded soldiers on straw-strewn bare boards in covered freight wagons. Public opinion critical of the lax treatment of the wounded in the Austro-Prussian War had prompted the Prussians to create a commission to examine the best way of transporting the wounded. As a result, they developed a somewhat improved version by adapting fourth-class coaches — which were easy to convert as they had no seats — as vestibuled trains, allowing medical teams to move around the train, and no fewer than twenty-one saw service during the war. They were still pretty crude affairs with patients dumped on the floor on straw palliasses as unaccountably the military authorities eschewed the more sophisticated suspended-stretcher system developed by the Americans in the Civil War. Nearly 90,000 Prussian wounded were transported in these trains during the Franco-Prussian War, with many remaining in these carriages for several days as the trains were not given the priority which the suffering of their passengers merited.

Towards the end of the century, there was much discussion about the best way of installing beds in the trains. The Americans favoured rubber loops into which the stretcher handles could be inserted while the Germans chose a hammock-like system and the Russians developed a method by which the stretchers were suspended on springs. Both the latter had their disadvantages, as the hammocks occasionally swung hard into the sides while the poor Russian wounded found themselves inadvertently trampolining. The Boer and Russo-Japanese wars had attracted much public interest in ambulance trains, as nursing the war wounded became a suitable occupation for titled, even royal, ladies. The Boer War saw the deployment of the well-fitted Princess Christian hospital train provided by the Red Cross and named after Queen Victoria's third daughter.

Given all this experience, it was quite extraordinary that none of the major combatants entered the First World War with a worked-out plan to cope with the wounded, despite all having intricate programmes to get the troops there in the first place. It was, yet again, an illustration of the military obsession with offence. Even the Germans, with their history of several conflicts during the railway age, and their reputation for being thorough and methodical, were woefully remiss, as an article in a medical magazine reported at the time on the transport of the wounded: "In the early part of November 1914 soldiers who had lain for days in trenches half full of water, and who had been exposed also to night frosts, were dispatched on long rail journeys in dirty trucks, as many as thirty men, probably suffering from dysentery, lying in each truck on a little straw, packed like sardines, without attention or protection from the cold." According to the author J. A. B. Hamilton, who fought in the war, "it is a strange fact that throughout the war Germans never quite caught up with their ambulance train needs".

The British started just as badly. There had been some thought devoted to the issue, but no action. As far back as 1905 there had been suggestions in the War Railway Council, the precursor of the Railway Executive Committee which ran the British railways during the conflict, that the major railway companies should provide ambulance trains to the military but an argument over costs resulted in the scheme being shelved. Therefore, bizarrely, when war broke out there were six ambulance train detachments of forty-five men

317

headed by two officers, but no trains for them. They went to France and after some delay the French provided a hundred goods wagons and a few passenger coaches which were made up into basic ambulance trains. The wagons were disinfected, and stretcher cases were laid on clean straw, but the provision fell far short even of the trains that had been provided in previous wars. A nurse, Sister Phillips, described the difficulties caused by the lack of connection between the wagons: "Climbing from coach to coach by way of the footboard was a practice absolutely forbidden . . . Frequently this means of passing from one coach to another was an absolute necessity in the interests of the patients. No doubt a French stationmaster in a little out of the way French village will probably remember to this day the sight that met his amazed gaze in the early hours of a beautiful September morning in 1914. An ambulance train was flying through his station with an English sister clinging like a limpet to the side of the train." This was muddling through at its British best (or worst), but gradually a fleet of ambulance trains was assembled by the French and British for the Western Front. The French gradually improved the trains in a haphazard way, with the medical staff commandeering suitable stock such as restaurant cars wherever they happened to see it, and adapting it to their purposes. Their endeavours resulted in a ramshackle series of trains, with coaches from different companies, with incompatible braking and lighting systems, and frequently supplied with whatever drugs and bandages could be bought from chemists en route. Not all coaches were suitable. The *wagons-lits* normally used on the *Orient Express* and originally hired at great expense to provide accommodation for officers, proved troublesome to repair and were soon discarded.

In October, the first British ambulance train was sent to France and the fleet eventually built up to thirty, some of which were paid for by the British Red Cross Society. Further trains were provided in other theatres of the war, such as Egypt and Salonika. Early trains could carry only up to 300 stretcher cases, but later versions were able to accommodate a total of 1,000, most of them lying down, and the best were the well-furnished Princess Christian trains. J. A. B. Hamilton recalls that the ambulance trains were comfortable, having travelled on one from Lille to Boulogne, but he could not have been seriously injured as, true trainspotter that he was, he spent the night "in an agony of speculation as to what sort of locomotive might be hauling us". He was able to find out in the morning by craning his neck out of his bunk when the huge train had stalled near Boulogne.

After the initial failure to make any provision, the number and placement of ambulance trains exercised the military authorities in some detail before every battle and undoubtedly the efficiency of the service improved. Hamilton recalls that at times the handling of the wounded did show the required urgency: "On the opening day of the Messines Ridge battle on June 7, 1917 . . . the mines [signalling the beginning of the assault] went off just before dawn, and at 2.15 on the same day the first wounded were arriving at Charing

Cross", presumably having made use of the boat train service that was by then in operation. They were luckier than the first arrivals from the battle of Antwerp in 1914, who, because of concern about spies, had been sent along the coast to Southampton as Dover was a military port.

Overall, more than 2.6 million British troops were transported in ambulance trains throughout the conflict. Once across the Channel, the wounded were carried in a separate fleet of twenty-seven trains that had quickly been provided by the train companies at the behest of the War Office, which had devised detailed plans before the war while failing to actually commission any trains. The first were ready within a few weeks of the outbreak of the war to greet the wounded off the boats at Dover and Southampton, further adding to the considerable loads on the domestic railways.

Indeed, the railways in Britain, which as mentioned previously were taken under the control of the Railway Executive Committee at the outbreak of war, were hugely overburdened throughout the conflict. After successfully transporting the British Expeditionary Force down to Southampton with commendable efficiency, the newly unified railways were faced with the awesome task of both catering for normal traffic and handling the massive military requirements. For the most part, the railways in Britain coped very well with the extra demands placed on them by the war. The load fell disproportionately on a few railways such as the London & South Western, which served Southampton and catered for no fewer than 20 million journeys by soldiers during the war, an average of 13,000 per day, and oddly, at the other end of the country, the Highland Railway, which served Cromarty Firth and Scapa Flow, two of the three main navy bases. All the supplies for the ships had to be carried on the railway, a single-track line that meanders through the Highlands, as well as, later in the war, the thousands of mines for the Northern Barrage, which stretched from the Orkneys to the coast of Norway and was designed to protect the British coastline from attack.

At first the railways were very keen to maintain a "business as usual" image to the public, which rather reflected the initial public mood since the war was on the other side of the Channel and those not directly affected continued as before. The railways boasted that they were providing "facilities as good as in June or in early July" and traffic to the Continent carried on as near normally as conditions would allow. Amazingly, the Great Eastern Railway managed to maintain its Harwich-Hook of Holland service throughout the war. The London, Brighton & South Coast continued to issue tickets to all kinds of European destinations in Italy, Switzerland and Spain via Newhaven-Dieppe. There were clearly not that many takers as the Brighton line enjoyed a boom in first-class travellers who might normally have gone to the Côte d'Azur for their holidays but now had to make do with the south coast. After initially cutting back services in response to fears about overcrowding on the lines by military traffic, many were soon restored and the companies even

321

resumed advertising and provided extra trains at Christmas as usual. There were just a few hints of the privations to come: the London & North Western cancelled the typewriting compartments it had installed on some of its London-Birmingham expresses and laid off the secretaries who provided the service. Wild rumours abounded. When a Liverpool-London express suffered a seventeen-hour delay at the end of August, a rumour swept through the country that the hold-up was due to the transport of Russian soldiers who had arrived in Scotland to help in the war effort. It was pure bunkum, but for several months thereafter anyone whose train was held up attributed the delay to the arrival of the Russians, which must have pleased the train companies, who would undoubtedly be delighted to have such an excuse today.

Priority was given to military traffic and the ability of the rail companies to maintain existing levels of passenger service merely demonstrated that there was considerable spare capacity in the railway network thanks to the fact that the British railways system, unlike its counterparts on the Continent, had been built with no central direction from the state but rather through the haphazard process of competition by the private companies. Therefore, the system had far more duplication than elsewhere, which inadvertently ensured that the network could cope with the extra demands placed on it during the war. Indeed, obscure railways which before the war had been financial basket cases suddenly found themselves overburdened with trains. One such was the Stratford-on-Avon & Midland

Junction, built primarily to carry ironstone but now becoming a useful route for mineral traffic between South Wales and the Midlands. Even the London Underground proved to be vital to the war effort as its City-widened lines, which connect King's Cross with stations south of the Thames, proved invaluable for war traffic going through the capital.

Gradually, though, the service deteriorated and cuts were made. The urgent demand at the end of 1916 for locomotives and rolling stock to be transferred abroad, together with a growing coal shortage, forced the British government to damp down the demand for civilian rail travel and consequently on 1 January 1917 sweeping cuts combined with fare rises of 50 per cent were introduced. Many dining cars were withdrawn, although sleeping cars were largely retained on the slightly dubious argument that government officials travelling on them needed a good night's sleep. The public felt that these carriages were largely provided for the well-off. Many services were curtailed or cancelled, others slowed down to save coal and more than 400 stations and 200 miles of branch lines closed, their tracks ripped up for transfer to France. Yet the passengers still kept coming as soldiers on leave spent precious days at the seaside or well-paid munitions workers enjoyed their new-found wealth. It might not have been comfortable — as Westwood put it, "government spokesmen talked of 'joy riders' and the need to eliminate them [but] by the end of the war there was little joy in riding the trains" — but everyone still wanted to use the railways.

Not only had the creature comforts been taken away, and blinds put up to avoid trains being spotted from the air — which passengers tended to lift irrespective of the injunctions not to — but there was the danger from air raids first by Zeppelin airships and later by aircraft. Initially all trains had to stop during a raid, but the authorities realized this was counter-productive. There were just over a hundred raids on Britain in the whole war, and while damage to railway property was widespread, it was superficial and only twenty-four railway workers were killed by bombs. The most exciting confrontation was an incident involving an attack by an airship in Suffolk, described by a local newspaper reporter as "a mad neck-to-neck race between the airship and a Great Eastern train. As the train dashed along at top speed, the Zeppelin dropped five bombs at the rushing train below. All the missiles fell wide of the mark and the train steamed into Bury St Edmunds unscathed." The pilot then apparently waved, admitting defeat. Much of the damage to the railways was quickly repaired, demonstrating, as we shall see in the next two chapters, how difficult it is for aircraft to put a line out of commission for any length of time.

It was the railways' own incompetence which at times proved far more damaging to their efficiency than bombing raids. This was particularly true of the freight service, which was frequently overstretched because of that old problem of empty wagons not being returned promptly. Whole lines became clogged up as sidings filled with wagons — sometimes for up to two years —

that were being kept "just in case" or with excess supplies ordered by companies worried that they might run out of vital materials, only to find there was nowhere to unload them. Government departments were the worst culprits, commandeering whole wagons to transport a single small box and trains to travel ridiculously small distances — a few hundred yards in one case — when a horse and cart, let alone a lorry, would have done the job far quicker. There were tales of tarpaulins and ropes, vital to protect goods in open wagons, going missing in huge quantities.

However, the worst aspect of the railways' performance was the decline in safety. The stress that the railways were put under inevitably led to an increase in collisions and accidents, and it was not happenstance that the worst disasters in the history of both the British and French railways, Quintinshill and Saint-Michel-de-Maurienne, involved troop trains in the First World War, and there was a third similar accident, also involving a troop train in Romania, which was probably the worst ever in European history.

The Romanian accident remains shrouded in mystery as not only did it occur during the war, when such incidents are routinely kept quiet, but it also happened in the remote eastern part of the country on what is now the border with Belarus and consequently precise details have never been ascertained. Nevertheless, from subsequent reports which have emerged there is little doubt that it was the deadliest accident in Europe and one of the worst in the history of the railways across the world. The Romanians had made

325

the mistake of entering the war belatedly on the Allied side in August 1916 in the light of Russian successes in Galicia and had hoped to keep the Central Powers out of their territory but, overwhelmed by superior forces, had instead soon found themselves retreating from the Germans' advance. Indeed, the speed of the German victory was the result of their intelligent exploitation of the available railway lines, as they moved troops swiftly by rail along the front to deliver a surprise attack on the foolhardy Romanians in what was later recognized as a logistical masterpiece.

Consequently, huge numbers of Russian soldiers and Romanian civilians fled the German onslaught providing the backdrop to the disaster. On 13 January 1917, a massive train with twenty-six carriages crowded with wounded Russian soldiers as well as civilians escaping from newly invaded parts of the country left the small station of Barnova towards the next stop at Ciurea, which was down a steep incline of 1 in 40. Soon after the start of the descent, it became apparent that the brakes were not working properly, probably because, unbeknown to the train crew, the connecting pipes between the carriages had been broken by passengers stepping on them. Without any help from the brakes on the coaches, the braking power of the two locomotives was not sufficient to prevent the train hurtling ever faster down the slope. Despite the efforts of the train crew, who put the locomotives in reverse and tried to sand the track to get a better grip, the coaches were derailed as they entered the station at Ciurea and inevitably burst into flames, causing carnage. Remarkably, one of the survivors, Nicolae Dunanreanu, wrote an account of the disaster and described how, as the train was speeding down the hill, "everywhere people and particularly soldiers, clambered on to the roofs, steps and buffers gripping each other in mad desperation. There was not even the smallest corner free, one could not even get both feet on a step nor a buffer and these desperate people seeking a relative or fleeing from the enemy who occupied more than half the country could not guess that a greater disaster soon awaited them." The ultimate death toll was thought to have exceeded 1,000, more than any other accident in the history of the railways in Europe, but no precise figure was ever issued by the authorities. Dunanreanu wrote only of seeing countless corpses on the day after the accident.

The French accident at Saint-Michel-de-Maurienne was also caused by a runaway train and remains by far the deadliest in western Europe to this day. It was the callousness and incompetence of the military, rather than any error or misjudgement by railwaymen, that caused the tragedy. There was an uncanny similarity with events in Ciurea, as the accident resulted from an overcrowded train descending a steep incline without sufficient braking power. A long train of nineteen carriages was heading over the Alps on the night of 12 December 1917 with more than 900 French soldiers who had fought with the Italians and were now anxious to get home for two weeks' leave over the Christmas period. Having come through the Mont Cenis tunnel, the train waited at Modane, preparing to descend into the valley below. It was held up for more than an hour to let through other trains, but before it set out there was a dispute over its progress. The train only had one locomotive, whereas normally there should have been two for such a heavy load, and to compound the problem only three of the carriages had air brakes while the rest had none or only hand-operated ones. The driver, Girard, told the stationmaster that he could not proceed without a second locomotive, but the only one available had been allocated to an ammunition train, and there was enormous pressure from the troops to get going. There was a demob-happy atmosphere in the station, made rowdier by the absence of the officers, who had departed on a faster train heading for Paris. Girard's protest was referred to the local traffic officer, a Capitaine Fayolle, who ordered the driver to proceed, threatening that he would be thrown in the *"forteresse"* if he refused. It was a classic case of the military trying to run the railway over the heads of the professionals and it was to have deadly consequences. Girard acquiesced reluctantly and the train departed for Saint-Michel-de-Maurienne, which is 1,000 feet lower, down an incline of 1 in 30, very steep for a railway. And far too steep for such a heavy train with just one locomotive's brakes to control it. The train began to gather speed uncontrollably and the brakes started overheating, becoming ineffective and igniting fires. Aboard, there was panic, with the lights going out and some soldiers even jumping onto the tracks, judging this was the best chance of survival. At a bend approaching the station on a bridge with a 25 mph speed limit, the train was hurtling down at three times that speed and the inevitable happened as the carriages were thrown off the bridge and plunged into the gorge below, with several bursting into flames. Relieved of its heavy load, the locomotive stayed on the tracks.

To be fair to Fayolle, it was not entirely his fault. The *poilus*, well tanked-up after hanging round for an hour in the bars at Modane while the other trains were being let through, were in no mood to wait and were unconcerned about such trivia as brakes and overcrowding. Every minute of their Christmas leave was precious and they were desperate to get back to their families and girlfriends. In the immediate aftermath of the disaster, 424 bodies were found, but the best estimate of the final death toll is 675, as many of the dead were incinerated in the ensuing fire, which took a day to burn out, and numerous survivors died from their wounds in distant hospitals.

Apart from the high death tolls, the accidents in France and Romania have other similarities. In both cases, the subsequent fire resulted in the number of casualties remaining unknown and both were kept secret by the respective authorities until after the conflict because of the supposed propaganda advantage it would have given the enemy. A more credible explanation is that neither government wanted the incompetence that led to these disasters to be exposed.

While the blame for Quintinshill, which was actually the earliest of these three accidents, can be firmly laid at the door of two signalmen whose sloppy practices were the immediate cause, it too was the result of the extraordinary strain on the rail network during the war. The section of the Caledonian Railway between Carlisle and Glasgow where the accident occurred was one of the busiest on the whole network, taking the majority of the huge amount of traffic between England and Scotland. The accident, near a small signal box at Quintinshill, in the vicinity of Gretna Junction, involved a triple collision on the morning of 22 May 1915. Because the two regular sleeper trains from London were late, as often happened, and the sidings on both sides were full with trains which had less priority than the expresses, a local train was directed to wait on the southbound track main line to let the overnights through. That in itself was not unusual but the signalmen then made a terrible mistake. They forgot that the local train was there, even though it was virtually in front of their window, and one of them had even just travelled to the signal box on it. Fatally, the signalman allowed through a troop train carrying 485 soldiers of the Royal Scots on their way from Scotland to Gallipoli in Turkey and it smashed into the local at 70 mph with such force that the carriages were telescoped into a third of their original length. The gas-lit carriages promptly burst into flames and, worse, one of the overnight sleepers smashed into the wreckage a minute later. The official death toll was 227 but this may be an underestimate as many bodies were burned beyond all recognition. The subsequent inquiry revealed not only an overworked signal box, but procedures that were lax in the extreme, with the two signalmen having a private arrangement about the timing of their changeover and sitting in the box chatting to the crew of the local when the fateful decision to allow through the troop train was made.

For the most part, though, the railways in Britain performed heroically throughout the conflict, but in America, the other country heavily involved in the war but on whose territory no battles were fought, their performance was patchier and did not improve until they were brought under government control. The American railroad companies were in a poor state at the outbreak of the war, beset on one side by strong trade unions demanding increased pay and reduced hours, and on the other by a government which, aware of the companies' unpopularity and strong monopoly position, was reluctant to allow them to increase their freight rates or fares. By the time the USA declared war on Germany in April 1917, the railroads had already seen an increase in traffic thanks to preparations for the conflict, but they were nevertheless in a parlous state, with many major companies in receivership or making heavy losses. The railroads were still the only effective form of long-distance travel, for both passengers and freight, and therefore it was essential that they worked efficiently once American troops and matériel were being despatched across the Atlantic. Initially, the railroads struggled. Not only did the government refuse to increase freight rates, but the failure of the railroad companies to co-operate with one another led to a vast waste of resources. Most notably, since there was no pooling arrangement of rolling stock, there were numerous trains pulling empty wagons which could have been used to transport other companies' freight.

The presidents of nearly 700 railroad companies eventually tried to co-ordinate their services by signing an agreement to operate like a unified "continental rail system". This proved impossible because of anti-trust legislation which prevented them working together too closely and the companies' readiness to exploit any competitive advantage gained as a result of this supposed co-operation. Their difficulties were compounded by the fact that all war freight was needed at a small number of eastern seaports, which were overflowing with wagons that could not be unloaded, partly as a result of the loss of shipping to attacks from German submarines. The efficiency of the whole network, measured in terms of wagon mileage per day, reduced by 20 per cent and was made worse by a misguided attempt to prioritize government freight which backfired badly. Thousands of government agents were despatched around the country with bundles of preference tags to give cars a right of way, but they were handed out so indiscriminately that 85 per cent of the wagons belonging to one company, Penn Central, were tagged. An analysis of the role of US railroads in the First World War recognized that the lessons of the American Civil War about the management of rail traffic had been "forgotten" and concluded: "This was not a breakdown in rail transport, but the result of abuse and mishandling of rail transport." By Christmas 1917, the situation had reached a crisis point, forcing the government to step in and assume control of the railroads. Many railroad bosses were replaced by federal appointees and decisions over the operation of trains were made by the National Railroad Administration. Rolling stock was pooled and priority given to wartime traffic. It worked, with distinct improvements to passenger as well as freight services, and both troops and matériel arrived in Europe on time. Nevertheless, in the land of free enterprise, and raw capitalism, it was a source of great shame for the railroad companies that it had taken nationalization to sort out their problems and, as we shall see in the next chapter, in the Second World War they were determined that they would not suffer the same humiliation.

On the other side of the Atlantic, as we saw in the previous chapter, the arrival of the Americans placed extra strain on the French railways. Their arrival prompted the final decisive stage of the war. The Germans were anxious that America's entry into the war would tip the balance of power in the Allies' favour. They called on fifty divisions (600,000 men) from the Eastern Front, who were now available thanks to Russia's collapse, and launched what was supposed to be a final offensive on 21 March 1918 against a British-held section of the front with the immediate target of capturing the key railway town of Amiens and with the ultimate goal of pushing the British back to the Channel. On the first day of the attack, the Germans, using stormtrooper tactics for the first time on the Western Front after their successful use in the east at the battle of Riga in September 1917, managed to advance up to twenty miles, helped by the early-morning fog which allowed them to go past the British machine guns unnoticed. However, the Germans did not get to Amiens as their attack petered out, at the cost of tens of thousands of their crack troops. They were hampered by advancing too far beyond their supply lines and by the difficulty of the terrain they were crossing, a morass of shell holes and mud. By this stage of the war, the Germans were also critically short of horses and had failed to mechanize their transport at anything like the rate of the Allies. Artillery, a vital component of the stormtrooper tactics, could not easily be moved forward and anything but the lightest loads proved too cumbersome for the pock-marked terrain. As John Keegan suggests, "the Somme may not have won the war for the British in 1916 but the obstacle zone it left helped to ensure that in 1918 they did not lose it". The German spring offensive may have failed in its objectives but it did break the long stalemate on the Western Front. However, while the war was no longer static, it could hardly be described as one of great movement either since the conditions were too difficult and the lines of communication too tenuous. According to A. J. P. Taylor, "the impetus of the German advance gradually ran down. Allied reserves arrived faster by train than the attacking infantry could move on foot." The Germans had run out of reserves to exploit their initial success and their manpower was severely depleted, notably by the influenza epidemic which had started to take a heavy toll on the battle-worn troops.

The British lost huge amounts of artillery and had to destroy or abandon 300 light-railway tractors and locomotives as their positions were overrun. It was ironic that once the need for the light railways had been accepted wholeheartedly by the government and military and massive resources were being devoted to them, the nature of the war changed. Nevertheless, in the southern section invaded by the Germans, where the entire line was lost, a whole new system of light railways was built up between May and July, demonstrating they were still considered a vital part of the supply line. The Germans launched four more attacks, each increasingly more desperate, culminating in the second battle of the Marne in July, whose failure finally passed the initiative to the Allies.

Although the Germans failed and the Allies realized this was their enemies' last throw of the dice, these attacks placed an enormous burden on Allied resources, which were also very much depleted. In particular, the French railway network was on its last legs. Not only had it to cope with the extra demands placed on it by the arriving US troops and their matériel, but "the permanent way, the locomotives and rolling stock were wearing out, the skilled railway personnel insufficient and tired, and the stocks of essential materials dangerously low".

The foundering of the German attack gave the Allies a couple of months to improve their railways, creating supply lines with yet more light railways, and repairing crucial parts of the standard-gauge network. They were waiting, too, for the American forces to build up and finally, in August, with the help of 1.3 million American troops, the Allies launched the hundred-day offensive, that would end the war. The first attack was early in the month at the battle of Amiens, where tanks proved to be the decisive factor in the victory.

It was not easy. Moving these huge armies with little effective transport posed insuperable problems and any rapid advance risked breaking the line of communication with the crucial railhead. The Allies' own supply lines were taxed to the maximum by their advance. The *gares régulatrices* system broke down as the huge demands placed on these stations was simply too much. Instead of all the goods and personnel being transferred at one station, other nearby stations were called into use with, for example, one being used for artillery, another for animals destined for slaughter, and a third for hospital and ambulance services.

Just as the Germans had found when they advanced, progress into country where roads and rail had been destroyed was slow. While the military planners had envisaged that light railways would play little part during the advance, in fact several of the advancing armies made heavy use of them and constructed new ones as they moved forward. Moreover, lengthy sections of 60cm railways abandoned by the Germans were taken over by the Allies.

There were, though, great difficulties in keeping the lines of communication open as the advance into previously held German territory progressed. While in previous offensives there had been several railheads to feed into the advance, now they tended to be lined up behind one another with few roads fit for lorries or light railways connecting them. The distances to be covered by the columns grew longer and road congestion more acute. By early November, the front was advancing faster than the roads could be reopened and the zone of country only passable by animal transport was rapidly widening. Progress was further hampered by numerous rail accidents, and derailments sometimes caused by delayed-action mines left by saboteurs. By the time of the armistice on 11 November, the most advanced British troops, the 4th Army, was fifty miles ahead of its railhead, and in the north the 5th Army was thirty miles ahead.

Shortly before the armistice, horse transport from the ammunition columns was being used to carry the loads forward and were taking seventy-two hours for what should have been a 24-hour journey. The official report on transportation concluded: "until the railways could deliver further forward and the roads could be made fit for MT [mechanized transport], it was no longer possible for the army to advance at full strength; little more than a thin screen to keep touch with the retreating enemy could have been kept supplied."

Some of the Allied leaders wanted to chase the Germans beyond the Hindenburg Line that they had built in 1916 as a defensive barrier to prevent any invasion of the Fatherland. However, as the Germans retreated and winter approached, the Allied leadership saw this would prolong the war into a fifth year since it would take time for the lines of communication to be established while railways and roads were constructed.

With no appetite back home to prolong the war, peace eventually became inevitable, stimulated by the inadequacy of the transport system. This hasty end to the war, strangely, left Germans still on French soil and no foreign troops on theirs, the source of the myth exploited by Hitler that Germany had not really lost the war. According to the official report on transportation: "The growing impossibility of railway and road reconstruction keeping pace with the rapid advance of the allies was undoubtedly an important factor in influencing the mind of General Foch when he agreed to accord an armistice." The war on the Western Front had, quite literally, run out of steam, but its rather unsatisfactory end contributed to the next one.

CHAPTER
NINE

Here We Go Again

The period between the two wars marked the true beginning of the motorized age. While before the First World War the ownership of automobiles had been confined to a small affluent minority and the railways still carried the bulk of freight even for short journeys, by the outbreak of the Second World War this had changed completely. Cars were commonplace and the lorry had become the transport of choice for many kinds of freight carriage. Coupled with the development of air transport, the railways were expected to play a much lesser role in the Second World War than in the First World War. The growing competition from air and road had restricted railway investment during the interwar years in all the combatant nations. While there had been improvements to signalling and rolling stock, many of the world's railways, largely built in the nineteenth century, were in desperate need of modernization and refurbishment, but little had been forthcoming because of the expectation that the car and the lorry would be the key to meeting future transport needs.

This assumption neglected a crucial advantage that railways had over motor transport — they used coal, still in most countries in plentiful supply even after the conflict broke out, while oil, frequently dependent on shipping, would become scarce. Neither Germany nor Britain had oil, and even the US was not self-sufficient, and therefore railways regained their place as the key mode of transport during the war precisely because they used old technology, still mostly based on coal, and had not been modernized. Fortunately, for the most part the railways were still serviceable and the networks still dense as the days of widespread closures would not start until after the Second World War.

Their role was, though, not the same as in the First World War. The Second World War was not a railway war in the way that the conflicts of the previous three quarters of a century had been because of the existence of the alternatives to rail transport and the development of more sophisticated weaponry. It was far more mobile as entrenched positions were now too vulnerable from the air and tanks to be sustained for long periods. Even when positions became fixed, railways were no longer needed to bring supplies right to the front, as trucks could do the job over short distances. Artillery was self-propelling or could be towed, reducing the need to carry it on trains. Nevertheless, the role of the railways remained central to the logistical needs of the combatants, because they were still unrivalled for the transport of heavy loads and for journeys of, say, more than 200 miles. Railways were still the workhorses, often unsung, of the logistics of war and where no lines were available, or as in Russia were insufficient, supply bottlenecks invariably developed. Roads had greatly improved in the quarter of a century since the First World War, but away from the main routes were still primitive. There were no motorways apart from the German *Autobahnen*, and even main highways were easily blocked by marching troops, as the Germans found to their cost when invading Russia. Cars and lorries now provided much of the basic transport needs for shorter trips, but to a large extent they replaced the horse rather than the railway. The railways were, therefore, again a crucial aspect of the conflict and their role, while often unappreciated, can hardly be overestimated. Even many of the fortresses of the Maginot Line, the series of concrete fortifications that were designed to protect France against German invasion, were supplied from depots up to thirty-five miles behind the line by 60cm railways, which went right into the larger ones.

As in the First World War, there was a long build-up during which the expectation of a conflict grew. German resentment about the settlement at the end of the First World War had led to Hitler's rise to power and the country's rearmament. Once Hitler invaded Czechoslovakia in 1938, war appeared inevitable despite Neville Chamberlain's infamous trip to Munich, and arrangements for a likely conflict began to be made across Europe. While there was no equivalent of the Schlieffen Plan, there had been considerable logistical preparation on both sides in the 1930s. In Britain, the railways were not in a particularly good

341

shape as competition from motor transport had begun to erode their market, while they were still required by government regulation to provide a universal service to all, which was expensive and often unremunerative. There had been insufficient investment in the interwar period and the railways had belatedly started a campaign for a "square deal" just before the war in an effort to be relieved of their "common carrier" obligations, which required them to transport any goods offered to them, from small parcels to lifeboats and circuses. Preparations for war had started as early as 1937 with, in that British way, the establishment of a committee to examine what protection and precautions were needed for the railway in the event of a war. Grants were made by the government to the Big Four railway companies, which had been created in the aftermath of the First World War, and London Transport to build up supplies of material to permit rapid repairs, to improve telegraph equipment, to develop lighting systems that could not be seen by aircraft and, interestingly, for preparations to move all four company headquarters out of London. Lighting was a particular obsession of the war planners and tests were even carried out early in 1939 to investigate whether it was possible to continue running services under blackout conditions. In 1938, work started on a public evacuation plan from the cities which was completed just two months before the outbreak of war. The scheme, which envisaged running 4,000 special trains, involved not only moving thousands of vulnerable people out of the cities, but also Britain's

342

cultural heritage in the British Museum, the Tate and other buildings was to be conveyed to a remote destination in Wales, where the artefacts were to be housed in specially adapted disused mines.

As in 1914, it was envisaged that a government committee consisting of senior railway managers would take over the railways as soon as war broke out. Again, the British railways excelled in the early stages of the war when they were called upon to deal with the expected huge increase in demand. On the very day that war was announced, 3 September 1939, huge numbers of people flocked to the railways — foreigners anxious to get home, holidaymakers cutting short their vacations, colonial civil servants heading for ships from Liverpool to get back to their postings. This was quickly followed by the evacuation of 1.3 million children and other vulnerable people out of London and a number of big cities. Ambulance trains which had been fitted out during the build-up to war were now used to ferry hospital patients from London and other major cities to safer locations. The first contingent of the British Expeditionary Force, 158,000 strong, was despatched to France over the next few weeks with a minimum of fuss. This time, realizing that there would be greatly increased demands on the railway, about half the normal train service was cancelled but again there was a great reluctance on the part of the British people to obey the injunctions not to travel. The pinnacle of the British railways' efforts in the early stages of the war was the unexpected task of having to cope with the rapid influx of 338,000 evacuees, many of whom were injured, from Dunkirk in May 1940. Virtually the whole of the Southern Railway network was reorganized to cope with the arrivals, with, for example, one line being devoted solely to stabling rolling stock in readiness to pick up the passengers.

The Dunkirk debacle was the nearest the war got to the British mainland, which meant that again the railways were not involved in front-line combat but on the Continent they played their now traditional role as the core of the logistics of war, a function which Hitler had fatally failed to grasp. Hitler was a car fanatic who understood their technology and how the engines worked, and had consequently focussed his country's transport infrastructure effort on the *Autobahnen*, the world's first motorways, rather than on building up the capacity of the railways. That was understandable given that it was very much in keeping with the *Zeitgeist* as railways were seen as an old-fashioned technology and the National Socialist emphasis on modernization naturally led them to embrace motor cars. The National Socialists did build innovatory diesel trains like the streamlined 100 mph *Fliegende Hamburger* ("Flying Hamburger"), but it was the Volkswagen Beetle and the white *Autobahnen* which were their showpieces.

This emphasis on rubber rather than steel tyres would severely constrain Germany's war effort. Worse, Hitler compounded the error by focussing on the roads rather than on the vehicles which were needed to run on them. Yet it was the railways which kept the German economy functioning. According to a study of the German economy before and during the war, "the dependence on transportation was multifaceted and self-reinforcing. It was the very heart of the Reich's military might." And it was the railways which were at the heart of the system, as they carried 90 per cent of the coal that was the basis of the nation's industrial output and 75 per cent of all freight.

One surprising aspect of the German Army in 1939 was the limited extent to which it was motorized. The British had dispensed with the horse apart from ceremonial duties, but the Germans surprisingly had made less progress in converting their army to motor vehicles. This was partly because of Hitler's lack of attention to detail, which meant he focussed on the more sexy hardware like tanks and aeroplanes, but was also a result of the German motor industry's inability to meet army requirements. According to van Creveld, "of 103 divisions available on the eve of the war, just 16 ... were fully motorised and thus to some extent independent of the railways". The rest of the army marched on foot while their supplies were, for the most part, carried in horse-drawn wagons as lorries could not cope with the demands of the army and, in any case, there were not enough of them. In the technological conditions of 1939, an astonishing "1,600 lorries would be required to equal the capacity of just one double-track railway line". Worse, trucks use up vast amounts of road space and require more fuel and people than an equivalent railway, greatly elongating the army's "train", which meant that in relation to payload, "the railway maintained its superiority at distances of over 200 miles ... however great the effort, there was little chance that motor vehicles would relieve, much less replace, trains as Germany's main form of transportation in the foreseeable future."

Hitler's focus on motorizing his army and his failure to see it through left the railways suffering from comparative neglect, with the result that there were fewer locomotives and wagons available in 1939 than there had been at the outbreak of the First World War. To a large extent, the marching German armies depended on scavenging trucks from the local populace — a move that increased antagonism towards the invaders — and, equally unpopular, even from their own civilians.

While the German invasions of Poland, and France and the Low Countries in 1939 and 1940 respectively, were astonishing victories, they exposed weaknesses in the Army's logistics. German advances were characterized by having two sections, a small rapid motorized advance party which quickly took over vast swathes of territory but lost contact with its supply line, and a much larger, slower-moving rear. This tactic was fine in these early assaults since they were successfully concluded rapidly enough not to require reinforcements and the prolonged maintenance of supply lines. In Poland, the destruction of the railways by the retreating Poles had been so complete that it was only the rapid surrender of their army that prevented a logistical bottleneck for the Germans, who lost about half their trucks to the atrocious roads on which they were wholly reliant. By January 1940, the supply organization at Army HQ (OKH) was forced to resort

to horse-drawn transport to make up the shortfall in available trucks. In France, the logistical failings did not escape Hitler's notice since they contributed to the decision of the Germans not to press home their advantage in their sweep through northern France. The armoured spearheads speeding over the Meuse towards Paris progressed faster than expected and, as the railways had all been destroyed by the French, lost contact with their supply lines, leaving a gap between the two flanks. Hitler called a halt to allow for the supply lines to be re-established, which is why the British Expeditionary Force was able to escape from the beaches of Dunkirk, an event which contributed much to the Allies' morale. Although the sabotaged railways were reinstated as soon as possible, there were too few *Eisenbahntruppen* to carry out the work quickly enough or to work the lines efficiently. There were frantic calls to requisition "all the lorries of Germany" but by the time they arrived the Dunkirk beaches had been cleared. Again, as in Poland, had the French not crumbled so quickly, the split between the two parts of the army could have been exploited by the Allies and the Germans would have been forced to stop and consolidate.

It was the invasion of Russia in the summer of 1941 where the logistical failings were to be cruelly exposed. In truth, however, Operation Barbarossa, the name given to the massive plan to invade Russia, was always doomed to suffer the same fate as all previous attempts to overcome the Great Bear. The Germans decided on a rather muddled three-pronged attack on a vast

1,400-mile front aimed respectively at Leningrad (formerly St Petersburg, then Petrograd), Moscow and Kiev, involving more than 3 million men, five times the number that Napoleon had at his disposal, and the largest invading army raised in the history of warfare. The basic orders for the operation, which van Creveld calls "a rambling and confused document", provided for an advance to the line Dvina-Smolensk-Dnieper, respectively 600, 700 and 900 miles away from the point of departure. Yet, each army group only had one railway line to supply it during the advance, with motorized transport expected to do the rest. It was simply impossible because of the massive shortfall of motorized transport. Not only was the fleet of trucks a ramshackle collection of vehicles of 2,000 different types largely purloined from occupied countries, but to replace rail with road movements to reach Moscow would have required "at least ten times the number of vehicles actually available". Operation Barbarossa was overwhelmed by the logic of its supply constraints and its failure changed the course of the war.

There was, therefore, no alternative to using Russia's sparse railway network and that was fraught with difficulties. Locomotives with boilers that kept functioning in the arctic conditions would have to be produced and track relaid because of the change in gauge between Germany and Russia. In other words, as Len Deighton puts it, "the speed of the advance would be limited to the speed at which a new railway could be built".

The plan for the German advance was therefore drawn up in the light of these logistical constraints. To be successful Russia had to be conquered before winter and to achieve that a series of optimistic assumptions were made by the German HQ. It was to be the apogee of the blitzkrieg method of warfare, the strategy that combined tanks, infantry and air power in a single overwhelming attack concentrating tremendous force at points of weakness in order to overcome the enemy quickly. The plan for Barbarossa envisaged the rapid motorized units of all three army groups speeding 300 miles into Russia and then pausing while new railways were built and supply depots created to prepare for the final assault further east. To this end, remarkably, the *Eisenbahntruppen*, charged with repairing and converting the railway, were sent ahead as part of the advance party, even before the territory where they were expected to work was properly secured. This contradicted normal military practice. As van Creveld puts it, "instead of the logistic apparatus following in the wake of operations, it was supposed to precede them, a procedure probably unique in the annals of modern war". Such expediencies were a measure of the desperation of the Germans, who grasped that the successful invasion of Russia depended entirely on their ability to supply their armies. And they couldn't. The attack was launched on 22 June, rather later than seemed wise given the short Russian summer. Military historians argue about whether the start had been fatally delayed by Hitler's last-minute decision to invade the Balkans to get the Italians off the hook in

Greece, where they were being beaten by a poorly equipped Greek army, or whether he always intended to begin the invasion on the longest day of the year. Initially, the Germans met only feeble resistance from the shell-shocked Russians, allowing the fast advance units to reach their targets within days. However, the unmetalled roads proved to be even worse than expected, and deteriorated in the face of unusually heavy rainfall during the first week of July. A quarter of vehicles had failed within three weeks of the start of the campaign. On the railways, the difference in gauge meant the invaders were heavily reliant on using captured rolling stock but the Russians took away the best locomotives and destroyed the rest, leaving only a few wagons and coaches behind.

Not surprisingly, the *Eisenbahntruppen* could not cope with the scale of their task and were beset by a host of difficulties. Undermanned and lacking requisite skills, they failed to carry out conversions and repairs thoroughly, tending only to provide the tracks without installing such vital equipment as platforms, workshops and engine sheds. They were forced to travel by road but were not given the priority they needed because the officers of the combat regiments did not understand the importance of their task. Changing the gauge was a slow and cumbersome job and proved to be the major obstacle for the efficiency of the lines of communication. While captured wagons could be adapted to standard gauge, it was impossible to convert locomotives and therefore, effectively, the Germans were always having to contend with two separate railway systems. At the point of change of gauge, which was advanced into Russia as quickly as possible and therefore had to be moved frequently, huge bottlenecks built up, at times delaying loads for two or three days.

Railways tend to have their own particular characteristics and the Russians had built theirs with lighter rails and fewer sleepers, with the result that the lines, even once converted, could not cope with the more modern but heavier German locomotives which were used on the sections where the gauge had been changed. German engines struggled in the winter, too, as they had not been built to withstand the extreme temperatures. Unlike the Russian engines, their pipework was external and in the harsh climate of the Russian steppe, far colder than anything ever experienced in Germany, the pipes quickly froze and burst, putting the locomotives out of action.

Shortages of fuel, both coal and petrol, were a perennial problem. Russian coal was inferior and therefore needed to be mixed with some imported fuel in order to power the German locomotives. To compound the supply difficulties, Russian petrol had such a low octane value that it was unusable for German vehicles. Even the horses were of the wrong kind. To pull their heavy wagons, the German army relied on strong draught horses, which proved unsuited to the cold conditions and required enormous quantities of forage. Amazingly, in order to ensure supplies could be carried, half the infantry divisions were equipped with small hand carts, *Panje* wagons, which meant the world's most modern army was dependent on a transport method familiar to Christ.

Each of the three German armies was accompanied by two armoured trains. The *Wehrmacht* had been rather unenthusiastic about armoured trains, especially after their failure during the invasion of Poland, where attempts to use them to spearhead attacks on key railway crossings over rivers were stymied when the Poles simply blew up the bridges. The Poles themselves deployed five armoured trains, which proved effective in several encounters with German *Panzer* (armoured) units, but three of them were destroyed by the *Luftwaffe*, demonstrating their vulnerability to air attack. Nevertheless, the *Wehrmacht* decided that they would be useful in the initial stages of Barbarossa to seize railway bridges and then, after conversion to the wider Russian gauge, to protect the long stretches of railway line from attacks by partisans, which as the Germans advanced deeper into Russia increased in both severity and effectiveness. The Germans used not only their own armoured trains but several captured from the Soviet forces, who had started the war with a far bigger fleet but lost many in the early battles of Barbarossa. Some of the trains used by the Germans were even protected with armoured cars, mostly French Panhards, converted to rail use and sent out in front of the train to reconnoitre the line and draw any fire.

Of the three armies that invaded Russia in theory the northern group led by Field Marshal von Leeb, which headed towards Leningrad, had the easiest task as it only needed to cover a distance of 500 miles from East

Prussia. And at first, helped by the good road and railway network in the Baltics, which had been prosperous independent states before their occupation by the Soviets in 1940, progress was remarkable, with the motorized units covering 200 miles in just five days. However, as the convoy headed north-east, the forests became denser and the roads fewer, and the supply trucks became entangled with the huge infantry columns marching ahead of them. Soon airlifts had to be organized to keep the forward troops supplied and although by 10 July the leading armoured troops led by General Max Reinhardt were within eighty miles of Leningrad, and were in the process of overwhelming the outer defence line of the city, launching an all-out attack proved impossible because the infantry was strung out over the Baltics and the tanks could not operate in the heavily wooded terrain. This was typical of many similar offensives in the Second World War in which the attacking armoured forces ran ahead of their logistical support that then failed because it was predominately road-based. By then the *Eisenbahntruppen* had converted 300 miles of railway but the railhead was still well behind the front and in any case the line was in such poor condition that it could only accommodate one train per day. The armoured troops therefore had to wait for supplies to arrive by road and for the transport situation to improve, and consequently the opportunity to take Leningrad swiftly was lost. Moreover, Russian resistance stiffened with numerous partisan attacks on German supply lines, making life difficult for the invaders, and in August heavy rain turned the roads into quagmires. By September, Hitler, recognizing that Leningrad could not be taken quickly, ordered the withdrawal of the *Panzer* tank unit, *Panzergruppe 4*, to join the assault on Moscow, leaving the *Luftwaffe* with the impossible task of trying to take the city. Van Creveld concludes that the strategy of the attack was fatally flawed at the outset: "It seems certain that Army Group North's best chance for capturing Leningrad came around the middle of July, when Reinhardt's corps had penetrated to within eighty miles of the city. At this time, however, supply difficulties ruled out any immediate resumption of the offensive." By the time any attack was possible, the citizens of Leningrad had built a series of fortifications, including anti-tank ditches, trenches and reinforced concrete emplacements that proved all but impenetrable during the siege, which lasted two and a half years and became one of the most deadly in human history.

The middle group, aimed at Moscow and led by Field Marshal von Bock, was by far the strongest force. While initially its supply difficulties were the least pronounced of the three army groups because it straddled the main Warsaw-Moscow railway that remained undamaged, they were to play a crucial role in the army's failure to reach Moscow. Indeed, the progress of the central army group was initially even more impressive than that of its counterpart to the north. The strategy was to create a series of pincer movements with Smolensk, about halfway to Moscow, as the target for the first stage of operations, but the usual difficulties of roads being blocked by streams of infantry and of insufficient railway capacity soon became apparent. There was a shortage of petrol exacerbated by the higher consumption of lorries on the atrocious roads and of spares, especially tyres, whereas on the railways there were the customary bottlenecks at the gauge changeover points. However, by and large there was reasonable progress until the Germans attempted to build up a supply base for the final attack on Moscow. Then it became clear that there was insufficient capacity to launch the assault on the Russian capital. Bock needed thirty trains per day to build up stocks whereas, at best, he was getting eighteen. Just as in the north, Hitler then changed the game plan, diverting resources — a tank unit, *Panzergruppe 3* — to the south, along with 5,000 tons of lorry capacity, to ensure that Kiev could be taken. It was a terrible mistake. While Ukraine was important in terms of resources — wheat, coal and oil — Moscow was the centre of the nation's communications and had the Germans been able to block it off, the Russians would no longer have been able to use the rail lines to transport troops between the north and south.

With the help of the extra panzers, Kiev soon fell but then another mistake resulted in the move eastwards being undertaken too hastily. Already the south group, which had been charged with taking Kiev and then crossing the Dnieper to capture the coalfields of Donetz and invading the Crimea, had been beset by wet weather that knocked out half its motor transport. Progress was also slowed by fiercer resistance from Russian partisans than faced by the other two groups.

355

Once Kiev had been encircled, the eastward move resumed on 1 October but it was greatly hampered by the destruction of the bridges over the Dnieper, which forced supplies to be shipped across the river. The Germans took over sections of the Russian railways but they were in a poor state and during October barely a quarter of scheduled trains arrived at the two easternmost railheads. Chaos on the Polish railways further back on the line of communication added to the supply difficulties. Therefore, the decision to resume the offensive proved premature as, without any effective railway support, there was no hope of reaching the Donetz Basin with its mineral riches before winter set in. Although the Germans captured Rostov in late November, their supply lines were overextended and they subsequently lost the town, the first time the German advance had been successfully repelled.

The attack by the centre group on Moscow finally began on 2 October after the *Panzer* division returned from Kiev, but it was too little, too late. One unit reached the suburbs, but the Germans' strength fell far short of the numbers needed to take the capital. There was a final hopeless attack on 1 December, which had no chance of success because of the lack of resources. The Red Army, which had the advantage of ski troops, counter-attacked, pushing the Germans back sixty miles by January, not only removing the immediate threat to their capital but, even more importantly in terms of morale, achieving their first large-scale success over the invading forces.

By the winter, therefore, all three prongs of the German advance were at a standstill far short of their objectives, and with little likelihood of achieving them. The Germans had to adapt to a war of attrition, for which they were not prepared, and which ultimately would be their undoing. As van Creveld concludes, "the German invasion of the Soviet Union was the largest military operation of all time, and the logistic problems involved of an order of magnitude that staggers the imagination". Yet, although the means at the disposal of the *Wehrmacht* were modest, the Germans came closer to their aims than might have been expected, which van Creveld attributes "less to the excellence of the preparations than to the determination of troops and commanders to give their all", making do with whatever means were made available to them. Indeed, during the initial phase of the attack, the supply shortages were greatly alleviated by the armies living off the land in the traditional manner, but once the frost set in, the conditions not only made transportation more difficult but the required level of supplies increased greatly. The most notorious failing was the lack of provision for winter coats and other cold-weather equipment for the troops advancing on Moscow, which resulted in thousands of men, fighting in their summer gear, freezing to death in the cold. There is much debate among historians as to whether this equipment was available or not, but van Creveld is convinced this is irrelevant because there were no means to deliver it: "The railroads, hopelessly inadequate to prepare the offensive on Moscow and to

357

sustain it after it had started, were in no state to tackle the additional task of bringing up winter equipment."

Ultimately, the Russian invasion was a step too far for the Germans, who even with everything in their favour and better preparation would probably not have succeeded simply because of the size of the task — the territory to be captured was some twenty times the size of the area conquered in western Europe and yet the German army deployed only 10 per cent more men and 30 per cent more tanks. Hitler's dithering and his changes in strategy, and the dogged resistance of the Russians, often using guerrilla tactics, undermined the advance further and made failure inevitable, but supply delays played a vital, if not decisive, role. The German supply lines were simply extended beyond their natural limit, as the optimism of the HQ generals who had prepared the assault came up against the reality of the Russian steppe. The effect of the logistical shortfalls was not just practical but extended to the morale of the troops. Arguments between different sections of the military over the need for transport led the *Luftwaffe* to protect their supply trains with machine-gun-toting guards ready to fire not at Russian partisans but at German troops keen to get hold of their equipment.

Throughout the campaign, the Red Army troops retained the advantages of fighting on their own territory, which had proved crucial to all defending armies since the start of the railway age. Cleverly, rather than building up huge supply dumps that risked being captured by the enemy, the Russian Army supplied its troops directly from trains at railway stations, a task which required a level of flexibility and operational experience of the particular lines that would never have been available to an invading force. The Russians had, too, ensured that they retained most of their rolling stock by transporting it eastwards in anticipation of the German attack, with the result that the railways still in their control enjoyed a surfeit of locomotives and wagons. According to Westwood, "by 1943, the Russian railway mileage had decreased by forty per cent, but the locomotive stock by only fifteen per cent".

Stalin, unlike Hitler, had long recognized the value of the railways and thanks to an extensive programme of investment in the interwar period the Russian system was in a much better state than at the onset of the previous war. While Hitler had been counting on the Russian system breaking down under the strain of retreating troops, it held up remarkably well. Indeed, the smooth running of the Russian railways was instrumental in allowing the rapid wholesale transfer of much of the nation's industry during the early days of the war from threatened western areas to the remote east, an evacuation conducted so efficiently that even frequent bombardment was unable to disrupt it. At times traffic was so great that signalling systems were ignored and trains simply followed one another down the track almost nose to tail.

Russian railwaymen were effectively conscripted as martial law was imposed on the railway system and those who failed in their jobs were liable to find themselves in front of a firing squad — but then so was anyone else. Later in the war, however, Stalin, grateful for the railway workers' efforts, created a series of special medals for railway workers, including one for "Distinguished Railway Clerk", presumably for issuing tickets to war widows while under fire. The Russians laid a staggering 4,500 miles of new track during the war, including a section of line that supplied the defenders at Stalingrad. The railways were crucial, too, to the defence of both Leningrad and Moscow. When all the railway lines to Leningrad were cut off by September 1941 — the Finns blocked communications from the north as they were fighting with the Germans — the "death" road across the frozen Lake Ladoga, so called because of the dangers of using it, became the last lifeline to the beleaguered city and was supplied from trains. Towards the end of the siege a railway was built across the ice, like on Lake Baikal in the Russo-Japanese War, but since the territory around the south of the lake was soon regained by the Russians, it was never actually used.

In Moscow, a circular line had been built around the city just before the war connecting the existing lines stretching fan-like out of the city and this proved vital in maintaining links between different parts of the country after the Germans cut off most of the main lines. When the Red Army went on the offensive, the Russian railway troops regauged thousands of miles of line — indeed some sections of track were regauged numerous times as territory was won and lost — including parts of the Polish and German rail networks. Indeed, Stalin travelled to the Potsdam peace conference in a Russian train.

360

The need for effective railways during the invasion was made all the greater because of that great barrier to smooth transport, mud, whose impact on the outcome of the war cannot be underestimated. Not only was it a frequent obstacle on the roads, but at times it even prevented tanks from moving. Undoubtedly, better roads would have improved the supply situation but not solved it. As Deighton suggests, "the virtual absence of paved roads meant that mud was an obstacle on a scale never encountered in Western Europe". Only more railways with greater capacity could have tipped the balance, something that was not within Hitler's ability to change. Each of the three army groups stalled after initial advances as they waited for the infantry to catch up, allowing the Russians to regroup or even counter-attack. Even if Hitler, as some of his generals recommended, had decided to focus all his forces on one target, Moscow, the lack of logistical capacity, especially railways, would have saved the city from invasion.

The failure to complete the invasion before the winter of 1941–2 set in proved to be the turning point of the war. There would be big battles such as Stalingrad and Kursk, and the siege of Leningrad would continue, but essentially the German advance was checked along a vast but not entirely stable front that stretched from the Baltic to the Black Sea, and when the war of movement resumed, it was a westward push by the Red Army rather than any continued advance by the Germans.

The last-ditch attack on Moscow coincided with another turning point, as it took place a few days before the Japanese bombing of Pearl Harbor in Hawaii on 7 December 1941, which propelled the US into the war. America was quickly put on a war footing and despite the fact that the country had embraced the automobile age more firmly than any other, the railroads were at the heart of their transportation system, carrying virtually all war traffic, both goods and personnel. During the Second World War, the American railroads carried 90 per cent of military freight and 97 per cent of all organized military passenger movements. In other words, railways were still very much the dominant form of transport. The President, Franklin D. Roosevelt, was well aware of this and within days of Pearl Harbor created the Office of Defense Transportation to co-ordinate all transport facilities and war traffic. This time the US railroads were determined not to suffer the humiliation of being taken over, as had happened in the First World War, and responded by complying with all the federal government's demands. Such co-operation was essential as the railroads were in a state of decline owing to the Depression and competition from motor transport. Compared with 1916, the railroad companies' rolling stock had been reduced by a third, although, on the positive side, locomotives were more powerful than a quarter of a century before and the surviving network was in better shape thanks to improved signalling and maintenance. With petrol and, particularly, rubber for tyres in short supply, the railroads were the only form of long-distance transport available.

During the four years of American involvement in the Second World War, the railroads carried 44 million troops in 114,000 special trains, twice the monthly average during the First World War. More freight, too, was carried than in the previous war and the railways also had to cope with a huge influx of civilian passengers, with the result that 1944 was the all-time record for the railroads with almost a billion passenger journeys. Yet, thanks to much better co-ordination by the railroads and the fact that both Pacific and Atlantic seaports were used, there were none of the bottlenecks which had forced the government to take over the railroads in the First World War. All this was made possible by the more efficient use of the system facilitated by co-operation rather than competition and, according to a military analyst, because the railroad companies had adhered to Haupt's rules of wartime railway operation: "There was a general observance of the vital doctrine 'no car shall be loaded without positive assurance that it can and will be promptly unloaded at destination'." Not surprisingly, the railroad companies enjoyed a boom in profits thanks to this extra traffic, but after 1945 they reverted to the cut-throat competition which had characterized their pre-war behaviour and soon found themselves back in the financial mire. They did, though, get a big thank-you from the military. General Brehon Somervell, the commander of the US Army Service Forces, later wrote about the vital role of the railroads: "The American railroads can take the greatest pride in their contribution to our victory. Without that contribution the war would have been prolonged for many months and even our ultimate success would have been jeopardized. The prolongation of the war would have meant the loss of thousands of additional lives . . ."

In Britain, after the excitement of the early evacuations and Dunkirk the railways settled down to a pattern of overuse that had typified their performance in the First World War. This time, however, matters were made worse because, right from the outset, the peacetime passenger train service was cut back in order to prioritize military movements and frequent air attacks on the rail network disrupted operations even further. The reduction in services meant that the remaining ones were overcrowded as, despite the injunctions not to travel, there was a desperate desire to do so and there was little alternative to rail given the strictness of the petrol rationing system. Travelling on the railways during the war was an increasingly grim experience owing to the delays and overcrowding, and there was not even any recourse to luxury for the more affluent as first class was soon abolished to allow for better use of the available space, followed towards the end of the war by the cessation of all restaurant car services. The latter had, in any case, been losing money during blackouts as an official report delicately explained: "It was also discovered on the restoration of the lighting after the termination of the warning that certain passengers found it convenient to leave the dining cars during such periods and thus relieve the dining car attendant of the necessity of making out their bills." Nor was it only the price of meals that was lost. The Blitz spirit did not preclude the odd bit of pilfering and the London, Midland & Scottish had to change the lighting system on its Glasgow trains because the cost of maintenance was soaring as a result of the theft of bulbs at the rate of 50,000 per year. Passengers were distinctly unruly in other ways, too, frequently lifting up the blackout blinds for a view out of the window, despite the dangers from air attack. The government's propaganda machine created an irritating priggish cartoon character called Billy Brown, who featured in several poster campaigns with horrible homilies, such as, in an effort to stop people removing the netting from railway windows:

I trust you'll pardon my correction,
That stuff is there for your protection

Graffiti artists frequently added the lines:

Thank you for your information
but I can't see the bloody station

Oddly, at other times, the public was so incensed about lights showing on railways that misguided vigilante groups threatened to remove signalling equipment from the lineside, prompting the authorities to issue a warning for them not to do so because of the potential dire consequences. Despite the deprivations of war, the authorities did find time to make sure that passengers on the Royal Train did not suffer inconvenience as train drivers were instructed, in the event of an air raid, to ensure that they stopped with "care being taken to see that the train is not suddenly brought to a stand" so that there were no royal bumps.

The British railways were, as in the First World War, hampered by labour shortages. This time, unlike in 1914, the government had made the railways a "reserved occupation" but nevertheless 60,000 railwaymen still signed up, many to join the railway regiments which were vital in repairing and maintaining lines that were essential for supplying the Army. In the First World War, there had been much debate and hesitation over employing women, who hitherto had rarely worked in the railways, but eventually more than 33,000 were taken on to fill a variety of jobs ranging from ticket collection to guard duty, though they were banned from driving trains and kept out of supervisory and managerial jobs. This time there was no debate about filling the gaps left by the men, and women were recruited in far greater numbers, with more than 100,000 employed by 1943, a sixth of the workforce.

All the difficulties of overuse that beset the rail network in the First World War were compounded by the bombing raids, notably the initial Blitz, which ran for a year from June 1940 until the invasion of Russia diverted the *Luftwaffe*, and the flying bomb attacks towards the end of the war in 1944–5. During the Blitz, although industrial centres around Britain such as Manchester, Liverpool, Hull and Newcastle were all bombed heavily at various times, the Southern Railway bore the brunt of the attacks, with a third of them aimed at the area it covered. According to the railway historian Ernest Carter, the most bombed station was the East End station of Poplar near the London docks, which endured 1,200 high-explosive bombs, 50,000 incendiary devices and fifty-two rocket attacks, although presumably that vast total includes ordnance which fell on the surrounding area. As a consequence of the Blitz, Londoners flocked to the Underground to protect themselves, and after initially banning people from sleeping there, the government relented and Tube stations became "the best shelters of them all", though they took a few hits, notably at Bank, Balham and Bounds Green, and the worst disaster was caused by a stampede in the station shelter at Bethnal Green.

Given the labour shortages, air raids, extra military traffic and overcrowding, delays on the railways were legion, measured in hours rather than minutes. Trains were initially stopped once the air raid sirens sounded but the authorities realized this caused chaos and put more people at risk, and consequently decided to allow traffic to continue at reduced speeds. It was not so much direct damage from bombs that resulted in delays but the rule which specified that any unexploded ordnance within 400 yards of a railway line resulted in the cessation of all traffic. Interestingly, in 1944, in order for the invasion of France not to be delayed in the face of anticipated heavy enemy attacks, the government relaxed rules about trains passing unexploded bombs so as not to hold up the service but kept this decision secret from the public.

One of the reasons for the small number of accidents caused by bombing was that the air raid warning system in fact worked very well and not many German planes managed to get through unnoticed. There were remarkably few instances of trains being involved in major derailments because of damage to the tracks, although in general the accident rate on the railways rose as a result of the blackout conditions that required, for example, signals to be at just 6 per cent of their normal brightness. Because so little information was given out, the public did not know what was happening on the railways or why particular rules were being enforced, and consequently "the railways were subjected to much unfair, unwarranted and unjustifiable opprobrium at the time, both by the public and the press". The government body which ran the railways, the Railway Executive Committee, was driven to publish a poster with doggerel explaining its dilemma over information that began:

In peace-time railways could explain
When fog or ice held up your train
But now the country's waging war
To tell you why's against the law . . .

The overall burden on the railways proved to be far greater than in the First World War, but this time it was Norfolk, rather than Scotland, where there was most extra traffic, because of the 150 bomber airfields sited there thanks to the county's proximity to Germany. The Southern Railway was inevitably the most heavily used of the four railway companies as it served the Channel ports, and its heavy density of lines gave flexibility by allowing diversionary routes when lines were damaged or overcrowded. Indeed, one calculation suggests there were no fewer than 136 different ways to reach Dover and Folkestone from the London area on the tracks of the Southern Railway. However, virtually every railway in the country was used in some respect for military purposes and as in the First World War many duplicate routes suddenly became essential supply lines. Most bizarrely, the tiny Romney, Hythe Dymchurch Railway, a thirteen-mile-long railway built in the late 1920s to the tiny 15in gauge on the Kent coast, was requisitioned and fitted with an armoured train sporting anti-tank rifles and machine guns, and was intensively used to carry supplies for the war effort, notably equipment for the pipeline under the ocean (PLUTO) which was vital in keeping the Normandy invasion force functioning until the French ports could be reopened. While a dozen armoured trains patrolled the Channel coast until 1943, after which an invasion was deemed unlikely, at Dover rail-mounted 9.2in guns were regularly hauled to a siding to lob a few shells half-heartedly over the Channel in the forlorn hope of hitting the corresponding German guns near Calais.

Another unusual line in the south-east which saw particularly heavy use, principally for training purposes, was the Longmoor Military Railway in Surrey, originally opened before the First World War and known until 1935 as the Woolmer Instructional Railway. During the First World War it was used to train thousands of railway troops and in 1916 a 60cm railway was installed because of the wider use of such railways on the front. At its peak, it had seventy miles of line and sidings, with, deliberately, a vast array of types of locomotive to offer a varied experience to the trainees. While it continued to be operational throughout the interwar period, usage increased enormously in the run-up to the Second World War. Indeed, the Army built numerous similar railways around the country both for training purposes and to carry ammunition and explosives. The largest was the Bicester Military Railway, and other notable ones included a narrow-gauge railway serving the explosives storehouses at Eastriggs near Carlisle, and the notorious line at the ammunition dump in the Savernake Forest in Wiltshire, where there was a huge explosion in July 1945.

Paradoxically the Germans never targeted the railway network itself in a systematic way believing, perhaps, that this would be ineffective. That view was strengthened by the remarkable recovery in Coventry, the subject of one of the *Luftwaffe*'s earliest major raids in November 1940. Although the city suffered devastation from an attack by more than 500 bombers, and while railway property suffered no fewer than 122 hits, the lines were operational again within a week, some within two days. According to an analysis of the German bombing campaign against Britain, "very few direct attacks were made with the railways as a definite target", and while indiscriminate bombing raids caused damage, "they made no large concentrated attack on a strategical junction or marshalling yard in this country". One theory, though seemingly unlikely, is that the Germans were reluctant to destroy the railway system as they would need it if they invaded. More likely, they did not have the resources or the ability to target the railway system specifically as it proved remarkably difficult to target a thin line of tracks without a guidance device. The Allies would come up against this problem in the later stages of the war, when attacks on the French rail network did not prevent the Germans bringing in reinforcements to resist the Allied advance after D-Day. As John Westwood concludes: "It is significant that the unaimed flying bomb of 1944 was as likely to cause serious railway damage as the aimed bomb of 1940." Indeed, by chance, the first V2, the more sophisticated version of the rockets aimed at Britain in the final stages of the war, happened to strike a railway line at Bethnal Green in the East End and several other rockets caused damage to railway property, including one which hit the track in front of a Kent Coast express, resulting in the death of several passengers.

Railways throughout the theatre of conflict were a target for attacks, especially by sabotage. It was a major tactic of the French Resistance, which from early 1943 began to launch daily attacks against the railways to prevent German movements. By the autumn of that year, around twenty acts of sabotage per day were being recorded, seriously hampering the Germans' ability to move supplies around the country. There were notable examples elsewhere in parts of Europe under occupation by the Germans. In Greece, virtually the whole 1,350-mile railway system was wrecked by sabotage. In November 1942, partisans, with help from

British paratroopers, blew up a series of three viaducts on the main Athens-Thessaloniki line, which helped inspire far wider resistance to the German invasion. The most spectacular part of this concerted wave of destruction was to the Gorgopotamus Viaduct as its 70ft spans crashed into the gorge below, but the most troublesome for the Germans proved to be the Asopos Viaduct, which was repaired by forced labour. However, the Polish and Greek labourers had deliberately undermined the foundations, and when the first locomotive was driven over the bridge, its central pier collapsed, ensuring the line was out of action for a further two months. Yugoslavia, which was invaded at the same time as Greece, also saw similar levels of railway sabotage by guerrilla forces and by the end of the war no line in the country was functioning. Even the Jersey islanders got in on the sabotage act, though only on a minor scale. The Jersey railways had been closed during the interwar period, but when the Germans invaded the island they reopened and extended the railways for military use while banning the local populace from travelling on them. The Jersey railways thus became the only part of the British rail network to be taken over by the Germans, and according to a history of the railways in the Second World War, "islander involvement was confined to children placing stones on the tracks and inflicting a series of minor derailments that interrupted operations briefly".

Despite all these attacks, there were no railway accidents on the scale of the three involving troops in the First World War, although there was one tragedy in Italy which was indirectly caused by wartime conditions. On the night of 2 March 1944, a freight train was carrying more than 400 people travelling illegally from Naples to a market town where fresh produce was on sale. The train struggled to climb up a steep incline in a tunnel out of the small Eboli station because of the weight of passengers and stalled, slowly releasing deadly carbon monoxide gas. Nearly all the passengers died, but, as with the enormous First World War disasters, the precise number is unknown because the disaster was kept secret at the time.

While the destruction of railways and rail equipment was a recurring feature of the Second World War, so were the construction of new lines and the expansion of existing ones for strategic purposes. The most impressive achievement was the expansion and refurbishment of the railways of the Arabian Gulf, in Iraq and Iran, which became a vital part of the war effort. In Iraq, the main line through the country had been cut in several places between Basra and Baghdad during the German-backed attempt by the Prime Minister, Rashid Ali, to oust the British. British forces arrived in Basra in May 1941 and Royal Engineers began the task of repairing the line, moving slowly northwards towards Baghdad and then up to Mosul supported by an armoured train. They eventually secured the whole railway, which connected with Turkey and Syria, for the British once more, effectively balking German plans to move further eastwards to reach the oilfields. More important strategically was gaining control of the Trans-Persian (Trans-Iranian) Railway, mentioned in Chapter Six, which had been finally completed by the Shah of Persia just as war broke out. Persia had tried to stay neutral in the war, but the need to guarantee oil supplies in the face of the German advances eastwards on both sides of the Mediterranean led the Allies to occupy the country in August 1941 with little resistance and to install a new leader, the son of the previous Shah, who had been supportive of the Axis (and who in turn would be ousted in 1979 by the Ayatollahs). The 865-mile Trans-Persian Railway was an obvious means to supply the Russian war effort while avoiding the perilous shipping route from the North Sea to Murmansk. With the roads being totally inadequate, the railway through Persia and on to Soviet-controlled Azerbaijan was the only viable alternative option. The line, however, was inadequate for the needs of the Allies and a huge improvement programme was immediately set in motion. Ironically, the only locomotives were of German manufacture but soon both British and American engines were brought to the line, which, along with most of the other rail equipment, had to be transported 15,000 miles across the world around the Cape of Good Hope to reach the Gulf. The very fact that the Allies were prepared to go to so much effort to establish this supply route demonstrated its vital importance. It was not easy. Whole new port facilities had to be installed on the Shatt al Arab waterway and connected to the line by a new extension built over marshes in the full heat of the summer. The

Trans-Persian had been one of the most ambitious railway schemes ever built, with a single-track line crossing swathes of desert, then climbing up and through both the Luristan and Elburz mountain ranges to reach a height of 7,000 feet with steep gradients and no fewer than 144 tunnels. New sidings, marshalling yards and, most important, numerous passing places were built with remarkable speed and the water supply, always a problem, greatly improved. Running conditions were virtually unique. On the same trip temperatures in the desert could reach 50^0 C while on the mountains they could plunge to 20 below freezing. Conditions were so harsh that the tenders of the imported locomotives had to be painted white to prevent the water inside becoming too hot for the engine to function.

Once the supply trains started rolling, they needed protection, especially in the bandit-infested mountain sections, where Indian troops had to be placed on permanent patrol duty and every train had armed guards. While initially the line was operated by the British, with many British drivers, the Americans soon took over, bringing with them diesel engines requisitioned from US railroads. These were more powerful and suitable for the steep sections in tunnels where steam locomotives often struggled to climb, putting the crews at risk of asphyxiation from carbon monoxide fumes. Another hazard was colliding with camels, which derailed at least one steam engine at full speed. The tremendous efforts to create this line of communication proved, however, worthwhile. The capacity of the railway had been just 200 tons per day, but thanks to the improvement it carried 5 million tons through to the Russians in under three years, a 25-fold increase on what would have been possible previously.

Lines were constructed elsewhere in the Middle East and in many parts of Europe during the war, but the most infamous line built in the war was the Burma-Siam railway. Soon after the Japanese captured Malaya and Burma in 1942 they decided to improve communication between the two countries as there were no adequate road or railway links. To build the 300-mile line through mountainous terrain and jungle, the Japanese drew on a labour force amounting to more than 250,000, most of whom were local people press-ganged into work but also including 61,000 British troops captured when the Japanese overran Singapore. The line, which was designed to link the Burmese and Siamese (now Thai) railway networks, was built simultaneously from both ends, Thanbyuzayat in Burma and Nong Pladuk in Siam, and was completed at breakneck speed in just sixteen months at a terrible human cost. The conditions on what became known as the Death Railway were so appalling that disease, starvation rations, lack of sanitation and the brutal behaviour of the Japanese and Korean overseers resulted in more than 100,000 workers perishing, including a quarter of the Allied prisoners. Similar suffering, but on a far smaller scale, occurred on the puppet Vichy government's short-lived project in 1941–2 to revive the scheme to build a Trans-Sahara railway that was intended to connect Dakar in Senegal with the Mediterranean. Prisoners, mostly foreign nationals who had the bad luck of being stranded in Dakar when the Vichy government took over, were forced to build the first section but the project was thankfully soon abandoned when its sheer unreality became apparent.

The death rate on the Burma railway was particularly high in the final stages of construction as the Japanese were desperate for the line to be completed. Robert Hardie, a doctor who was captured at Singapore and wrote a book about his time as a prisoner, described how even sick men were made to work extremely long hours: "They are being worked very hard and very savagely [on the railway] — from 7.30a.m. to 9 or 10p.m. every day. Unfit men just collapse if they are sent up." All that on just seven ounces of rice per day, often with no vegetables, let alone meat.

When the line opened in October 1943, it was a vital part of the Japanese line of communication because the Burma front had become a key supply route when the Japanese lost control of the South China Sea. It would not be until the following year that the Allies re-established a foothold in Burma and the capture of the Myitkynia station allowed them to use the railway to advance towards the Japanese. According to Ernest Carter, the lack of roads meant that many cars and lorries were adapted for railway use: "As soon as they came on the line, American engineers fitted flanged wheels to a couple of army jeeps and put them at each end of half a dozen wagons to form a push-pull train." He even reports that one of the commanders of the

British forces, General Francis Festing, was seen to be driving his own jeep along the track ahead of his men. After the war, most of the railway was quickly abandoned as it was in poor condition, though a section of about eighty miles was brought up to standard and remains in use today.

On the other side of the Burmese front, there was much railway activity, too. To counter the threat of the Japanese advancing towards India and possibly through Bengal to the port of Chittagong, the Allies needed to strengthen the supply line to the Chinese, under Chiang Kaishek, who were fighting with the Allies. The principal supply route from Calcutta was cumbersome and slow, a 600-mile-long railway that had been built to serve the tea plantations of Assam. A standard-gauge railway struck north to Parbatipur on the foothills of the Himalayas, and then a metre-gauge line continued across Eastern Bengal to the banks of the Brahmaputra river, where there was only a ferry to connect with another narrow-gauge railway, which wound up the valley to Dimapur, the supply base in the north-eastern corner of Assam. The Allied forces in China were supplied by an airlift over the Himalayas from airfields close to the north-east end of the railway. According to the historian of the line, John Thomas, "the fate of India and to a degree the British Empire depended on this slender line of communication", which was inevitably slow given that goods had to be manhandled three times between the various modes of transportation.

To speed the flow of goods on the line, 400 British railway troops were brought over in early 1943, followed at the start of 1944 by ten times that number of Americans. By improving the line and building passing loops to accommodate the massive trains of 120 wagons pulled by imported locomotives, the capacity of the railway increased more than tenfold, from just 600 to 7,000 tons per day. Relations between the British, the Americans and the Indians were, however, not always cordial as the Americans tended to view the railway as solely a military operation, whereas the British, intending to stay in India after the war, were keen also to retain it for civilian use, while the Indians tried to insist that the regular "mail train" should take precedence over the military traffic. Cultural differences caused numerous difficulties: "An American officer commanding a troop train pulled the communication cord as his train was leaving Sealdah main station in Calcutta because there was no toilet paper on board." The Americans tended to commandeer the best coaches for use in sidings as offices for their control staff. Moreover, the military controllers of the line cut corners, resulting in a tenfold increase in accidents with smashed wagons and broken locomotives littering the side of the track. To compound the difficulties, disease severely reduced the effectiveness of the imported railway troops, and there were frequent attacks on the trains from the guerrilla army of the Indian resistance movement. The sabotage was easy but effective. According to Lieutenant Colonel Anthony Mains, an officer who helped protect the railway, "the modus operandi was extremely simple and the only tool required was a long handled spanner . . . The wreckers would merely remove one or more fishplates [the connecting plates holding lengths of rail together], usually on a curve, and the centrifugal force generated by the trains would distort the track and derailment followed." Nevertheless, despite all these difficulties, and the fact that a proposed bridge over the Brahmaputra river was never completed, the supply route proved successful, and was essential in the construction of a series of new roads through the mountains to replace the airlifts.

It was not only railway lines that were hastily constructed in the war, Britain, the US and Germany all produced vast quantities of standard locomotives, mostly based on pre-war freight designs. These "Austerity" locomotives were designed in a minimalist style to ensure they were cheap and efficient to build. More than 6,700 of the basic German *Kriegslok* were produced as they had the advantage of only taking 8,000 man-hours to build, a third of the time that their more sophisticated predecessors required. After the start of Operation Barbarossa, Hitler recognized the need for more locomotives and demanded that 15,000 be constructed, and Hermann Göring decreed that locomotive production should, with the oil industry, have priority over all other armament projects. The US produced nearly 800 locomotives of a type designed by the Corps of Engineers that came to be known as "MacArthur" and these were despatched to several theatres of the war, notably Normandy after the D-Day landings, and also saw service in Africa, India, Burma and even Australia. In Britain, the War Department built and owned over a thousand "Austerity" locos and a clutch of shunting locomotives, many of which were transferred to British Railways in the 1950s, but, as with the German war locomotives, others ended up all over the world.

Hitler liked technology and expended much effort, fruitless as it turned out, on developing the V1 and V2 rockets that were launched towards Britain in the final stages of the war, but he was also obsessed with producing guns that could destroy enemy positions from a great distance. Inevitably, these had to be rail-mounted and in 1941 Germany constructed two enormous 800mm guns intended for use against Gibraltar, but Franco would not allow them to cross Spanish territory. Instead, one was despatched to the Crimea, where it helped to destroy the fortifications of the naval base at Sevastopol, which, as a result, was soon abandoned by the Russians. It was, though, an impractical piece of artillery since it required 1,400 men and two 110-ton cranes to assemble. To spread its huge weight of 1,350 tons, it had to be supported on forty axles, and as with so much ultra-heavy artillery the resources devoted to building it far outweighed its value. It arrived at Sevastopol right at the end of the ten-month siege, required a purpose-built railway network, fired only forty-eight rounds and needed massive amounts of maintenance to keep it operational. Not surprisingly, after this modest record, there is no confirmation that it was ever used again, though there is some evidence of it being fired against the Poles in the Warsaw uprising of 1944.

While railways across the various theatres were, as we have seen, put to intensive use, the preparations for the Normandy landings of D-Day, 6 June 1944, provided the railways with their sternest test. In Britain, these had been going on for several months, hampered by the need to retain a high level of secrecy. Britain's railways, already overworked, went into overdrive, and a series of tiny stations in the south-west with wonderfully quaint names straight out of *The Titfield Thunderbolt* like Dinton, Tisbury, Woodbury and Bridstowe, which in normal times barely saw a handful of passengers in a day, suddenly became major rail centres as supplies were stockpiled and US troops despatched to remote corners of the country for training. By March 1944, special trains were already being run and by the beginning of June there had been over 30,000 such services, concentrated in the southern part of Britain. In the month after the start of the landings, Britain's railways had the busiest period in their history, with 600 extra troop, freight and ambulance trains per day, all concentrated on the Channel ports. The Midland South Western Junction Railway from Cirencester and Swindon to Andover, for example, a single-track line cutting across the Downs, did a heroic job of carrying far more traffic than ever before, like countless other similar railways which had largely fallen into virtual disuse in peacetime.

Once the soldiers reached the other side of the Channel, they had to re-create a railway network almost from scratch. Already the importance of re-establishing railways to support an invasion force had been acknowledged by the Americans, who within two days of landing in Sicily in July 1943 had a team of railway troops beginning work on reconstructing wrecked lines, a pattern that was followed as the Americans progressed up through Italy. The Germans had taken over the French railways, which had been nationalized just before the war, in 1940, having deliberately avoided damaging them during the invasion as they were aware of their future usefulness. After the invasion of France, the railways were operated under German control by French railwaymen and became a centre of resistance since railway workers could travel without suspicion, enabling them to garner information and carry messages. Most famously, messengers were regularly carried in and out of Vichy France, which controlled the southern part of the country, in the tender water tank of the locomotive used to haul the special train of the collaborationist president between Paris and Vichy.

There was much passive resistance, too, as the French railway workers could easily amend paperwork or lose documentation to ensure that freight was sent to the wrong destination. There were all kinds of ways of delaying services. Locomotives were run directly into the pit of a turntable, or allowed to run out of steam, or coal was dumped on the tracks instead of the furnace. It was only in 1943 that the active sabotage mentioned above started being carried out both by Resistance guerrillas and railway workers themselves. In the countryside, trains were easily derailed, while inside railway installations more sophisticated disruption was carried out to disable trains. The Germans took to escorting their key services with armoured trains carrying troops who, like Trotsky's Red Army, could chase down any members of the Resistance who had stopped the train. The smooth operation of the French railways was further hindered by the despatch of tens of thousands of railway workers to replace German railwaymen sent to the front.

In 1944, as D-Day approached, sabotage and derailments were coordinated from London to ensure there was maximum disruption to German efforts to resist the landings. The French railways were systematically bombed while the Resistance was instructed to supplement the destruction. Because of the difficulties of targeting railway installations without destroying the towns adjoining them, bombing was mainly confined to marshalling yards and major junctions while the Resistance was charged with immobilizing the French locomotive stock and destroying vital bridges. This division of tasks not only ensured the thorough wrecking of the railway network, but saved many urban areas, notably large swathes of central Paris surrounding the stations, from being damaged: "Instead, a few well-informed, brave railwaymen, supplied with moderate quantities of explosives, were able to paralyse rail traffic in the Paris area." The Germans were greatly hampered by this destruction, which continued after D-Day with the Resistance carefully targeting its attacks in order to prevent reinforcements reaching Normandy.

Consequently, when the Allies landed in June 1944, there was effectively no railway system in France and a map of the railways as they were on D-Day shows a series of short lines with no semblance of a network and virtually every river crossing destroyed. In retreating, the Germans were particularly thorough at wrecking any lines that the Resistance and the Allied bombers had left intact, using a device called a router (pronounced as in grouter), a huge hook mounted on a flat wagon and dragged along by a train, ripping up and breaking the middle of the sleepers. It was, in truth, little more than a more powerful version of the devices employed to similar effect in the American Civil War nearly a century previously, but much more effective and quick. More complex parts of the railway, such as junctions and crossovers, were simply blown up.

The Allies, however, needed the railways and a process of reconstruction started as soon as they landed. Within a month, a rail line was in operation from Cherbourg to Carentan, thirty-one miles away, and reconstruction took place so near to the front lines that on occasion the unfortunate railway troops found themselves being shelled by the enemy and had to beat a hasty retreat. River crossings where the bridges had invariably been blown presented the greatest obstacle and temporary structures were quickly strung across the water. On the Seine, for example, a bridge together with a quarter of a mile of new railway was laid in just fourteen days at Le Manoir, near Pont de l'Arche. This temporary line opened on 22 September and was the railway route supplying forces operating in the north for the next two months, even though it could not withstand the weight of locomotives, with the result that wagons had to be propelled over it by hand.

There was no time to install signalling on the reconstructed lines, which meant that the heavy traffic attracted onto them had to be controlled by a primitive system of "permissive working" involving flags and boards, rather like the early railways of the middle of the nineteenth century. Inevitably there were frequent accidents caused by drivers bemused by the system. In order to make up for the lack of sufficient railways, a kind of rail system on rubber tyres was set up to bring supplies rapidly from the Channel ports to the front. Called the Red Ball Express, it involved, at its peak, 6,000 trucks that were given sole access to two routes between Cherbourg and Chartres, principally to carry POL — petrol, oil, lubricants — for the army in eastern France, which had far outrun its supply line. It operated through a strict set of rules: drivers could not exceed 25 mph, no overtaking was allowed and at ten minutes before every hour the entire convoy was to stop for a rest. Broken-down trucks were simply pushed aside to await repair. In other words, the system had all the characteristics, even the name, of a rail service, except that it was operated by trucks. The 165-mile-long Red Ball Express was, for a couple of months, a vital part of the line of communication carrying up to 12,500 tonnes per day, but it became self-defeating as the armies progressed east since the trucks consumed so much fuel themselves. While Red Ball was recognized as a remarkably efficient operation, the massive resources it consumed highlighted the limitations of lorry transport for long-distance haulage. The lack of road capacity and the shortage of lorries ensured rail was still the only viable mode to supply such massive military movements, as an analysis of transport in the Second World War explained: "The advance of the armies was thus retarded because only rail transport could provide the needed volume of supply." Gradually, as lines were repaired, more freight was transferred to the railways, with banners on the front of the engine proclaiming "Toot Sweet", a corruption of the French *tout de suite*, in order to ensure they received priority.

The railways played a vital role in the Battle of the Bulge, the last major set-piece confrontation of the war and a clash that turned into one of the bloodiest battles on the Western Front. Fought principally in the Ardennes forests of south-eastern Belgium, it was the last major counter-offensive by the Germans and raged for five weeks as 1944 turned into 1945 with both sides being hamstrung by continuing supply difficulties that were compounded by the severe wintry conditions. The Germans were so short of fuel that anything that could not be transported directly to the front by rail was put on horse-drawn wagons. The Allies had been forced to pause in their advance towards Germany while the railways were repaired and supplies became available from the port of Antwerp, which had been reclaimed by the Allies in November but took a month to become operational. The Germans saw this as an opportunity to counter-attack, using the poor weather as cover since they had all but lost the battle in the air. The Americans, taken by surprise as a result of the Germans' ban on radio communications, were forced to shift troops around with great haste. Fortunately, there was a railway line available and within forty-eight hours of the attack four divisions of the 3rd Army had been moved across the front into the south flank of the bulge to support General Patton's counter-offensive. According to the military historian Van Fleet, "this feat was achieved against the handicap of heavy snow which had to be cleared by hand shovelling and against enemy air opposition. Ammunition was delivered sometimes right to the guns by rail."

While the French railways had been wrecked by a combination of the Resistance and Allied aircraft, the Allies had to rely on attacks from the air to destroy the German ones and that showed how difficult it was to wreck railways without the availability of precision-guided munitions. The Germans had, however, the advantage that they had been on a war footing throughout the 1930s and therefore their railway system was far better able to withstand attacks than those of Britain or France. This was made apparent by a post-war visit to Germany by civil defence officers keen to learn the lessons of the conflict, presumably in anticipation of another one. The strict British officialese language in the report, published in 1947, cannot disguise the deep-set jealousy and even awe of the officials at the thoroughness of the German preparations to protect their railways during the war. The report provides, too, an insight into how well the

Germans coped with their logistical problems until the concerted efforts of the Allies put the German transport system out of commission. The officers were particularly impressed by "the large number of alternative routes available and the generous nature of the facilities provided and the spaciousness of the layouts on running lines at junctions in passenger stations and goods depots and marshalling yards". In order to recover quickly after an attack, huge stockpiles of materials had been stored around the country. Bridges, retaining walls, signal boxes, stations, and railway offices had all been built to resist bomb damage and the officers noted that many of these were still standing, showing signs that they had withstood attacks. Whereas British railway workers struggled in their goods yards in the dark — and were killed by the score as a result in accidents, "the Germans were able to keep lighting at their yards and stations far longer than in the UK because radar gave them better warning of impending attacks". The German railways, the Deutsche Reichsbahn, were also able to withstand the early Allied bombing attacks because the raids were highly concentrated but did not last long and tended to be switched from area to area after a few nights. Therefore the railways could be suspended for a short time and then trains temporarily diverted to alternative routes. Consequently, "a shutdown of services for more than a temporary period of say from 2–3 days was rarely necessary, owing to the existence of so many alternative goods stations and yards". The one error, admitted by the officers' German hosts, was that there

389

were not enough triangular junctions — such junctions can continue functioning even if part of them are destroyed — and their conventional junctions proved to be a weak point in the system.

The basic premise on which the German railways operated was that the "show must go on". Train operation was maintained until considerable numbers of enemy aircraft were in the immediate vicinity. Attacks by single aircraft were generally ignored as maintenance of traffic flow was considered to justify the slight risk. Trains in main-line stations were ordered to leave as soon as possible after an attack began as they were less vulnerable on tracks in the open air.

After attacks, huge resources of manpower, including prisoners and forced slave labour, were thrown at the repair work, and all railway personnel were expected to report for immediate duty. At Hamm, for example, which suffered more than 1,300 hits in a raid on the night of 22 April 1944 (inevitably nicknamed the Hamm and Egg run), 6,000 workers were commandeered almost immediately. A through-track was restored within twenty-four hours of the attack and by the end of six weeks, with the workforce increased to nearly 10,000, the yard, which had been specifically targeted in the raid, was working almost to full capacity.

One clever tactic used across Germany throughout the war was to install railway camouflage: fake bomb craters were dug and flimsy artificial bridges were flung across rivers while mounds of earth and debris were left scattered to suggest that repairs had not been carried out. Decoy targets were provided at a number of less important yards and were deliberately lit to attract the bombers away from more significant areas. Another brilliant innovation which helped the speedy recovery of the railways was the mobile signal box. The Germans built 300 of these boxes, which were despatched with great speed on express passenger trains as soon as damage was reported. They resembled ordinary freight wagons and, placed on sleepers, could be set up within just five hours of their arrival.

The post-war visiting British civil defence officers concluded that "the German railway was never, as a whole, short of motive power, rolling stock, materials or manpower, until 1943 when the destruction was enormous. Even then in many instances, the shortages were often due to the administrative breakdown and to distributional problems rather than to any lack of material as such." The Germans had created vast numbers of spare marshalling yards, so that alternatives could easily be used should one be destroyed, and that was to prove essential in keeping the railways moving once the air attacks intensified. Nor were the railways in the beginning a specific target but rather they were "incidental to the main attack". It was only from April 1944, when the bombing was directed specifically against railway installations as part of the plan to disrupt communications prior to invasion, that the ability of the system to function began to be seriously undermined: "The situation became such that no repair organisation could restore working sufficiently so as to enable the German railway to carry that quantity of traffic and to deliver it with the speed necessary to maintain industrial production and a successful army in the field."

All of this explains one of the mysteries of the war — why it took so much effort to destroy the German communication systems from the air. According to an American analysis of the effect of bombing on Germany's economy, "it took 9,000 aircraft in Operation Clarion to knock out about three quarters of German production of railway trucks between the spring of 1944 and March 1945." On the other hand, it required massive diversion of German resources to provide both the air defence and operational staff to keep the railways running. Right at the end of the war, in 1945, the British started using massive "Tallboy" bombs, weighing up to 10 tons, to destroy railway infrastructure such as tunnels and viaducts, and had these been available earlier, the bombing campaign might have taken its toll more quickly.

On the other hand, the transportation system might have done even better, as suggested in a contemporary report by the *Daily Telegraph*, which in September 1944 highlighted Hitler's mistake in favouring roads: "Up to the present there has been no actual breakdown of the German railway system. But it is very clear that in the last, the crucial, phase of the war, Hitler is suffering the consequences of one of his less spectacular but most important miscalculations. He has at his disposal the finest road system any country ever possessed — but he lacks the petrol to use it." Moreover, the motorways had been funded by profits from the German railways, and the *Daily Telegraph* concluded: "If all the gigantic expenditure of money and effort which went into the building of the great trunk roads had been allotted instead to the railways, they would at least have started the war at the highest pitch of efficiency and they might still be highly efficient today." Hitler, in other words, might have resisted longer had he focussed more on the railways and less on building roads for which he did not have sufficient vehicles or fuel.

If, as demonstrated above, the efficiency of the railways was key to the German war effort, it was also essential for carrying out the greatest crime of the Second World War, the despatch of millions of Jews and other victims of the Holocaust to the concentration and death camps. Just as war could not have been conducted on such a huge scale without the railways, the sheer number and speed of the deportations would have been quite impossible through road transport alone. The railways not only enabled vastly greater numbers to be transported, but since the victims were locked into freight railway wagons, the Germans needed far less manpower to supervise and transport them, which was a crucial factor in enabling so many people to be carried in a relatively short period of time. Not only did the method of transport save manpower and trucks, but crucially fuel, which was ever in short supply for the German war effort. It was telling that there were bigger arguments within the German leadership over the transport needs required to carry out the policy than there were over its morality.

The first trains, in October 1941, between Germany and Poland (and further east to Riga), were principally to move German Jews out of Germany into ghettos where the previous inhabitants had been eliminated. The despatch of Jews direct to Auschwitz and the other death camps for extermination began in the spring of 1942 and the flow intensified over the next two years and then began to slow after the Allies landed in northern France, although the last recorded train was in March 1945. The deportations were carried out on an industrial scale and in an extremely calculated manner. For the most part, freight wagons were used, though in places where the Germans were keen to maintain the myth that the Jews were simply being "resettled in the east", the victims travelled in third-class carriages. Cruelly, most of the deportees were forced to buy a one-way ticket, with children being charged half fare.

In order to carry out the transportation of the victims, basic calculations had to be made by the railway authorities in order to ensure that the camps received the number of people that could be "processed" — mostly, of course, murdered on arrival. Each freight wagon could accommodate fifty people but they were usually filled with 100 or even 150, with the result that many people died before reaching the camps. No food or water was provided, and only a bucket as a latrine, and since the wagons had no protection from the heat or cold, conditions soon became intolerable whatever the weather conditions outside. In order for the trains to proceed reasonably quickly once they were on the main line, they were limited to fifty-five wagons each. The average journey time was more than four days as the trains were given the least priority and consequently were frequently stabled in sidings for days at a time while freight and troop services were allowed to pass through. The longest journey involved a train of Jews from Corfu, who were transferred to a train on the mainland which then took eighteen days to reach its destination. By the time it reached the camp, there were only corpses on board. The total number of people transported in the trains, as ascertained from the detailed records kept by the German and Polish state railway companies, was about 8 million, packed into 1,600 trains.

The deportations would not have been possible without the co-operation of the various countries' rail companies, notably the French state railway, SNCF, but also its counterparts in the Netherlands and Belgium, and there were severe recriminations against these companies after the war. According to a report in the *Jerusalem Post*, 200,000 German railway employees alone were involved in the deportations and "10,000 to 20,000 were responsible for mass murders but were never prosecuted".

As this grim crime demonstrates, as with all aspects of its operation, the Deutsche Reichsbahn was nothing if not efficient. Its remarkable ability to survive the Allied onslaught for so long meant that its ultimate collapse was all the more devastating. The redundancy built into the German railways before the war, with much deliberate duplication of facilities, and the priority given to maintaining the coal supply, which was the lifeblood of the system, ensured that the railways had continued functioning far beyond expectations throughout the conflict. Because they had managed to survive so long under such difficult circumstances, when they finally did collapse, virtually the whole system fell apart with frightening speed. The Germans hastened the process by destroying lines in front of the invading forces, notably blowing up all the bridges across the Rhine, with the exception of the Remagen bridge captured in March 1945, which was only partly destroyed, leaving it able to carry wagons, though not locomotives, until it collapsed ten days later. The first replacement bridge over the Rhine at Wessel was completed in ten days and within a month it was carrying nearly fifty trains per day. The destruction of the German railways, nevertheless, was again a handicap to the Allied invaders and slowed their progress on numerous occasions. From beginning to end, therefore, the railways or the lack of them played an important part in the progress of the Second World War. Surprisingly, despite the growing sophistication of aircraft and missiles, the railways would still play a part in several conflicts of the second half of the twentieth century.

CHAPTER
TEN

Blood on the Tracks

Those damn Commies. One can almost feel the irritation of General James Van Fleet, the commander of the US and UN forces in the Korean War, as he describes the way that the North Koreans managed to keep their railways operating despite two periods of intense bombardment by the Americans aimed at destroying their railway supply lines. His account is a blend of exasperation tinged with begrudging admiration and respect for the enemy: "How could the Chinese Communist armies in Korea supply themselves in hostile territory 200 miles from their Manchurian base in the face of the terrific interdiction program of the USAF and Naval Air? . . . We knew they were getting the bulk of their supplies by rail. We knew the location of all rail lines. We had air and naval supremacy. But in spite of all our air and naval interdiction attacks, their railroads continued to keep them supplied, even to the point of building up reserves for offensive actions. How could they do it?"

As the general suggests, the railways played a key role in the Korean War, which may have been the first war of the Cold War era but in most respects was an old-fashioned conflict fought through infantry attacks backed by air cover and even, at times, involving troops dug into trenches. Korea was divided, without reference to the Korean people, in the aftermath of the Second World War and it was the China-supported Communist North's attempt to invade the South which triggered the war in June 1950. In the first phase, the Communists took over nearly all the Korean peninsula. Over the next three years, they would be gradually forced back to a dividing line along the 38th Parallel by United Nations forces which mainly consisted of South Korean and US troops, though they included a sizeable contingent of nearly 100,000 soldiers from Britain and Australia, as well as men from more than a dozen other nations. Although the Americans and South Koreans had blown up railway bridges as they retreated southward in the face of the North Korean onslaught, it did not take long for the invaders to have supply trains up and running on those lines. The North Koreans were supplied from Manchuria, part of China, which under the rules of engagement was out of bounds to United Nations bombers and consequently the railways were vital in bringing supplies down south.

The key to the strategy of pushing the Communists back north towards China was to destroy their supply lines from their base in Manchuria and this led the Americans to launch two massive aerial attacks targeted at the railways, called, hubristically, Operation Strangle and Operation Saturate. In fact, they managed neither. Despite being supplemented by a naval blockade and long-range gunfire from ships, the bombing campaigns proved ineffectual. The lessons of the Second World War had not been learnt. According to an examination of the operation by a military analyst, "the planners simply asserted that air attacks could make sufficient cuts in rail lines to stem the flow of supplies. This assumption ignored the recent experiences of . . . rail interdiction efforts in World War II, which showed that cutting rail lines was extremely difficult and that, until a new munition was developed, this was not a particularly effective technique when compared with the effort involved in achieving those cuts." As the British and Americans had discovered when attacking Germany at the end of the war, railway lines were difficult to destroy solely from the air. And so it proved again.

The US military had originally intended to target roads but then realized that the railways were far more important in the line of communication. If the railways were blocked they calculated that a fleet of 6,000 trucks would be needed to replace the 120 freight wagons carrying the 2,400 tons of supplies needed daily. And the North Koreans simply did not have that number of trucks, and, as ever, the roads were in a poor condition. Consequently, the first bombing operation aimed at destroying these lines, Strangle, was launched in August 1951. For the first three months it seemed to go well but that was mainly because supporting ground forces followed up the aerial attacks, and the seasonal rains added to the difficulties of operating the railway. Once the ground forces withdrew, however, the effectiveness of the air attacks greatly diminished. Only one in four sorties resulted in any damage to the railways and only an eighth of the 500lb bombs fell anywhere near the tracks. Moreover, more than one aircraft per day was being lost in the raids. As Operation Strangle entered the Korean winter, the results were even worse because the bombs simply skidded along the frozen ground and exploded harmlessly, littering the countryside with shrapnel but leaving the rail lines untouched.

Even worse for the American attackers was the speed with which any damage they did cause was quickly reinstated. Or appeared to be. Wrecked bridges were replaced or, if that proved too difficult, a new line was built to by-pass the wreckage. With an almost infinite amount of Korean and Chinese manpower to call on, supplies were simply manhandled past any obstruction in the line and transferred from one set of wagons to another. Van Fleet, however, kept on being informed by his aides, who, like all staff officers before them, had over-optimism in their DNA, of the good news that the railway had been put out of commission for a long time: "Repeatedly I was assured by my own staff and by the Air Force and Naval Air, often supported by photographs, that 'a mile or more of rails at critical points' or 'the bridges at Sinanju' were 'out for good'. But always a few days later, locomotives pulling trains were operating at these very locations. In short, we were witnessing this time to our own military disadvantage and frustration, another demonstration of the capacity, the durability, and the flexibility of railroads under war conditions."

Partly this was because the Communists proved very clever at fooling the US forces into thinking that the bombing was more effective than it was. Bridges were made to look wrecked by having removable spans taken out during the day and replaced at night; by-pass crossings over rivers were hidden with camouflage and trains sheltered in tunnels at night. The deception worked. The post-war reports later criticized the military commanders for failing to spot that much of the photographic evidence of destruction was nothing of the sort, rather reminiscent of the famous Iraq weapons of mass destruction dossier.

Operation Strangle had been intended to last only a month and a half, and after four months, at the end of 1951, there were calls within the military leadership to stop the waste of resources and wind it up. Instead, a new programme, Saturate, was launched. It was a more comprehensive attempt to bomb the supply lines out of existence by operating at night when the trains ran, as well as during the day. However, there were only the resources to attack a limited number of targets, and most of the railway lines were left intact. Again, any damage was repaired quickly and Saturate was deemed another failure. In total, the Americans flew a staggering 172,000 missions of reconnaissance and bombing, and fired 230,000 rounds of ammunition on "interdiction" flights aimed at disrupting the Communists' supply lines. Van Fleet, still exasperated half a decade later when writing his report on the performance of the air force in the Korean War, recalled how "we dive bombed and skip-bombed, we shelled with heavy naval guns, we cannonaded with ground artillery, we strafed with rockets and machine guns, we organized sabotage and guerrilla attacks. But we never stopped the Red railroads from delivering ammunition and supplies ... At no time, except locally and temporarily, did the enemy limit his combat effort because of supply considerations. By every index, the Communists were able to steadily increase their flow of supplies to the front lines." As John Westwood, the author of *Railways at War*, put it: "In this contest, in which the latest air and naval weapons were deployed against the railway system of North Korea, the railways emerged a clear winner." The Americans had, too, probably overestimated the level of supplies needed for a lightly armed Asian army, which meant that the enemy's troops could survive with far fewer trains than had been estimated.

The United Nations forces themselves made heavy use of the railways remaining in their hands during the conflict. The reinforcements and supplies which were landed at Inchon on the west coast were all immediately transferred by rail to the front lines and bases on railway wagons pulled by locomotives brought over on the ships. It was, by all accounts, an incredibly efficient operation, unhampered by bombing raids since the United Nations forces dominated the air.

In the early stages of the Vietnam War, too, the railways were perceived by both sides as the crucial transport lifeline. In particular, the 1,100-mile line between Saigon and Hanoi that stretches parallel to the coast for much of the country was much fought over.

The initial conflict in Vietnam, which pitted the colonial power, the French, against the Chinese-supported Viet Minh seeking independence, began as the Second World War ended and throughout the conflict the government struggled to retain control of the railways. The French were acting as a proxy for the United Nations and the other main Western countries who wanted to maintain the colonial presence in south-east Asia but struggled to retain the area which they had occupied nearly a century previously. The railways were, according to a contemporary report written in 1953 by an American journalist, Paul Wohl, "the backbone of United Nations defenses against Russia's Stalin and China's Mao in Southeast Asia. Had it not been for these railroads, the French together with the Vietnam administration of their puppet, the former Annamese emperor Bao Dai, might have been thrown into the sea by the guerrillas who have the support of a large part of the intensely nationalistic population."

It was, however, a struggle. Less than half the Saigon-Hanoi line was functioning and remained under French control, and running trains required huge military support. The French had lost most of the inland regions to the insurgents but, in order to maintain supplies to parts of the country still under their control, needed to run trains along the line. While for the most part the line hugs the coast, at times it veers inland and operating on those sections involved running through guerrilla-controlled areas. Therefore, rather than sending a train alone along the railway, the

French ran convoys of half a dozen trains consisting of both passenger and freight cars dubbed *rafale* ("gust of wind"), with the president's former train now converted into a mobile hospital at the core. Confined to a maximum of 25 mph through fear that round the next curve there might be a gaping hole rather than a bridge, these trains only ran during the day, guarded by an armoured freight wagon at the front and an armoured train in the rear. Being French, these extraordinary convoys included *wagons-cuisines* complete with chef in white headgear flanked by an assistant and a butler. For the Vietnamese travelling in the train, there were "one or two more *wagon-cuisines*, complete with rijstafel [a lavish feast based on rice] and chop sticks and additional detachments of fighting culinary specialists".

At night, the trains stopped "in special encampments with barricades and watch towers established at convenient points between terminals where the convoy is re-arranged for shelter and defense", and the whole set-up, as Wohl rightly points out, was "not so different from the one adopted in this country [the US] in the days of the great trek to the West when covered wagons were lined up for the night". There was indeed a kind of Wild West spirit about these trains and their commanders, who gained a legendary reputation for getting through the enemy lines. Like the wagon trains, they were constantly being attacked, bombed, mined or faced with boulders rolled onto the tracks. Several trains were damaged but, according to Wohl, "new units constantly are being equipped in Saigon and Hanoi" so that *la rafale* could "safely go on during the day".

The armoured support trains were crucial for the convoys' survival and patrolled the line at night: "Vietnam railway engineers believe that without these nocturnal train patrols which whisk ghostlike through dark rice paddies and jungles, suddenly lighting up the track or stopping for inspections and forays, the rail service could not have been carried on." The Viet Minh themselves had a few armoured trains and at one point two such trains from opposing sides met on the track and shot at one another across a vale where thick jungle growth had invaded the right of way. Wohl is probably not far off the mark in describing it as an event "unique in railway history" but his evocative description may just be slightly over the top: "As the beams of the searchlights swept through the mangrove brush and guns flashed and thundered, swarms of screaming birds rose into the night, and for seconds the swish and rustle of panicky gazelles, wild pigs and zebu bulls drowned out the clanking of the moving trains . . . After a few minutes the gunfire stopped. Either the distance between the Vietnam and the Vietminh tracks was too great or the gunners did not aim right in the confusion. The purpose of either train was not to fight the other but to clear the track. Mission accomplished, they returned to base."

The control of Vietnam's railways was crucial to the wider battle between the Western and Communist forces. According to Wohl, writing at the time of the engagement, "the United Nations long range strategy in

405

this struggle is to reopen the routes from the sea into the interior, while the communist aim is to extend their land transportation system into Southeast Asia to the Gulf of Siam and the Bay of Bengal. Both the United Nations and the communist strategies hinge upon control of the Vietnam railroads."

Soon, though, it was all over for the French. They could not retain their tenuous supply line on the railway and, with the war becoming increasingly unpopular at home, they left after being decisively defeated at Dien Bien Phu in May 1954, the remarkable battle where the guerrilla army of the Viet Minh came out of the jungle to triumph over the French. The Saigon-Hanoi railway was left in a sorry state, with huge sections of line missing, removed by the Viet Minh to build lines in the territory they occupied. When the Americans started arriving in force in the early 1960s in support of the pro-West South Vietnamese regime against the Viet Cong insurgents, they immediately recognized the importance of the line and funded the reconstruction of tracks on the 600-mile section between Saigon and Hué, close to the 17th Parallel, the border between North and South. However, it proved impossible to provide a reliable service because of the constant attacks by Viet Cong forces — no fewer than 800 between 1961 and 1964 alone — and soon large sections of the track had to be abandoned. It meant that road transport, ever vulnerable to ambush in the Vietnamese countryside, became the principal line of communication, along with expensive helicopters, for the American war effort.

Once the war escalated, the Americans frequently targeted the northern section of the main line between Hanoi and the border under Communist control, but again many sections remained in use thanks to rapid repair. However, the railways were a secondary route as most supplies were sent along the famous Ho Chi Minh trail, a jungle pathway that was gradually expanded into a road able to take the trucks supplied by the Russians and Chinese. By the end of the war, the railway on both sides of the border was virtually derelict, requiring a massive effort to bring it back into use involving reconstructing more than 1,300 bridges and twenty-seven tunnels. With almost limitless supplies of labour available, this huge task was carried out remarkably quickly and the first train on the hugely symbolic "Reunification Express" ran on the final day of 1976, just twenty months after the Americans had suffered the humiliation of fleeing their embassy in Saigon.

Between the Korean and Vietnamese wars, India and Pakistan had briefly been at each other's throats when Bangladesh separated off from Pakistan in 1971, and railways were inevitably involved. The Indians, rather suspiciously, had completed a railway crossing over the Ganges at Farakka a month before the outbreak of the war, eliminating a bottleneck on the route between India and what would become Bangladesh. According to John Westwood, a senior railway official said that without the crossing "it would have been well-nigh impossible to have moved the necessary troops and supplies". When the Indian Army invaded Bangladesh, railway personnel quickly repaired damaged routes, including laying a 25-mile line through to the town of Jessore in just ten days. While this brief war showed that railways were still important for the military in this type of conflict which involved substantial movement of troops, it was one of the last times that the logistics of war were dependent on them.

Armoured trains, too, were still used long after it may have been considered that sophisticated aerial weaponry would have made them redundant. In the post-war period, the Russians retained their long-standing interest in these behemoths. In the 1960s, they deployed sophisticated versions of armoured trains along the Chinese border to deter any possible attack during a period of tension between the two biggest Communist nations. They were also used by the Russian military in various campaigns against separatist insurgents, notably in 1990 against Azeri nationalists and in both Chechen wars of the 1990s and early 2000s. Remarkably, the Russian government, in February 2010, announced that it intended to put two armoured trains back in service in order to fight insurgents in the North Caucasus. This was in response to a series of terrorist attacks against railways in Russia mostly by Chechen or other separatist groups.

The Russians, too, were involved in the development of mobile rail-based missile launchers, which can be seen to be a sophisticated version of an armoured train. There was a brief flourish of interest in this concept by both America and Russia towards the end of the Cold War, when the two superpowers both began to work on railway-based intercontinental ballistic missiles mounted on armoured trains, which had the obvious advantage of mobility over the silos used for most of these weapons. The Russians spent the 1970s developing a highly sophisticated system with missiles that were capable of being launched from both silos and trains. After considerable difficulties, and the scrapping of several prototype models, a formidable rail-based weapon was produced. In 1987, the Soviets deployed launchers for the SS-24 missile, which were nuclear-armed rockets with a payload equivalent to more than 550,000 tonnes of TNT and capable of reaching the US with their range of 6,000 miles. Apparently only one test missile was ever fired from a rail-based launcher and, according to Russian news sources, it reached its target in Kamchatka, in eastern Russia, without the US spy satellites being able to ascertain the whereabouts of the train from which it had been launched.

The trains were unremarkable in appearance as each one consisted only of three missile launch cars, two or three diesel locomotives, an electrical power generating car, a command and control car, and two support and accommodation cars, and consequently spy satellites could not distinguish them from ordinary freight traffic. Most of the time, the rail launchers were kept in special sidings, but they were able to start rolling at a moment's notice and could cover up to 600 miles per day, making detection virtually impossible. They were capable of travelling on most of the Soviet rail network, but would not have been capable of firing on sections, like much of the Trans-Siberian, which were electrified with overhead wires.

Even with access to information released since the end of the Cold War, it is somewhat unclear how many trains were ever built. There were thirty-five missiles and trains were designed to carry up to three each, implying that around a dozen were deployed. The trains were eventually scrapped in favour of road- or silo-based systems in 2005, to the surprise of some Russian military commentators such as Yury Zaitsev, a research adviser at the Russian Academy of Engineering Sciences, who felt that rail offered undoubted advantages because road-based launchers, capable of only very slow movement, were "a sitting duck" while "a rail network, on the other hand, can ensure missile systems" stealthy movement. When the Americans considered building a rail-based missile system based on the Russian model, they concluded that "there was only a 10 per cent probability of 150 Satan missiles hitting 25 rail missile complexes (twice the number Russia had at the time) spread on a railroad network of 75,000 miles". This demonstrated the effectiveness of this type of system and therefore Zaitsev concluded that it could only be the high cost of maintenance which caused the Russians to scrap rail-based missiles.

In contrast, the US efforts to put missiles on trains did not get very far, although there were two abortive schemes. The idea of installing missiles on trains was first mooted in the US in 1959 and a test was carried out to assess whether the vibrations on the tracks would affect the mechanism. This seems to have been

410

successful and a plan was announced for thirty trains, each with three Minuteman missiles, but the scheme was scrapped on the grounds of cost by the incoming administration of President John F. Kennedy in 1961. A similar scheme was revived in December 1986, when President Ronald Reagan announced that there was to be a "rail garrison" system for basing part of the so-called Peacekeeper Intercontinental Ballistic Missile force. In order to make the hundred-strong missile system less vulnerable to attack, half the missiles were to be mounted on a set of twenty-five trains, which would each have two locomotives, two security cars, two missile launch cars, a control car, a fuel car and a maintenance car. The trains were to be parked in shelters located on air force bases throughout the continental United States but would be ever ready to be dispersed in the event of an attack. The project was developed for five years but scrapped in 1991 before deployment as Cold War tensions eased.

In the 1980s, Britain also decided on a mobile missile launch system for its nuclear warheads but instead of basing it on the railways, deployed its Trident nuclear missiles on tremendously expensive submarines, on the grounds that the UK was rather too small to hide rail-based launchers and that, in any case, turning the country into the equivalent of a huge aircraft carrier would have been unacceptable to the British public. However, the British government did request the state-owned British Railways to make civil defence preparations for nuclear war in the mid-1950s. Old carriages, mostly from the 1920s and 1930s, were fitted with modern communications equipment to act as mobile emergency control offices and communication centres for government officials in the event of a nuclear war. These works were carried out in secret but later it emerged that at least four of these trains had been formed in 1962, following the Cuban Missile Crisis. They were moved around between half a dozen secret locations, including Faversham, Tunbridge Wells, Derby and York, but appear to have been returned to British Rail in the early 1980s and at least three survive as passenger coaches on preserved lines.

Missile trains were the swansong of the military use of railways. There is the odd exception, with armoured trains still being deployed in Russia, which is forever beset with insurgents, and in North Korea, where Kim Jong-il travels around his country in his personal one, but that is more a neat commentary on just how much the Dear Leader trusts his fellow countryfolk rather than on the effectiveness of such use of the railways. Military equipment and tanks are occasionally carried on railways, and troops may still sometimes be moved around on trains, but in truth railways will never again be fundamental to the way conflicts are fought. General Van Fleet may have been wrong when he wrote in the late 1950s: "No form or combination of forms of transport appears likely to challenge the key place of railroads in the military logistical picture . . . military planners know they must look to railroads for the great bulk of the military requirement for transport in the future as in the past." However, that merely illustrates the military's perennial mistake of forever fighting the last war when predicting the needs for the next one. Van Fleet was not alone in his mistake.

Just as the military took so long to exploit fully the value of the railways, they were also slow to realize when the rules of the game had changed completely. Railways did play a crucial part in what was known as TTW (transition to war) planning by both NATO and the Warsaw Pact in the Cold War. Rail remained integral to the preparations of both sides in the wargame exercises of the Cold War when NATO actively prepared for an invasion of Europe by the Soviet Union. For example, the dimension of NATO tanks was determined by their ability to be transported on railways, which was the only way to move them rapidly over long distances and preserve their battleworthiness prior to fighting. And rail was used by the Russians to transport tanks during the Hungarian and Czech crises of 1956 and 1968 respectively.

Yet, the age of the railway war was coming to an end and, inevitably, military leaders began to understand that a different form of warfare was becoming necessary because of technological developments in both weaponry and transport. Warfare is now mostly conducted through the use of sophisticated weaponry that can be targeted with unerring accuracy, even if it goes wrong on occasion and wipes out innocent wedding guests or Chinese embassy officials. Large-scale set-piece warfare involving massive armies of hundreds of thousands of men on both sides has become impossible with the development of ever more sophisticated aerial weaponry, delivered both by aircraft

413

and by missile launchers. The trenches of the Somme would today be wiped out by a few well-aimed rockets probably fired from drones at no cost of life to the side dominating the air. Nothing better illustrates the changing nature of warfare than the death toll in the Afghan war which, after many years, still amounts to far fewer than the number killed in just one day in a typical First World War battle. With far smaller armies being deployed, there is no longer any need for railways to transport troops and, in any case, transport methods have greatly improved. Huge troop-carrying aircraft can ferry soldiers around the world with remarkable speed and once in the war zone, with tarred roads now almost universal, they can be carried long distances in modern trucks or, in unsafe areas, flown in by helicopter. The other type of modern war, the guerrilla insurgency, offers little role for the railways apart from, as we have seen, the deployment of the occasional armoured train, but even then only if the insurgents do not have access to anti-tank weaponry. Such wars have, however, proved very destructive to railways in various places. Railways are ultimately easy to sabotage and therefore are an obvious target for insurgents. In parts of the world, notably in African countries such as the Congo and Angola, where the government forces are not strong enough to prevent these attacks, whole railway systems have been put out of commission more or less permanently by warfare.

It was not happenstance that railways changed the nature of war. They were tailor-made for it. To ensure safety and to operate efficiently to a timetable, railways need military discipline. Right from the beginning, they attracted military personnel and were run like private armies, with uniforms and a clear distinction between officers and men. They were the first large corporations and consequently developed their own police forces. Their rules and regulations became enshrined in law. In a practical sense, too, they were eminently suitable for military use. They maintained and renewed their own equipment, from engine sheds and stations, to locomotives and the track. They were familiar with the challenge of repairing damage from accidents and natural disasters promptly, and they employed permanent maintenance teams who could easily be called upon to respond to military attacks. They were flexible, able to adapt by operating on alternative routes or even creating by-passes to circumvent obstacles. They were often built with military objectives in mind or at least with strategic aims being taken into account when routes were selected. For example, two of the world's greatest railway projects, the American transcontinental across the US completed in 1869, and the Trans-Siberian, which triggered the Russo-Japanese conflict of 1904–5, had military objectives.

For about a century, broadly from the Crimean War to the Korean, railways were an essential part of the conduct of war. This age of the railway war may only seem like a short episode in the long history of warfare, but it was a period in which several of the bloodiest conflicts in history took place. And that was no coincidence. The railways enabled carnage on that scale to take place, from delivering large numbers of men and unprecedented quantities of ammunition to the front lines, to moving troops around theatres of war rapidly, and taking away the wounded and the dying efficiently in ambulance trains.

While the age of the military railway is now over thanks to technological changes in both weaponry and transport, for more than a century the railways determined the nature, size and length of wars, but what about the outcome of these wars? There is no doubt that on numerous occasions the railways — or, more accurately, the effective use of the railways — were crucial in giving one side in the war an advantage over the other. That strange little railway from Balaklava, the first genuine military line, was certainly helpful in breaking the siege of Sevastopol but was probably not decisive to the outcome. In the first genuine railway war, the American Civil War, the North's better railways were certainly helpful but it is very difficult to assess whether they were decisive since the North would probably have won anyway as it had industrial and economic might on its side. Its better railways were simply a reflection of its more advanced state of economic development.

The ability of the Prussians to reach the battle of Königgrätz more quickly than the Austrians was important, too, but probably more in ensuring the war was short than in determining its outcome since the Austrians were pretty hopeless militarily, as they demonstrated later in the First World War. In the Franco-Prussian War, the side with the better railways lost. However, that merely highlighted the fact that it was not good enough simply to have superior equipment — true of weaponry, too — but it was vital to employ it to best effect. The result, therefore, was more the product of the chaos on the French railways at the beginning of the war, which immediately put the country at a disadvantage.

In the colonial wars waged by Britain, the railways probably were decisive. It is doubtful if the British would have been able to subdue the Mahdi in Sudan, let alone the Boers in South Africa, without them. Certainly, Churchill had no doubts about that. As for the Russo-Japanese War, it would never have happened without the railway which was not only a *casus belli* but the only means by which the Russians could reach Manchuria, where the conflict took place.

As for the two world wars, it is undeniable that they could not have been fought with such devastating consequences without the railways to deliver more and more men and supplies with unrelenting efficiency. If the railways were not responsible for the outbreak of the First World War, their availability — or lack of it — was crucial at every stage and they were undoubtedly fundamental in creating the ghastly and prolonged nature of the conflict. At the outset, the Germans were helped by having a superior railway system tailored to launching an offensive, but ultimately they were unable to make that advantage tell because the railway war only lasted a few weeks. While the Germans initially won the war of movement, France, after absorbing the initial shock of the invasion, survived and eventually prevailed. All that meticulous planning by Schlieffen

417

and Moltke came to little because they had underestimated the logistical constraints of the railway age. Nor did having the best line of communication guarantee success. The battle of Verdun, for example, showed that the side with an inferior supply route could resist an attack provided sufficient resources were devoted to improving it. More important than the relative strength of each railway system was the fact that at the stage of technology pertaining at the time of the First World War, the defending side in any battle had a natural advantage thanks to the railways. Moreover, by simply allowing armies to become bigger, the railways made it more difficult for an attacker to gain a decisive advantage. Larger defending armies with good logistical support just proved harder to destroy. The First World War demonstrated this in spades, and it was only the mechanisation of warfare that allowed the tables to be turned a little as tanks began to be able to overrun fixed positions.

Remarkably, though, even the Second World War was essentially decided during the period of attrition between Russia and Germany rather than during the phases of movement. Operation Barbarossa demonstrated that railways were, even in the middle of the twentieth century, still the key component of military logistics. The Germans would undoubtedly have fared better if their troops had arrived after a train journey rather than having to march several hundred miles through hostile countryside. They may well have been able to capture Leningrad or Moscow before the winter set in, enabling them to retain the initiative that was lost in the snow of the winter of 1941, thereby greatly prolonging the war. Nevertheless, ultimately, even with a series of rail lines to support them, the Germans would probably have been overcome by the sheer scale of their task, as had been all invaders of Russia before them. Oddly, too, they were defeated when the Russians made use of an unexpected means of transport: the ski.

Even if it is difficult to pin down precisely the influence of the railways on outcomes of the various conflicts during the age of the railway war, it is impossible not to recognize the way in which they became an integral part of warfare. The railways formed an extraordinary backdrop to war for more than a hundred years, most notably, of course, in the most devastating of the railway conflicts, the First World War. The images are striking, searing even, and have never left us. The troop trains covered with patriotic slogans early in the war but later filled with soldiers sat rather more quietly, having become more aware of the realities of fighting; the endless freight trains carrying war material through the night to overworked railheads, where countless men worked round the clock to make sense of the chaos of supplying fronts whose appetite for ammunition, food, equipment and home comforts was insatiable; the tiny light railways which appeared to be nothing more than slightly expanded versions of Hornby Dublo trains housed in countless attics but which proved to be essential in keeping those fronts supplied; the railway tracks twisted at impossible angles by the destructive forces of war and yet which were put back with remarkable speed through almost superhuman effort; the spick and span hospital trains waiting behind the front before an attack, with an aura of antiseptic cleanliness that can almost be sniffed from those staged photographs of matronly nurses who knew that within hours they would be toiling among the dead and the maimed soldiers, and which then, remarkably, could remove these broken men hundreds of miles out of further harm's way in a matter of hours; the express trains carrying generals and their staff to urgent assignments overriding every other train; and even bearded King George V, sitting next to a general on the front of a tiny four-seater carriage of a 60cm railway visiting a forest being cut down for duckboards; and so much more.

During a period of around a hundred years, trains and railways were inseparable from war. And rightly so. Without them, as we have seen countless times, industrial-scale warfare would have been impossible. This darker side of the history of railways is in danger of being forgotten. Railways have brought us so much. As demonstrated in my previous book, *Blood, Iron & Gold*, they were the agents of modernization, spreading industrialization and transforming the way people lived more radically than any other invention before or since. Yet, as this book highlights on almost every page, this wonderful invention, which brought the world cheap and easy transport for the first time, was also responsible for the deaths of millions of people. Industrial-scale warfare, and therefore industrial-scale carnage, would not have been possible without the iron road.

That role has now all but ended because ultimately railways proved too inflexible to maintain their usefulness for military purposes in a motorized age. Railways need an expensive and heavy infrastructure to support them — track, stations, sidings, signalling, locomotives, carriages and so on — and yet they cannot go where there are no tracks. It was inevitable that eventually motorized transport would take over, but it took a long time because the advantages of railways in transporting large quantities of both freight and people remained unparalleled, which is why they still thrive today. However, with the demise of mass industrial-scale warfare, they are no longer required for military purposes. Much blood was spilt on the tracks but, thankfully, railways will never again be called upon to be the engines of war.

Also available in ISIS Large Print:

Blood, Iron & Gold

Christian Wolmar

Blood, Iron and Gold reveals the huge impact of the railways as they spread rapidly across the world, linking cities that had hitherto been isolated, stimulating both economic growth and social change on an unprecedented scale.

From Panama to the Punjab, Christian Wolmar describes the vision and determination of the pioneers who developed railways that would one day span continents, as well as the labour of the navvies who built this global network.

Wolmar shows how cultures were enriched — and destroyed — by the unrelenting construction and how they had a vital role in civil conflict, as well as in two world wars. Indeed, the global expansion of the railways was key to the spread of modernity and the making of the modern world.

ISBN 978-0-7531-5249-2 (hb)
ISBN 978-0-7531-5250-8 (pb)

Fire & Steam

Christian Wolmar

The opening of the pioneering Liverpool & Manchester Railway in 1830 marked the beginning of the railway network's vital role in changing the face of Britain. *Fire & Steam* celebrates the vision of the ambitious Victorian pioneers who developed this revolutionary transport system and the navvies who cut through the land to enable a country-wide railway to emerge.

The rise of the steam train allowed goods and people to circulate around Britain as never before, stimulating the growth of towns and industrialisation. Workers and day-trippers flocked to the stations as railway mania grew and businessmen clamoured to invest in this expanding industry.

From the early days of steam to electrification, via the railways' magnificent contribution in two world wars, the chequered history of British Rail and the buoyant future of the train, *Fire & Steam* examines the importance of the railway and how it helped to form the Britain of today.

ISBN 978-0-7531-5683-4 (hb)
ISBN 978-0-7531-5684-1 (pb)

Wings

Patrick Bishop

The Royal Air Force is synonymous with its heroic achievements in the summer of 1940, when Winston Churchill's "famous few" held Göering's Luftwaffe at bay in the Battle of Britain, thereby changing the course of the war. For much of the 20th century, warplanes were fixed in the world's imagination, a symbol of the modern era. But within the space of a hundred years, military aviation has morphed from the exotic to the mundane. An activity which was charged with danger is now carried out by computers and unpiloted drones.

Aviators have always seemed different from soldiers and sailors — more adventurous, questing and imaginative. In both world wars air aces dominated each side's propaganda, capturing hearts and dreams. Writing with verve, passion and sheer narrative aplomb, Patrick Bishop brings us a rich and compelling account of military flying from its heroic early days to the present.

ISBN 978-0-7531-5326-0 (hb)
ISBN 978-0-7531-5327-7 (pb)

Target Tirpitz

Patrick Bishop

Tirpitz was the pride of Hitler's navy, the largest and most powerful battleship in Europe. To Churchill she was "the Beast", a menace to Britain's supply lines. To those who sailed in her she seemed impregnable, an "Iron Castle" that could withstand any bomb or torpedo. Tirpitz rarely fired her monster guns. She did not need to. This warship haunted the imaginations of the men directing Britain's war. Plan after plan was hatched to send her to the bottom.

In the end it was Bomber Command who finished her off. In the autumn of 1944, Wing Commander James "Willie" Tait, led Lancasters from 617 Squadron — the famous "Dambusters'" — and 9 Squadron on a series of raids that stretched endurance, skill and bravery to the limit. It ended with the destruction of the battleship that had come to symbolise the hubris of Hitler's Germany.

ISBN 978-0-7531-5316-1 (hb)
ISBN 978-0-7531-5317-8 (pb)

Raiders

Ross Kemp

Six raids that changed the course of history

Operation Judgement: one of the most spectacular efforts of World War Two, where obsolete British biplanes attacked the Italian fleet in Taranto.

Operation Archery: the first true combined operation carried out by all three British forces. This successful raid persuaded Hitler that the Allies were planning a full-scale invasion.

Operation Biting: a cross-Channel raid into France that was the first major attack by the British Airborne Division and its first battle honour.

Operation Gunnerside: a dramatic demolition assault on Hitler's atomic bomb plant in Norway.

Operation Chariot: the British amphibious attack on the Normandie dry dock at St Nazaire in German-occupied France.

Operation Deadstick: the story of the first Allies into the fray on D-Day, tasked with seizing and holding two bridges to prevent an armoured German counter-attack.

ISBN 978-0-7531-5334-5 (hb)
ISBN 978-0-7531-5335-2 (pb)

ISIS publish a wide range of books in large print, from fiction to biography. Any suggestions for books you would like to see in large print or audio are always welcome. Please send to the Editorial Department at:

ISIS Publishing Limited
7 Centremead
Osney Mead
Oxford OX2 0ES

A full list of titles is available free of charge from:

Ulverscroft Large Print Books Limited

(UK)
The Green
Bradgate Road, Anstey
Leicester LE7 7FU
Tel: (0116) 236 4325

(Australia)
P.O. Box 314
St Leonards
NSW 1590
Tel: (02) 9436 2622

(USA)
P.O. Box 1230
West Seneca
N.Y. 14224-1230
Tel: (716) 674 4270

(Canada)
P.O. Box 80038
Burlington
Ontario L7L 6B1
Tel: (905) 637 8734

(New Zealand)
P.O. Box 456
Feilding
Tel: (06) 323 6828

Details of **ISIS** complete and unabridged audio books are also available from these offices. Alternatively, contact your local library for details of their collection of **ISIS** large print and unabridged audio books.